Keyboard for Commercial Music Production

*To all the friends, family, and mentors that pushed me
to turn ideas into a first edition.*

To Julie - thank you for always seeing me as salt of the earth.

Keyboard for Commercial Music Production

Essential Skills for Music Producers, Songwriters, Audio Engineers, Studio Composers, and Creative Musicians

Andy Villemez

ROWMAN & LITTLEFIELD
Lanham • Boulder • New York • London

Published by Rowman & Littlefield
An imprint of The Rowman & Littlefield Publishing Group, Inc.
4501 Forbes Boulevard, Suite 200, Lanham, Maryland 20706
www.rowman.com

86-90 Paul Street, London EC2A 4NE

Copyright © 2025 by The Rowman & Littlefield Publishing Group, Inc.

All rights reserved. No part of this book may be reproduced in any form or by any electronic or mechanical means, including information storage and retrieval systems, without written permission from the publisher, except by a reviewer who may quote passages in a review.

British Library Cataloguing in Publication Information Available

Library of Congress Cataloging-in-Publication Data

Library of Congress Control Number: 2024947096
ISBN 979-8-8818-0022-2 (cloth : alk. paper)
ISBN 979-8-8818-0023-9 (paperback)
ISBN 979-8-8818-0024-6 (electronic)

♾️™ The paper used in this publication meets the minimum requirements of American National Standard for Information Sciences—Permanence of Paper for Printed Library Materials, ANSI/NISO Z39.48-1992.

Contents

Preface	ix
Foundations	x
UNIT ONE	**1**
Five-Finger Patterns	2
Practicing Five-Finger Patterns	3
Music for Reading (Treble)	5
Music for Reading (Bass)	6
Music for Reading (Grand Staff)	7
Triads 101	9
Practicing Triads	10
Lead Sheet Reading	11
Chord Charts	15
Introduction to Rhythm Exercises	18
Solo Repertoire:	23
"Morning Coffee"	23
"Cave of Wonders"	24
"Jumpin'"	25
Introduction to Harmonization	26
Identifying Triads by Ear	28
Melodic Playback	30
Unit One Melodies for Playback: Instructor Page	31
ADVANCED TOPICS I: How the Pros Practice	**32**
Practice Strategy Worksheet	35
UNIT TWO	**37**
Building Major and Minor Scales	38
The Foundations of Scale Practice	41
Scale Groupings	42
Practicing Scales: Essential Patterns and Variations	46
Scalar Melodies and Basslines	47
Music for Reading	49
Lead Sheet Reading	51
Unit Two Rhythm Training	54
Diatonic Triads and Nashville Numbers	59

Chord Charts	61
Chord Functions and Harmonization	64
Melodies to Harmonize	66
Reharmonization Using Simple Substitution	68
Melodies to Harmonize (and Reharmonize)	70
Unit Two Diatonic Triads Playback	72
Unit Two Melodies for Playback	73

UNIT THREE — 75

Chord Inversions	76
Practicing Chord Inversions	77
Expanded Scale Practice (Group 1 and 2)	79
Intro to Keyboard Style	83
Keyboard Style Reading	84
Lead Sheets:	86
"Dreamer"	86
"House of the Rising Sun"	87
Keyboard Style with Chord Charts	88
Common Chord Progressions with Triads	91
Harmonization with Target Chords and Types of Cadences	93
Unit Three Diatonic Triads Playback	97
Unit Three Melodies for Playback	98
Unit Three Rhythm Training	99
Twinkle Twinkle Challenge	104
Solo Repertoire: "Petite Prelude"	105
Composing with Chord Inversions	106

ADVANCED TOPICS II: Understanding Performance Mistakes — 107

UNIT FOUR — 111

Scale Fingering Review	112
Expanded Scale Practice (Group 3)	113
Technique: Introduction to Hanon	116
Music for Reading (Riffs and Basslines)	118
Solo Repertoire:	120
"Song Without Words"	120
"Forward"	121
"Around the Corner"	122
"Samba"	123

"Samba" (Duet)	124
Lead Sheet Reading	126
Creating Basic Accompaniment Patterns	128
Common Chord Progressions with Triads	130
Chord Charts with Accompaniment Patterns	131
Harmonization with Mode Mixture	134
Melodies to Harmonize	138
Unit Four Diatonic Triads Playback	140
Unit Four Melodies for Playback	141
Unit Four Rhythm Training	142
UNIT FIVE	**147**
Introduction to 7th Chords	148
7th Chord Building	149
Identifying 7th Chords	150
Practicing 7th Chords	151
Lead Sheets with 7th Chords	152
Keyboard Style with 7th Chords	154
Lead Sheet Reading with 7th Chords	
"Blue Skies"	158
"The New World"	159
Chord Charts with 7th Chords	161
Common Chord Progressions with 7th Chords	163
Diatonic 7th Chords in Major Keys	164
7th Chord Functions and Harmonization	165
Unit Five Rhythm Training	169
Solo Repertoire:	
"Piazza"	174
"Adieu"	175
Unit Five Harmonic Playback	176
Unit Five Melodies for Playback	177
ADVANCED TOPICS III: Writing Great Melodies	**178**
UNIT SIX	**183**
Transilient Scales	184
Building Pentatonic Scales	186
Building Blues Scales	187
Practicing Transilient Scales	188

Riffs and Melodies with Transilient Scales	190
7th Chord Inversions	192
Practicing 7th Chord Inversions	193
Lead Sheets with 7th Chords	194
Chord Charts with 7th Chords	196
Diatonic Chord Exercises and Secondary Chords	199
Harmonization Using Secondary Chords and Displacement	203
Unit Six Rhythm Training with Beat Patterns	209
Lead Sheet Ensembles	211
"Laying Low"	211
"Low Tide"	214
Solo Repertoire:	216
"Good Times"	216
"Mini Gymnopedie"	218
Final Project: Arranging a Tune	219
Acknowledgements	224

Preface

Keyboard for Commercial Music Production is designed to equip songwriters, music producers, arrangers, and audio engineers with a well-rounded musical foundation so they can have fluency in performance and efficient creativity in their workflow. While originally intended for use in a collegiate group piano lab, the content in this text can be adapted for private lessons, as well.

Each of the text's six units emphasize concepts that aid in performance, but also those that facilitate the interaction between a music producer and their chosen digital audio workstation software. These concepts include but are not limited to music reading, melodic and harmonic playback, harmonic theory, rhythmic feel, harmonization, basic improvisation, and composing. Technique, repertoire, chord charts, and lead sheets are designed to reinforce the concepts in that unit.

While each unit is organized by concepts, this text is not meant to be used as a "page by page" method. It is recommended that instructors use materials à la carte based on their students' needs.

Each unit of *Keyboard for Commercial Music Production* begins with a summary of concepts and activities for study. After completing Unit One, instructors may plan on mixing materials from subsequent units based on student learning objectives and engagement.

While this book was designed for students that have some experience with foundational musical concepts, a brief "Foundations" unit is placed before Unit One for those students that need a review of music fundamentals.

 Foundations

Sitting at the Keyboard

No matter the keyboard with which you're interacting, there are principles for healthy technique. Review these points before approaching or sitting at a keyboard.

- TREE TRUNK: Maintain an upright posture that isn't rigid or held. Our torso should be allowed to move like a tree in the wind.
- GROUNDED: Keep your heels rooted to the floor (even if using the pedals).
- ALIGNED: Align the middle of your torso with the middle of the keyboard.

Hand Position and Finger Numbers

Imagine your hands outstretched in front of you. You're given a baseball in each hand, and your fingers mold to the shape of the ball. The most efficient hand position at the keyboard has curved fingers and a thumb that rests on its side. Curved fingers allow us to utilize the hand's natural arch, and it allows the thumb to pass under the fingers or the fingers to pass over the thumb.

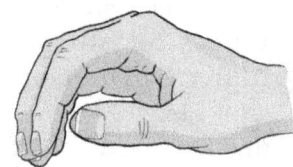

Unlike some other instruments, the piano starts numbering its fingers from the thumb and moves outward. The fingers of the left and right hands are numbered as shown in the illustration.

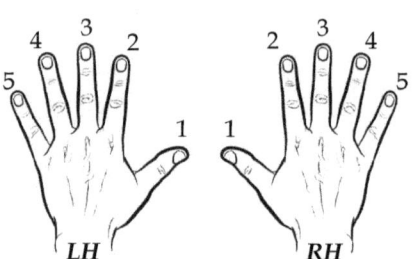

The Keyboard

The keyboard has two distinct visual patterns that players utilize to navigate. First, you can see white keys and black keys. Second, you will notice the black keys organized in groups of twos and threes. As you move down and to the left, sounds get lower. As you move up and to the right, sounds get higher.

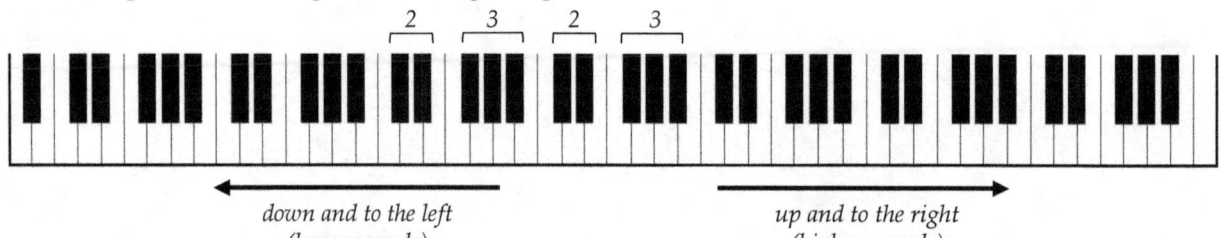

down and to the left
(lower sounds)

up and to the right
(higher sounds)

Naming the White Keys

White keys on the keyboard are named *A-B-C-D-E-F-G*. Also known as the musical alphabet, that pattern of letter names repeats across the entire length of the keyboard you use. Full-size keyboards have 88-keys with *A* being the lowest note and *C* being the highest.

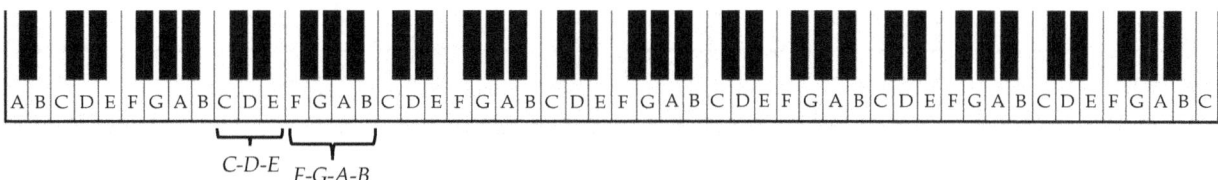

In order to see the keyboard in smaller sections, it is helpful to separate the white keys into groups of C-D-E and F-G-A-B. Groups of C-D-E surround the group of two black keys. Groups of F-G-A-B surround the group of three black keys.

Half Steps and Whole Steps

The smallest distance between two keys at the piano is a **half step**. You can identify a half step by moving from one note to the note *immediately* next to it without skipping any in between. A **whole step** in music is made of two half steps.

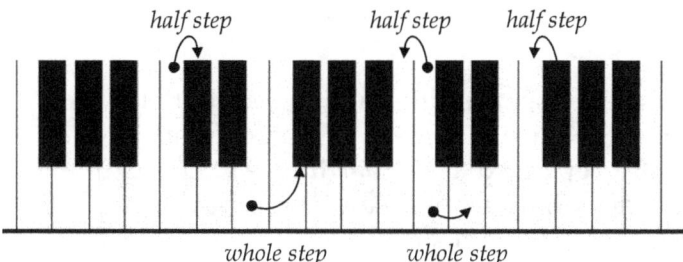

Naming the Black Keys

Black keys are identified with either a **sharp** (#) or **flat** (♭) sign. A sharp occurs when a note is raised a half step. For example, a G raised a half step becomes a G-sharp (G#). A flat occurs when a note is lowered a half step. For example, a G lowered a half step becomes a G-flat (G♭). Because black keys are surrounded by white keys, this results in black keys having the ability to be identified by a flat or a sharp.

Note Values and Rhythmic Notation

Rhythm in music refers to the patterns of sounds and silences we hear in a song. These patterns are notated through the notes and rests indicated below. Study their names, symbols, and relationships to one another.

	Note Values	Rest Values
Whole	𝅝	𝄻
Half	𝅗𝅥 𝅗𝅥	𝄼 𝄼
Quarter	♩ ♩ ♩ ♩	𝄽 𝄽 𝄽 𝄽
8th	♫ ♫ ♫ ♫ *or* ♪♪ ♪♪ ♪♪ ♪♪	𝄾𝄾 𝄾𝄾 𝄾𝄾 𝄾𝄾
16th	♬♬ ♬♬ ♬♬ ♬♬ *or* ♪♪♪♪ ♪♪♪♪ ♪♪♪♪ ♪♪♪♪	𝄿𝄿𝄿𝄿 𝄿𝄿𝄿𝄿 𝄿𝄿𝄿𝄿 𝄿𝄿𝄿𝄿
Dots	Adding a dot next to a note increases its value by half ♩. = ♩ + ♪ 𝅗𝅥. = 𝅗𝅥 + ♩	𝄼. = 𝄼 + 𝄽 𝄾. = 𝄾 + 𝄿

Music is organized in patterns, including rhythm. Most often, it is grouped in multiples of two (**duple time**) or three (**triple time**). In notated music, each grouping is called a **measure**. Measures are separated by a **barline**. At the beginning of pieces is a **time signature,** which indicates how many beats per measure (top number) and what note value receives one beat (bottom number).

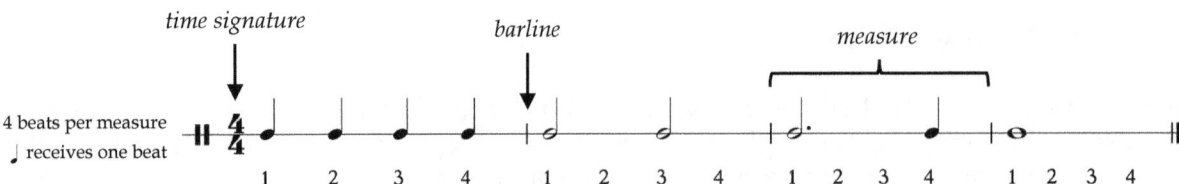

Duple Time Examples:

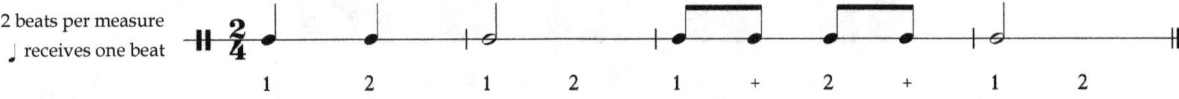

Common time, notated with a **C** in place of a time signature, means the same as $\frac{4}{4}$ time.

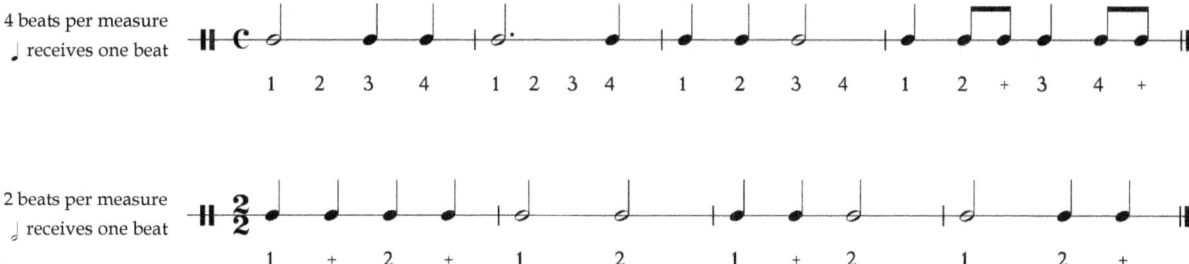

Cut time, notated with a **¢** in place of a time signature, means the same as $\frac{2}{2}$ time.

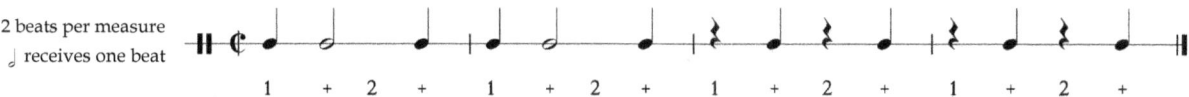

Triple Time Examples:

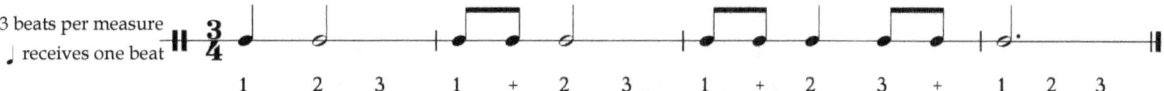

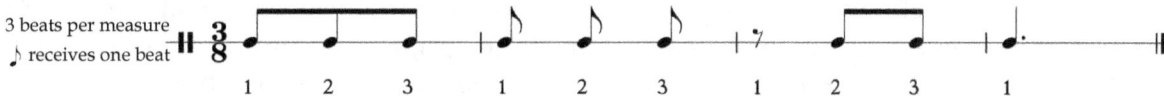

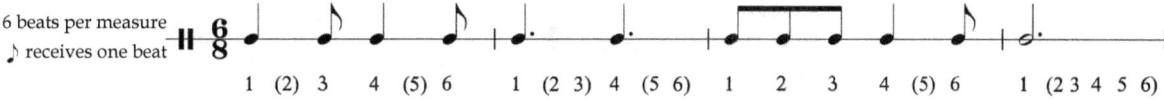

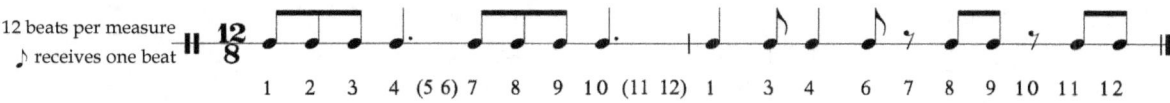

Beat vs. Pulse

Pulse:
For most kinds of music, especially Western music, you are able to find a heartbeat to a song and tap your foot along with it. You're not looking at a score or analyzing anything, you are feeling something steady and regular. This is the pulse—the feeling of the heartbeat in a song.

Beat:
While pulse is a feeling, the beat is a measurement of time. Most, if not all of the music you will study and perform will have a time signature like the example below. The time signature tells us that there are four beats per measure (the top number) and the quarter note receives one beat (the bottom number).

In the above example, the pulse and the beat are the same. We feel the heartbeat as a quarter note *and* a quarter note receives one beat. The example below, however, shows a case where the pulse and beat are not the same.

The time signature shows six beats per measure with the 8th note receiving one beat. Unless the tempo is very slow, we will feel the music in groups of three beats which is the equivalent of a dotted quarter note. The beat is measured in 8th notes, but the pulse is a dotted quarter note. You can feel this by counting all six beats while putting a small emphasis on beats one and four.

$$\mathit{1} - 2 - 3 - \mathit{4} - 5 - 6$$

The feel of a song (i.e., the pulse) can change in the middle depending on the musical characteristics you hear. This makes the pulse slightly subjective, but the beat will be objective as it is shown in time signature.

Music Reading

Music is notated on a **staff** consisting of five parallel lines and the spaces between them. Each line and space represents a specific letter name and note on the keyboard.

The Staff

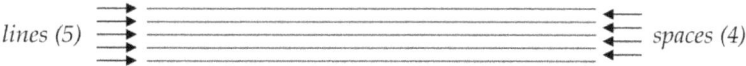

A **clef** is a symbol at the beginning of a staff that tells us which lines and spaces represent certain letter names. The two most common clefs are **bass** and **treble.** The bass clef indicates where the *f* below middle C is. The treble clef indicates where the *g* above middle C is.

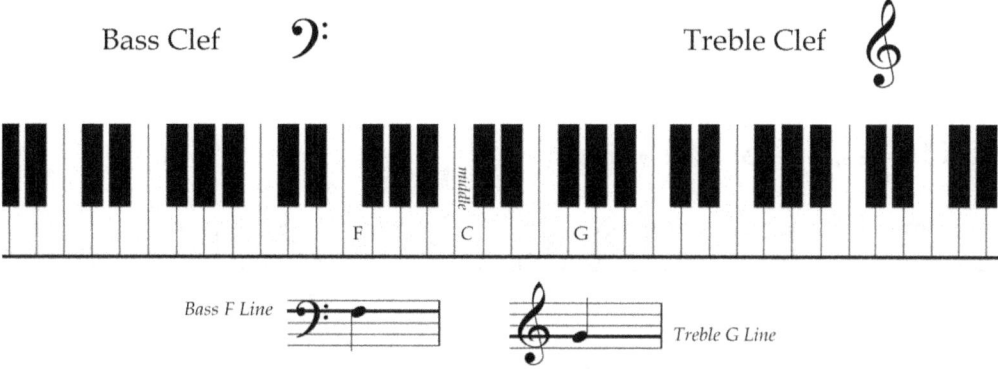

The Grand Staff

In fully notated keyboard music, two clefs are combined to form the **grand staff.** Usually, the upper staff indicates what the right hand will play, and the lower staff indicates what the left hand will play.

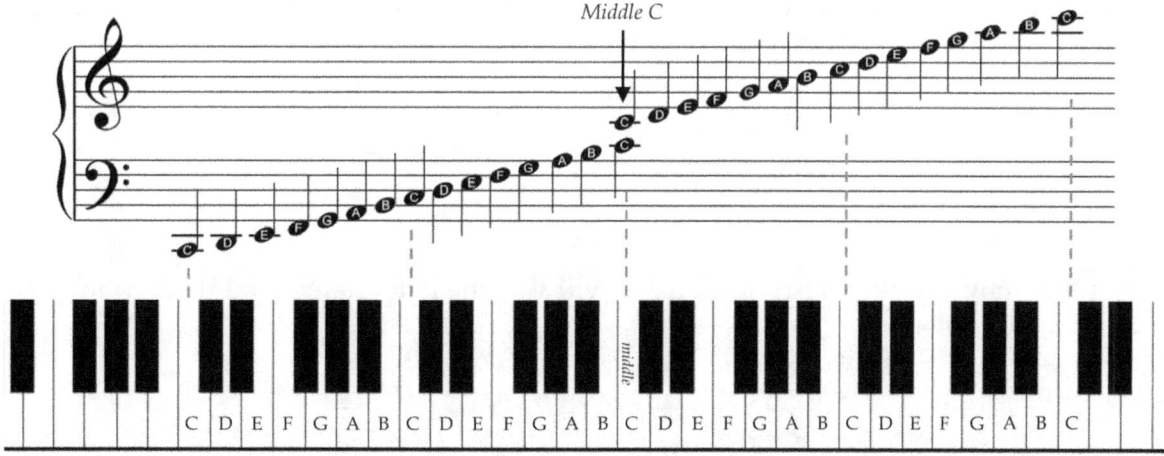

Foundations

Name and play the following notes.

Repeated Notes, Steps, and Skips

While knowing the letter name of every note is important, playing music also involves observing the shape of a melody and the distances between notes, also known as **intervals.**

Notes that **repeat** will stay on the same line or space.

Notes that move by **step** (also called a 2nd) go to the next letter name either up or down. Steps will always move from a line to a space or a space to a line.

Notes that move by **skip** (also called a 3rd) will *skip* one letter name (and usually a finger) moving up or down.

Basic Articulations

Articulation in music refers to the combination of effects like length, attack, and decay, that can change the sound of a note. You can think of articulation of notes the same way we think about articulation of speech. We can make a single word sound a variety of ways and the same is true of a single note on an instrument.

While technically there's an endless number of articulations, notated music uses two basic types – **legato** and **staccato**.

Legato refers to notes that sound *smooth and connected*. It is notated with a slur, a curved line that runs above or below the notes that should sound smooth and connected.

Staccato refers to notes that sound *short and detached*. It is notated with a dot above or below (not to the side) a note that should sound short and detached.

Foundations

Music Fundamentals: Review

Write in the counts for the following rhythms. Tap (both the rhythm AND the pulse) and count each example.

Before playing the following examples:
- count and tap each exercise.
- study each exercise for notes that repeat, step, or skip.

Unit One

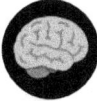     

- ❏ **Five-Finger Patterns**
- ❏ **Treble and Bass Clef Reading**
- ❏ **Triads 101**
- ❏ **Lead Sheet Reading**
- ❏ **Chord Charts**
- ❏ **Introduction to Rhythm Exercises**
- ❏ **Solo Repertoire**
- ❏ **Harmonization**
- ❏ **Identifying Triads by Ear**
- ❏ **Melodic Playback**

Notes:

Five-Finger Patterns

Also known as a **pentascale**, a five-finger pattern is a collection of five notes that serves as the starting point for a lot of musical and keyboard concepts. Before you run, you walk. Before you play four-octave scales hands together, you play five-finger patterns.

The first note of any five-finger pattern is called the tonic note, or simply **tonic**. This is also the letter name you'll identify each as pattern as. The example below uses C as the tonic note.

Building Major Pentascales

All major five-finger patterns are made of the same sequence of whole steps and half steps.

Tonic – Whole Step – Whole Step – Half Step – Whole Step

C Major Pentascale

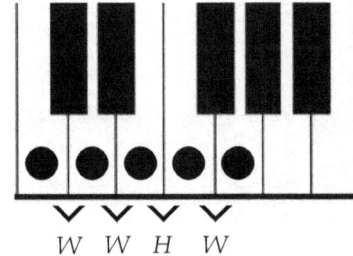 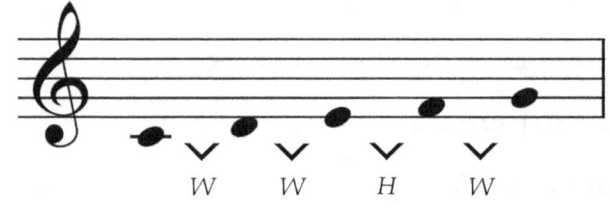

Building Minor Pentascales

All minor five-finger patterns are made of the same sequence of whole steps and half steps.

Tonic – Whole Step – Half Step – Whole Step – Whole Step

C Minor Pentascale

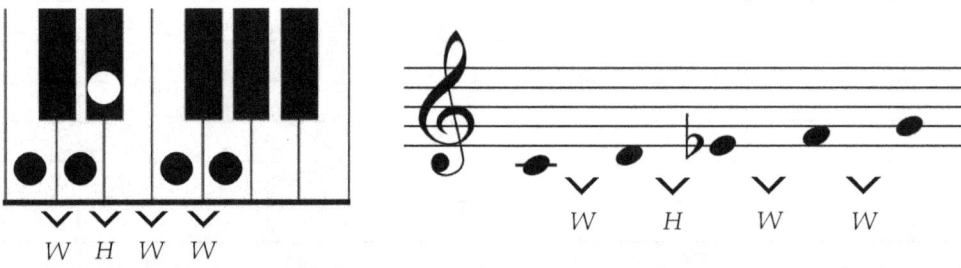

> **Next Steps:**
> Find the major and minor five-finger patterns that start on D, E, F, G, A, and B.

2   Unit 1

Practicing Five-Finger Patterns

Basic Practice Pattern

C Major

Essential Variations

Practice exercises are like tools in a tool belt. Choosing the right ones for the goals you have will help you make *more* progress *more* quickly.

Legato

Staccato

Combining Articulations

a. Two-note groups

b. Three-note groups

c. Legato RH with staccato LH

d. Staccato RH with legato LH

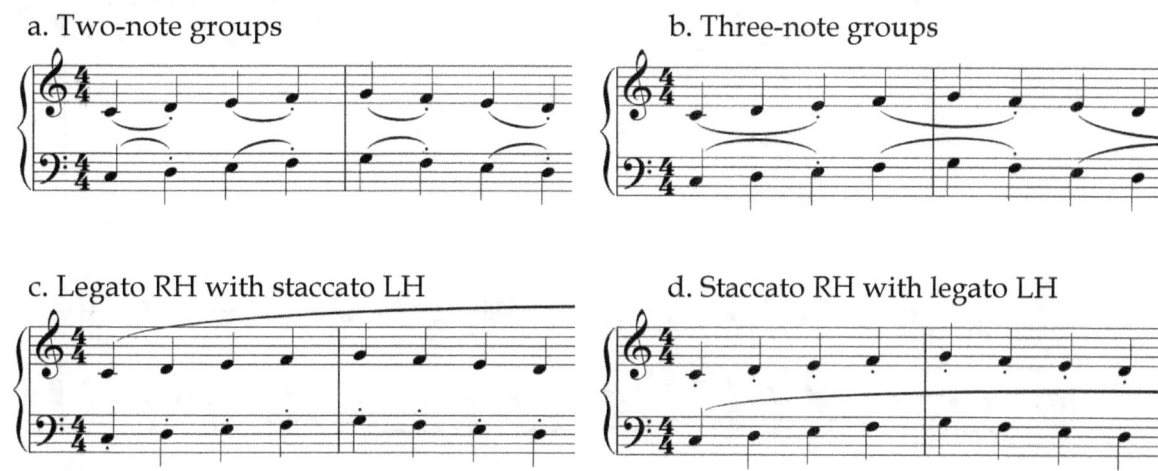

Essential Variations – Part 2

After becoming more comfortable with the variations on the previous page, you can incorporate more variations in texture and rhythm. The examples below use the F Major pattern.

2 against 1

a.

1 against 2

b.

Repeated Notes

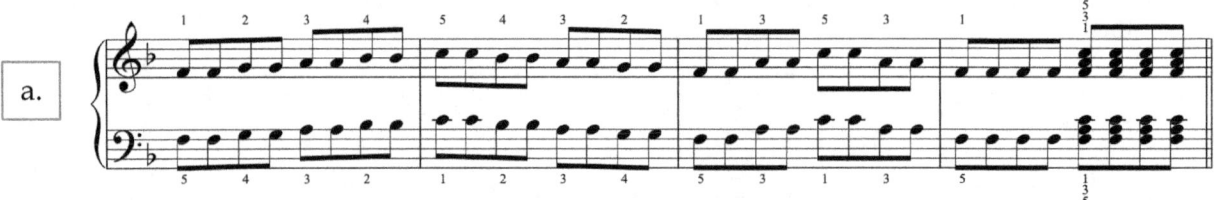

a.

b.

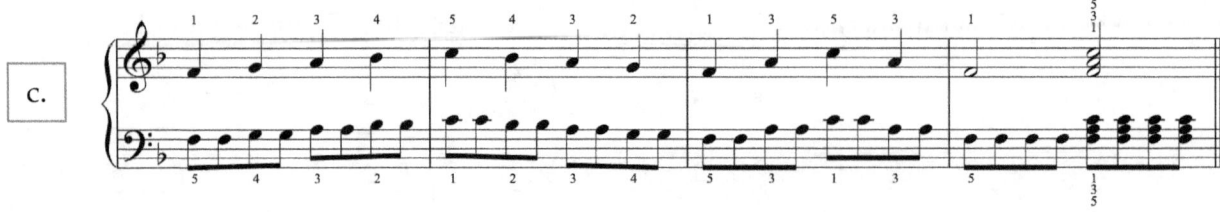

c.

Music for Reading (Treble)

For each melody:

1. Identify the major or minor five-finger pattern being used.
2. Scan the example for intervals, articulation, and dynamics.
3. Play with a steady pulse.
4. Practice recording each melody using a digital audio workstation (DAW).

Chord names above each melody may be used by instructors for creating accompaniment patterns.

1
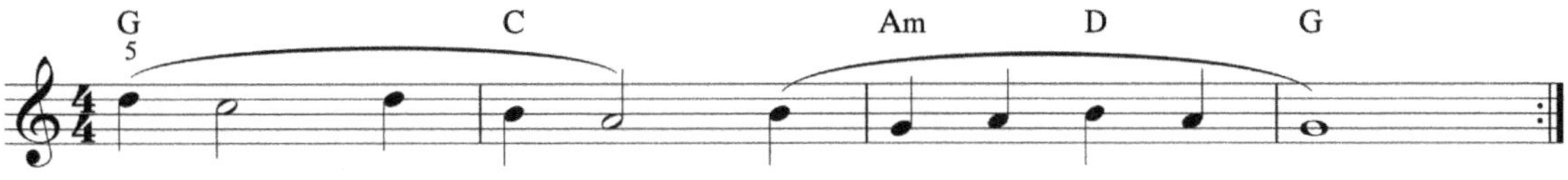

2
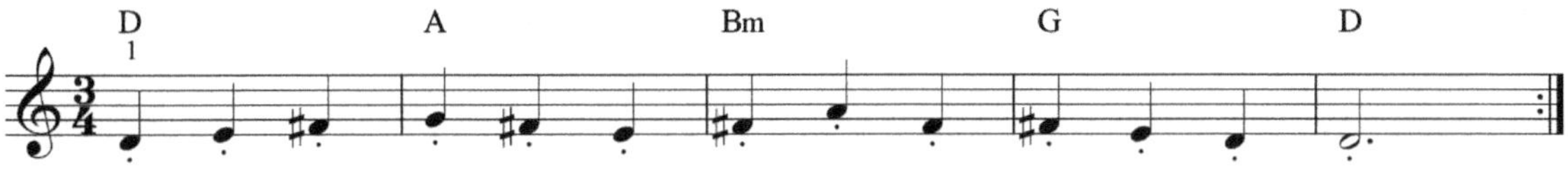

3
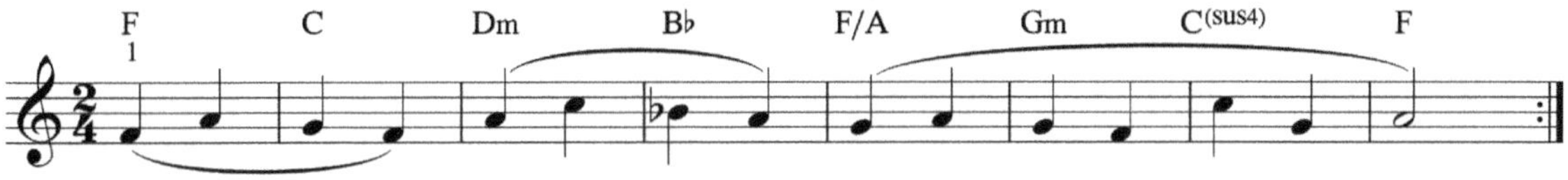

4
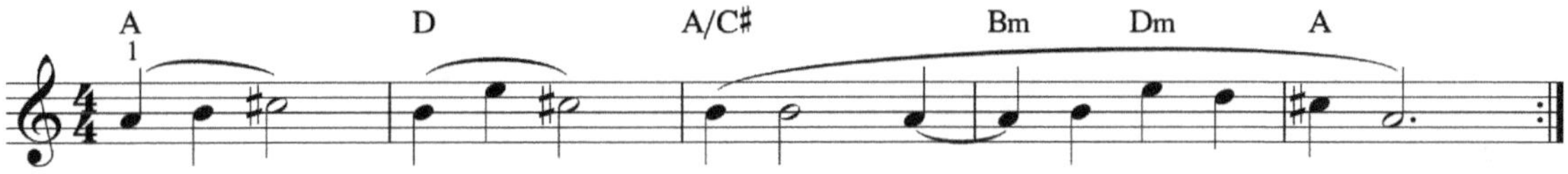

5
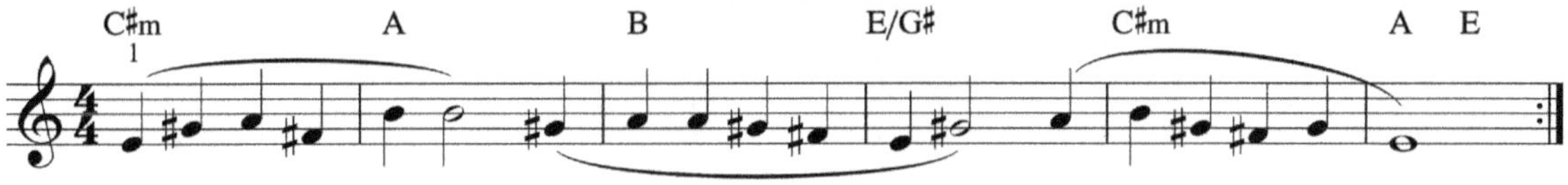

6
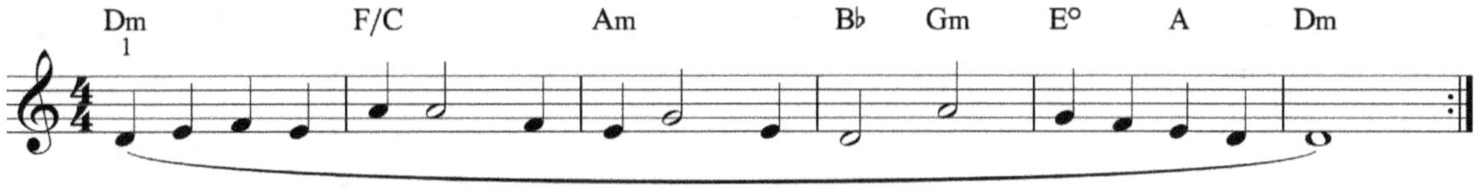

7
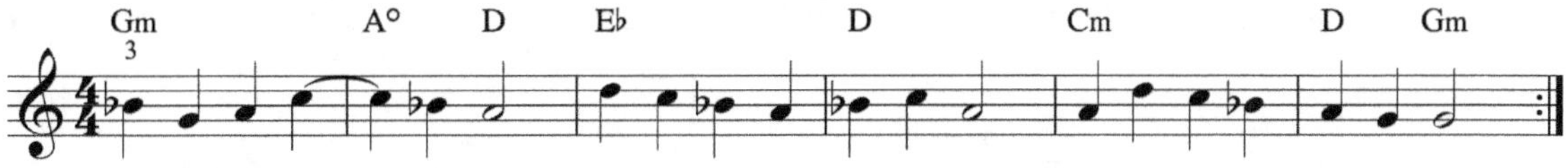

8
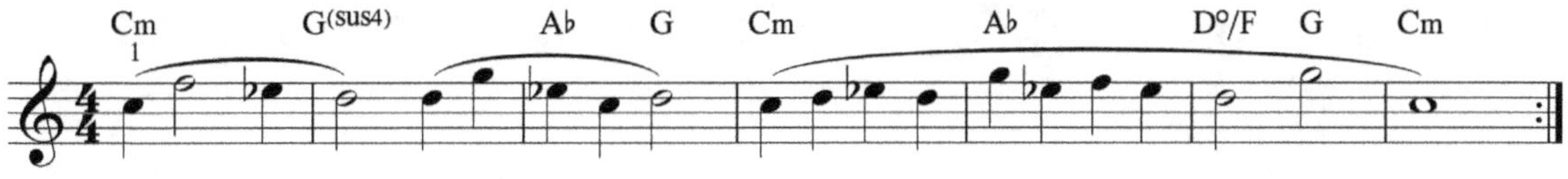

Music for Reading (Bass)

For each melody:

1. Identify the major or minor five-finger pattern being used.
2. Scan the example for intervals, articulation, and dynamics.
3. Play with a steady pulse.
4. Practice recording each melody using your DAW of choice.

1
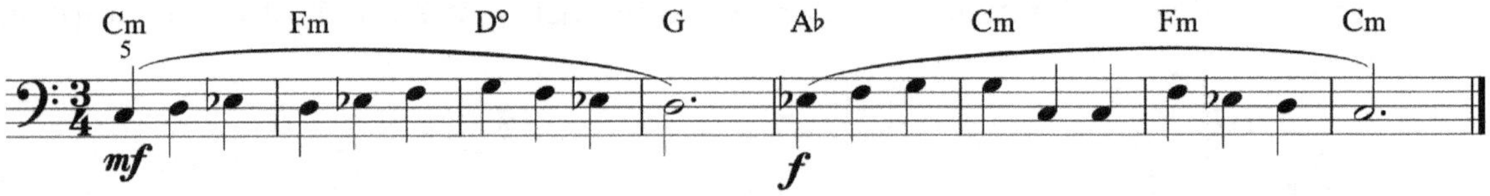

2
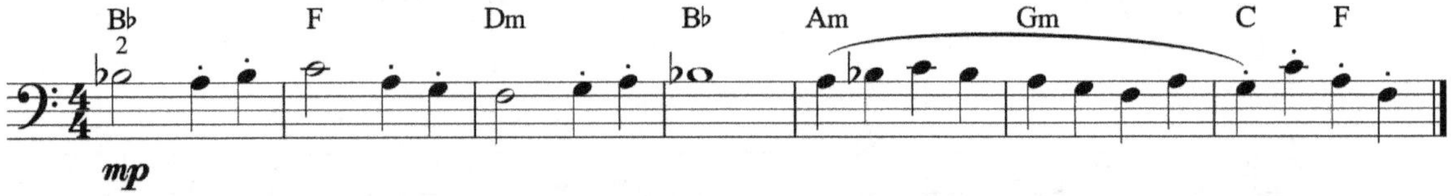

3
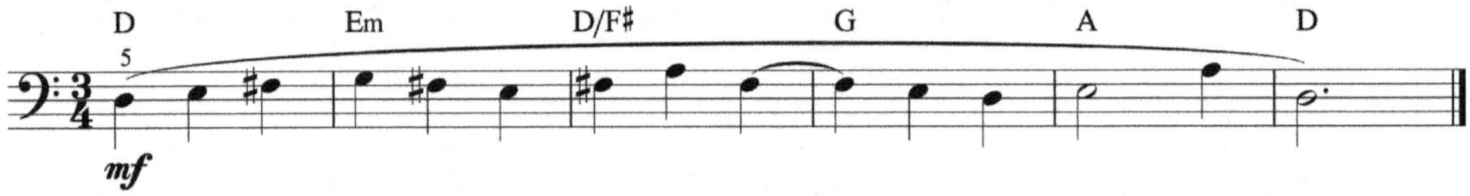

4
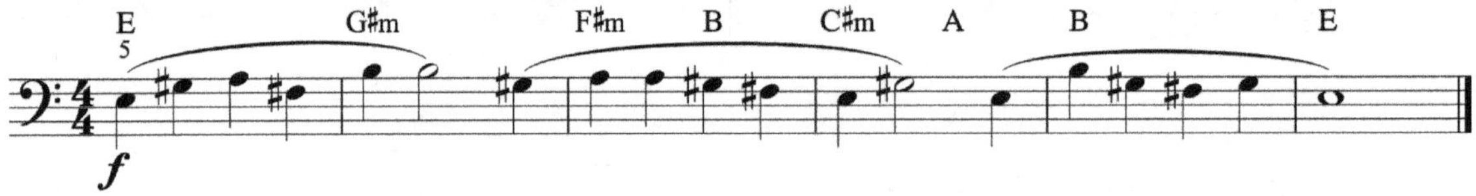

5
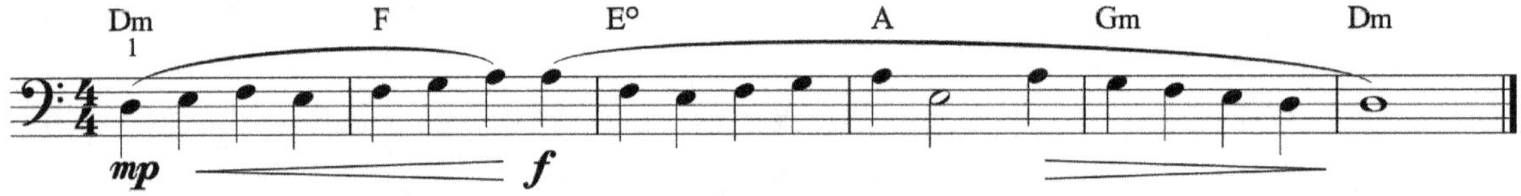

6
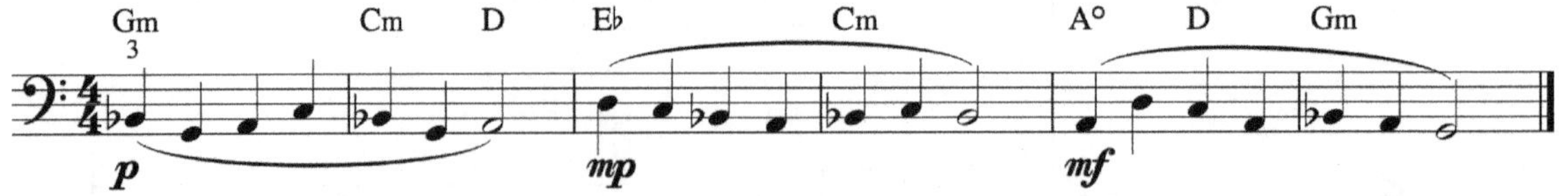

7
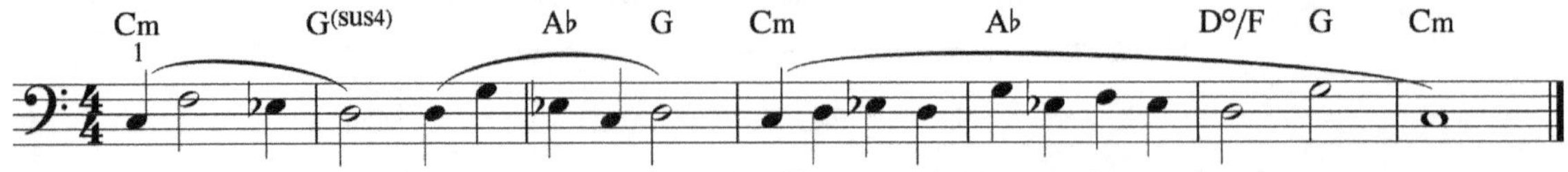

8
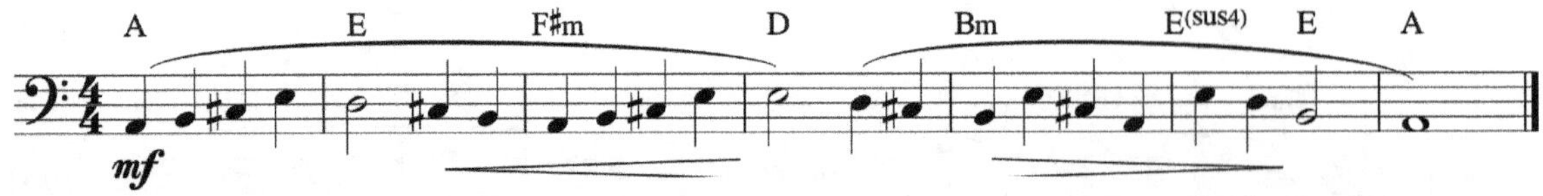

Music for Reading (Grand Staff)

Triads 101

If you know how to build five-finger patterns, you can build any triad. All formulas in this book use the major five-finger pattern (or major scale in later units) as its reference point.

All triads are built using the interval of a 3rd. That means when you spell them in root position, you will always skip one (and only one) letter name for each note. For example, all triads with a root note of F will be spelled F - A - C. The only differences between the different types of triads will be added sharps or flats that are used with the 2nd or 3rd note of the triad.

PRIMARY TRIADS

Major Triad

Formula*: 1 - 3 - 5

Example in F

F - A - C

Minor Triad

Formula: 1 - b3 - 5

F - Ab - C

Diminished Triad

Formula: 1 - b3 - b5

F - Ab - Cb

Augmented Triad

Formula: 1 - 3 - #5

F - A - C#

*The flat and sharp signs in the formula only indicate a note should be lowered or raised a half step. They do not mean that the change will result in a note needing a flat or sharp sign. For example, an F-sharp lowered a half step results in an F, not an F-flat.

 **Practicing Triads**

Four Triad Chord Progression

Use this chord progression to cycle through all four types of triads built on the same root note. All triads will use fingers *1-3-5* in each hand. Practice playing through this progression on all twelve notes starting hands separately.

Example 1: Triads Built on C

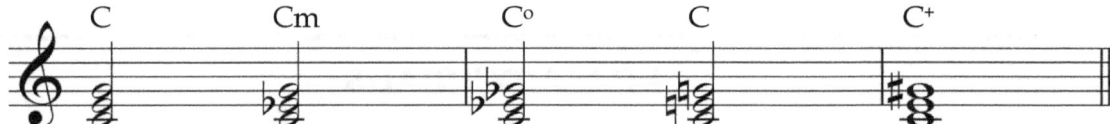

Essential Variations

> **Next Steps:**
> In your daily practice, don't feel the need to practice all twelve keys with all essential variations every day. Instead, choose three chord progressions that feel very different from one another (i.e., C, E, and Bb). Practice the progression and variations in those keys. Choose three new keys every few days.

 # Lead Sheet Reading

A lead sheet is a common form of notation for a song in jazz and popular music. It contains two elements: a notated melody and chords that go along with it. This kind of notation is a minimal set of instructions—usually the "bare bones" of a song. It requires the keyboardist to make their own decisions on how to add texture and voicing.

Interpreting Lead Sheets

The simplest interpretation of a lead sheet is in a texture demonstrated below. In this texture, the RH plays the exact melody line while the LH plays blocked chords usually in closed voicing (the notes of the chord are as close to together as possible). When playing in this texture, do your best to play the LH chords in the "Golden Chord Area" shown below. As you go lower than this area, the chords sound muddy, and as you go higher, the chords don't provide enough support.

Left Hand "Golden Chord Area"

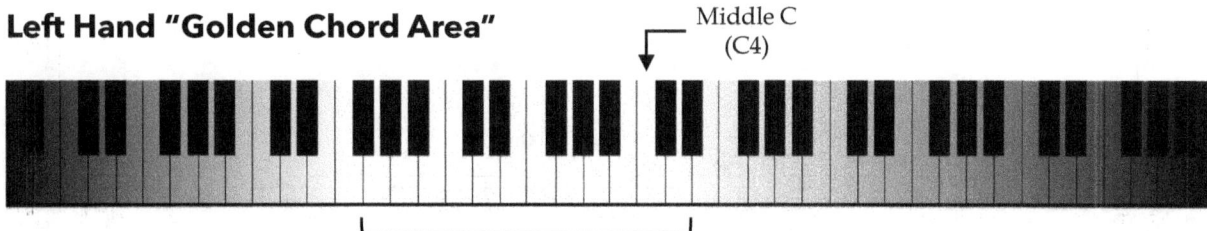

Example

The example below demonstrates what a typical lead sheet looks like and how a keyboardist would execute it with the LH playing chord tones and the RH playing the notated melody.

What You See

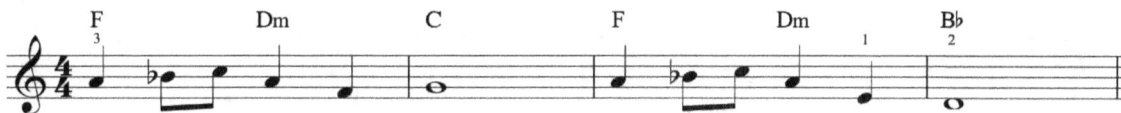

What You Play

LH adds chords in "Golden Chord Area"

Practice the following lead sheets in reverse keyboard style. Before diving in with both hands, make sure you can do the following:
1. Find and play the given chords with the LH in the "Golden Chord Area."
2. Play the RH melody by itself without breaking the pulse. (Write in fingerings if needed.)

Before diving headfirst into the lead sheets below, practice finding the chords in root position with the LH. When you have a choice to go up or down to the next chord, think about the shortest distance to the next chord and what will help you stay in the "Golden Chord Area."

Chord Charts

Unlike a lead sheet, chord charts do not have a notated melody. Typically, they will have only chord names (often written above the lyrics). In addition to chord names, the following charts have the harmonic rhythm notated so you know where a chord change takes place in a measure. **You will use a different texture to play these than you did practicing lead sheets.** In these chord charts, all chord tones will be played in the RH and only root/bass notes in the LH.

Reading Accompaniment Patterns

This unit uses two common accompaniment patterns—**blocked chord** accompaniment and **broken chord** accompaniment. The example below shows what both accompaniment patterns look and sound like with the same chord progression.

Example:

What You See:

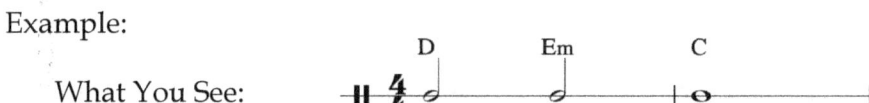

What You Could Play:

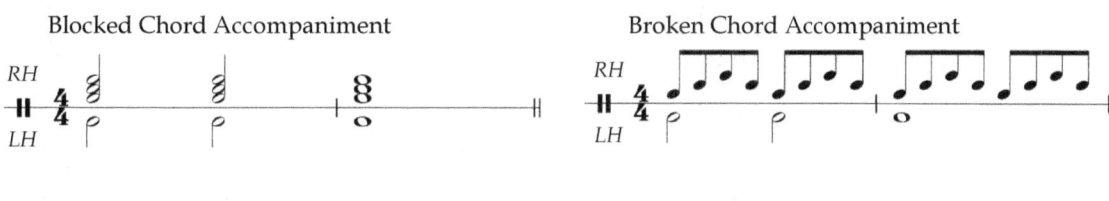

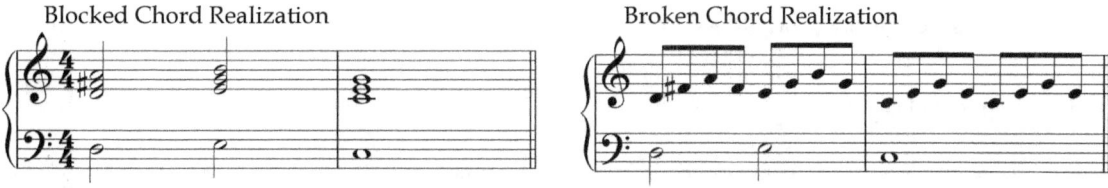

1. You can hear a chord progression like exercise 1 in the song "Elastic Heart" as performed by Sia.

KEY: A   Pop Ballad (♩ = 70)

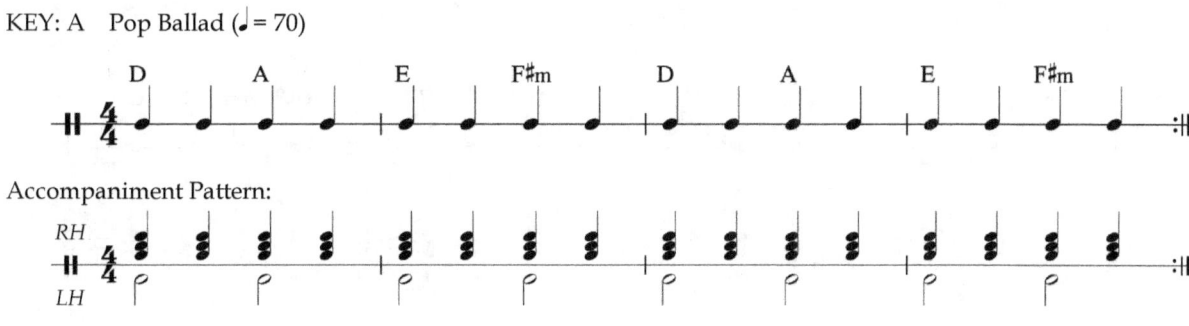

Accompaniment Pattern:

Unit 1   15

Exercise 2 uses a variation on the blocked chord accompaniment commonly used in reggae. The RH chords will be played on off beats 2 and 4.

2 You can hear a chord progression like exercise 2 in the song "All That She Wants" as performed by Ace of Base.

KEY: C   Reggae Pop (♩ = 85)

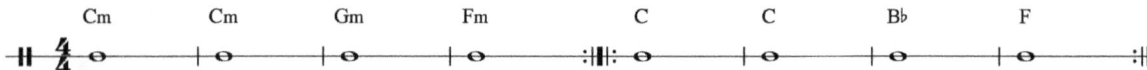

Accompaniment Pattern(s):

Building Sus Chords

Two triads that are not built in thirds are called **suspended** chords. They replace the third of a triad (the middle note of a triad) with either a perfect fourth or major second from the root. Use the chart below as a guide to the two types of sus chords.

Chord Quality	Formula	Example		Notations
Suspended 4	1 - 4 - 5	C^{sus}	C-F-G	C^{sus}, C^{sus4}
Suspended 2	1 - 2 - 5	C^{sus2}	C-D-G	C^{sus2}

3 You can hear a chord progression like exercise 3 in the song "Stay With Me" as performed by Sam Smith.

KEY: C   Pop Ballad (♩ = 85)

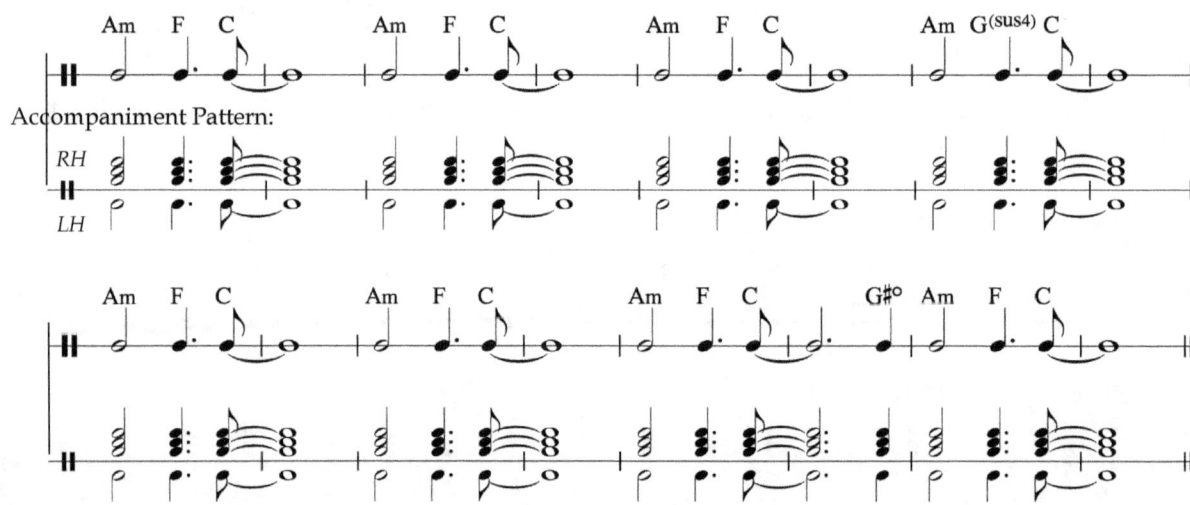

Unit 1

Exercise 4 uses both a broken *and* blocked chord accompaniment pattern in different parts of the song. Notice how the broken chord accompaniment pattern has a different rhythm and feel than on page 15.

4. You can hear a chord progression like exercise 4 in the song "Hallelujah" as performed by Jeff Buckley.

KEY: C   Folk Alternative Rock ($\quarternote = 60$)

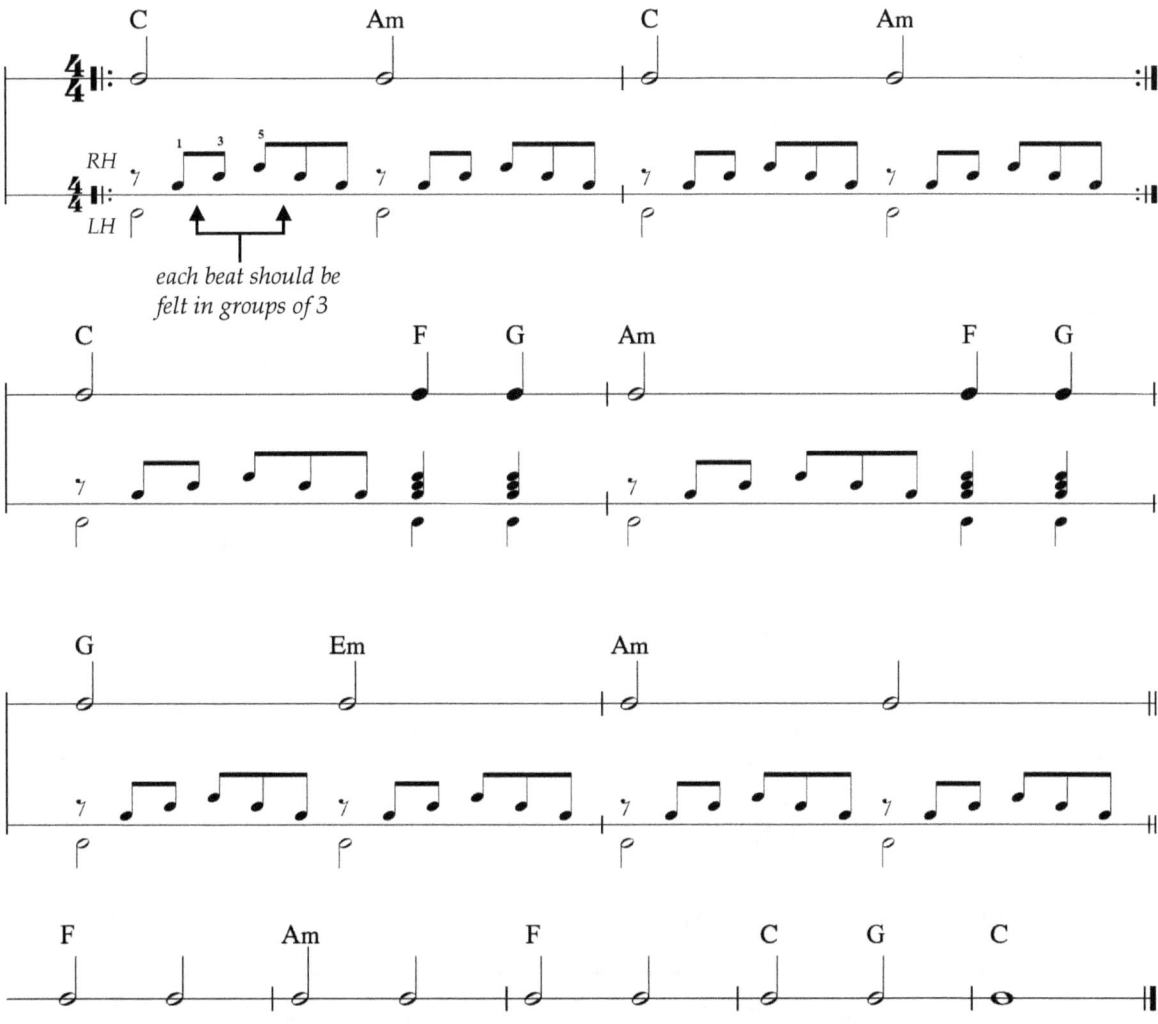

Continue broken chord accompaniment to the end.

Unit 1

Introduction to Rhythm Exercises

The ability to read rhythmic notation fluently, establish and maintain a steady pulse, and build a groove is the foundation for professional life as a musician. These exercises are designed to assist in learning not only rhythmic patterns, but also performance mindset, practice tools, and self-discipline. Units are organized with one or two rhythmic concepts in mind while increasing in difficulty.

Each unit contains four types of exercises:

1. One-part rhythm exercises with pulse indicated

2. Two-part or duet rhythm exercises

3. Four-part rhythm ensembles

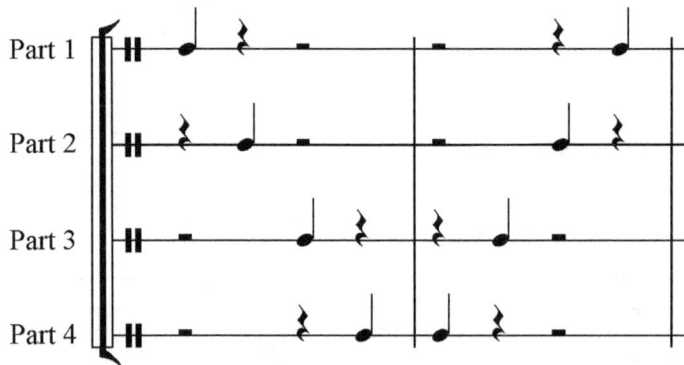

4. Drumbeat exercises (not contained in Unit 1)

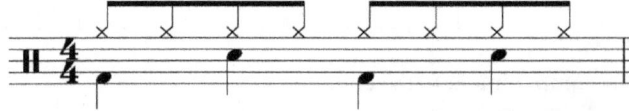

It is important to work on rhythm **individually and in pairs or groups**. Collaboration is an honest teacher in and of itself.

How to Use These Exercises

There are no limits to how these examples might be used, but below are guidelines for increasing your rhythm reading skills, as well as the other concepts mentioned in the first paragraph above. Each exercise should be performed with two elements—the pulse and the rhythm part(s). For example, you might choose to tap the pulse with your foot while tapping the rhythm part on a thigh. Alternatively, you could tap the pulse and say the rhythm out loud using "ta" or another syllable. In two-part rhythms, you could tap the pulse with the left foot and use the LH and RH for each of the rhythm parts, respectively. Throughout the exercises, the steadiness of the pulse should be your primary concern. These exercises are not necessarily meant to be practiced to perfection. It is most important to cultivate an ability to read rhythms, make mistakes, and recover all while maintaining a rock-solid pulse.

In summary, use the guidelines below as a benchmark for "completing" exercises:

1. Your primary goal is fluency, not perfection.
Very rarely do we achieve anything close to our idea of a perfect performance, so we should be training ourselves for practical situations. If you perform something perfectly, that's wonderful, but the mark of a mature musician is how they handle their mistakes. A "completed" exercise is not devoid of challenge, but it should feel like you made it through with minimal bumps and bruises. Think of fluency the same way you might think about language. How much of what you're saying (i.e., performing) is automatic, or does it take a lot of thought to think about the words and phrases you want to use? How much preparation and mental energy does it take? A lot of musical concepts, especially rhythm, can be thought of the same way. Ultimately, these concepts should feel as natural and automatic as possible. (NB: Natural and automatic do not mean perfect.)

2. Prioritize the pulse.
In these exercises, do not go back to correct your mistakes. Maintain the pulse and where you are in the exercise without stopping. After you've finished, analyze where you made a mistake and attempt to fix it the next time through. Allow yourself to make mistakes, but do not allow your mistakes to affect the pulse.

3. Don't stop.
I repeat, don't stop in the middle of the exercise for any reason. If the rhythm is too hard, you can still maintain a pulse and pick up wherever is easiest. It is far better to be silent for two measures while maintaining the pulse than it is to give up in the middle of the exercise.

Understanding Your Mistakes

Imagine if you had the power to know why and how you just made a mistake, or even multiple mistakes. How much more quickly would you be able to practice, learn, and gain fluency in all your work? These rhythm exercises can help you practice finding those reasons for mistakes so you can develop a mature consistency in your practice and performing. Every mistake you make, ask why and how. For more on understanding your mistakes, visit Advanced Topics II on "Understanding Performance Mistakes."

Single-Part Rhythms

For all rhythm exercises:
1. Your primary is goal is fluency, not perfection.
2. Prioritize the pulse.
3. Don't stop.

Two-Part Rhythms

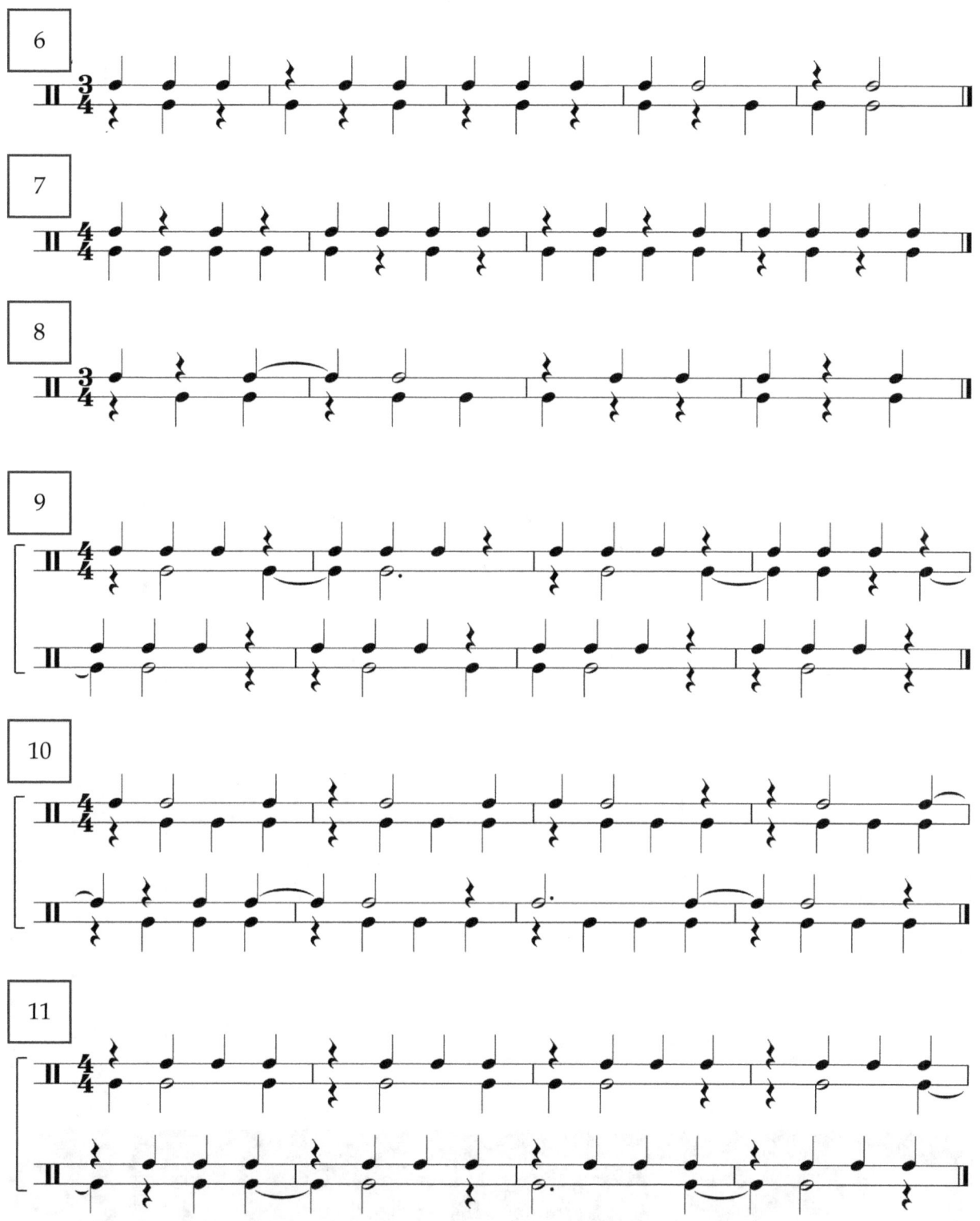

Rhythm Ensemble

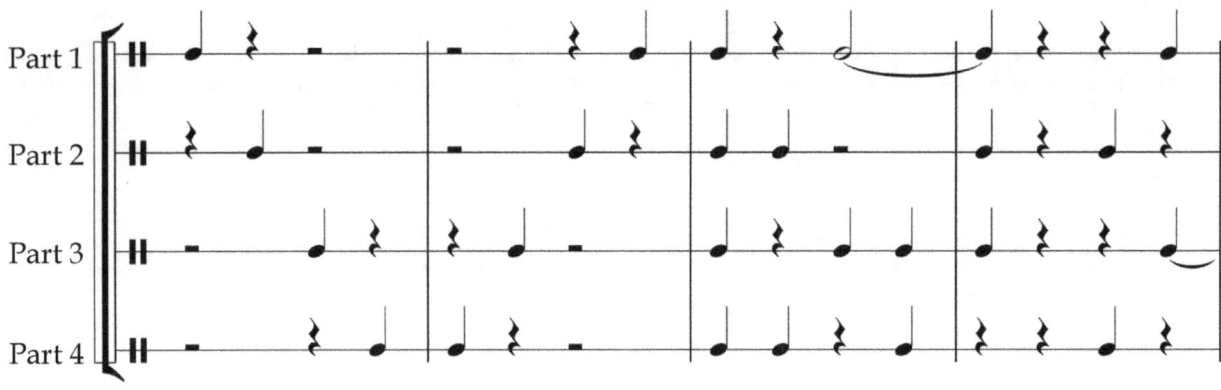

Practice Variations and Challenges:
1. For individual work, practice different two-part combinations.
2. For paired or group work, assign alternating measures.

Solo Repertoire

Morning Coffee

Moderately fast but smooth (♩ = 200)

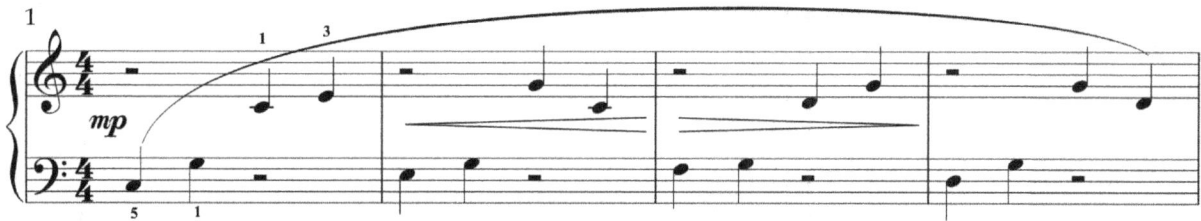

Next Steps:
Transpose this piece to other five-finger patterns.

Cave of Wonders

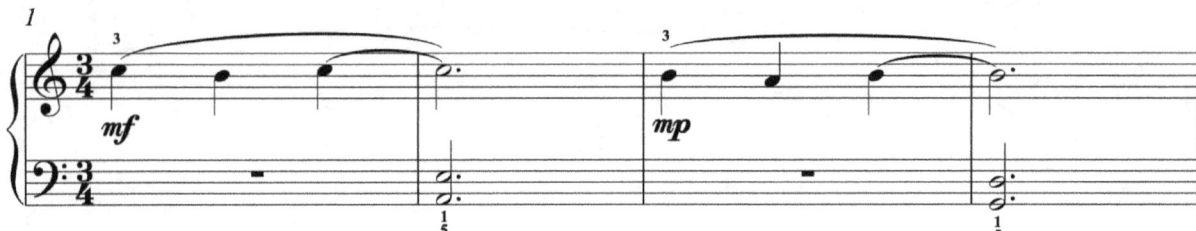
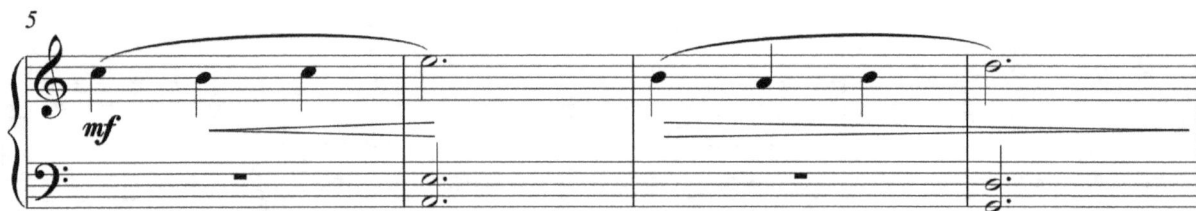
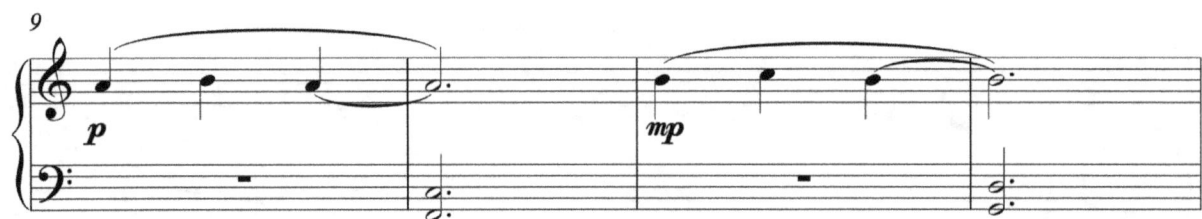

Next Steps: Add chord symbols above the staff where harmonies change.

Practice Preparation

In the piece below, there are quick and frequent hand position changes. Identify and mark each hand position change.

Introduction to Harmonization

Harmonization is the process of adding chords underneath a melody to color it in familiar or unique ways. The exercises in this book will give you mental and physical facility in the process of harmonizing a melody so you can create personalized combinations for your own compositions. We're not looking for definitive harmonizations for each melody, but rather working toward being able to produce as many possibilities as quickly as possible with an awareness of how your harmonic choices will affect the melody and the subsequent listening experience.

Example Melody:

Chord Options: F, G^{min}, A^{min}, B^b, C, D^{min}, E^{dim}

Example Harmonizations: play the following examples (RH melody and LH root position chords) to get a sense of how the harmonizations affect how we hear the melody.

Example 1:

Example 2:

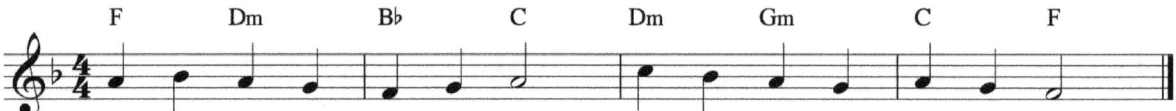

Example 3:

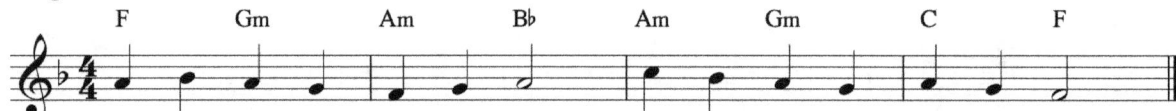

Questions for Reflection/Discussion:
1. How do the different harmonizations affect how we hear the melody?
2. Which chords support melody notes that are non-chord tones?
3. Where do chords add, suspend, or take away energy? Where are there points of rest?

Harmonize the example melody in a new way using a combination of your own. Refer to the chord options box at the top of the page.

26   Unit 1

Complete two harmonizations for each melody. Practice performing your harmonizations with the RH playing the melody and the LH playing root position blocked chords.

Guidelines:
1. Try to hear the sound, or "color," of the harmonies with the melody in your head before playing them.
2. If something sounds new or different, that doesn't mean it is incorrect or bad.
3. Think about how your chords add or take away energy. They can also be points of rest without sounding like we've arrived at "home" (aka tonic).

1. KEY: C Major
   Chord Options: C, D^{min}, E^{min}, F, G, A^{min}, B^{dim}

2. KEY: A Major
   Chord Options: A, B^{min}, $C^{\#min}$, D, E, $F^{\#min}$, $G^{\#dim}$

3. KEY: D Minor
   Chord Options: D^{min}, E^{dim}, F, G^{min}, A, $B^\flat$, C, $C^{\#dim}$

Unit 1

 # Identifying Triads by Ear

Hearing and playing back harmonies in various textures is an essential skill for the contemporary musician. Identifying harmonies is a combination of recognizing intervals within the chord and more general characteristics produced by the combination of those intervals (i.e., does the chord sound open, happy, dark, glassy, etc.?).

Guidelines:

Hear the chord multiple times before attempting to identify and/or play.

Just like in melodic playback, you need to try to develop an accurate version of the harmony in your "mind's ear" before attempting to play. This version is what you can "hear" in your head. This ends up being the version you use to recreate on a keyboard. If the version in your head is fuzzy or inaccurate, your attempt at playing it will be, as well.

Don't guess randomly. (Wrong and Strong!)

This just wastes time and builds bad habits. You will need to make educated guesses throughout the process of chord identification, but there is a big difference between trying a chord with purpose and guessing randomly. Make a strong choice for strong reasons as to why you think you're hearing a certain chord. Try it then repeat that process.

Create your own descriptive language for identifying chords.

All chords are made of the same building blocks—intervals. Hearing intervals is the key to identifying chords. However, we will use nonmusical terms to describe the effect a chord has. These terms might not be the way you would describe what you're hearing. That is understandable, but you will need to develop your own language so you can describe what you are hearing and identify it again in the future.

Listen for energy and stability.

Identifying characteristics of chords becomes easier when you ask how much energy a chord has. Does it feel like you could end a piece on this chord? Does it feel the chord is pushing us forward or keeping us where we are?

Primary Triad Characteristics

Use the chart below as a guide to describing and identifying triads by ear. Additional reflective questions that help differentiate chords as you listen are below.

- Would you end a song with this chord?
- Does the chord need resolution? If so, does it want to resolve up or down?

Triad	Intervals	Descriptors	Energy
Major	m3 / M3	open sunny happy bright looking up	stable low energy
Minor	M3 / m3	closed dark sad looking down	stable low energy
Diminished	m3 / m3	tense collapsing dramatic "train tracks"	unstable high energy
Augmented	M3 / M3	leaning opening expanding "question mark"	unstable medium-high energy

 **Melodic Playback**

Hearing and playing back melodies is an essential skill for the contemporary musician. The goal of these exercises is to increase your mind's capacity for memorizing and recalling different aspects of the music you hear while gaining more facility and comfort at the keyboard. Core musicianship skills like this are meant to increase the speed and efficiency of your workflow.

Guidelines:

Hear the riff/melody in its entirety multiple times before attempting to play.

You must attempt to develop an accurate version of the melody in your "mind's ear" before attempting to play. This version is what you can "hear" in your head. This ends up being the version you use to recreate the melody on a keyboard. If the version in your head is fuzzy or inaccurate, your attempt at playing it will be, as well.

Don't try to play more than you can remember.

This just wastes time. Allow your capacity to remember more to develop over time. In addition, allow multiple hearings to strengthen the version you can hear in your head.

Focus on direction and intervals/scale degrees.

All melodies are made of the same building blocks — intervals. Hearing intervals is key to knowing where you made mistakes. Hearing the overall shape of a melody is key to being able to remember larger passages.

Make aggressive mistakes. (Wrong and Strong)

The worst way to approach these exercises is by guessing your way through each note. Be purposeful in what notes you choose and make a concerted effort to figure out why you made a mistake. You'll notice examples getting much easier when you own your mistakes and go at each exercise without timidness.

Use the exercises on the next page to practice playing back melodies using the principles above.

Unit One Melodies for Playback   INSTRUCTOR PAGE

Guidelines for drilling playback:
1. Give the hand position (but not major/minor) of the example along with playing the tonic chord.
2. Count in one measure before playing.

ADVANCED TOPICS I:
HOW THE PROS PRACTICE

"Practice isn't the thing you do once you're good. It's the thing you do that makes you good." — Malcolm Gladwell

Practicing is a skill, and it needs planning and reflection. The musicians that make the most progress are rarely the ones who have the most talent; it's the ones who have found out how to practice with strategy and purpose. With however much time you have, practice can be revelatory, especially with the right mindset. It can also be difficult without guiding principles and tools to fall back on when troubleshooting is needed. There are a myriad of resources on practicing, workflow, routines, and habits. Great practice can look different from session to session and especially musician to musician, but there are still elements they all share. While this advanced topic will not be an exhaustive conversation on practice and skill development, it shares practical principles for getting the most out of your practice.

Planning

For any skill you want to improve, practice is needed to get there. And how you strategize, plan, and structure your practice has a significant effect on your success. So where do we start? **We start with what we can control, and we acknowledge the things out of our control.** We should be attempting to optimize our productivity through the structure and environment of our practice. Let's start with curating your environment.

An ill-equipped practice space can undermine everything you are attempting to accomplish. What tools (that you're aware of) enable efficient practice for you? Do you enjoy the comfort of pencil and paper, or do you embrace all things digital? Make a list of essentials for yourself, and don't leave out the obvious. The following page has a sample list of essentials.

My Essential Practice Tools:

_____

_____

_____

_____

_____

_____

My Practice Essentials:

- Pencil, highlighters, and Post-its
- bottle of water
- timer/clock
- metronome
- music score(s)
- as much quiet and privacy as possible
- copy of practice record/plan
- acoustic piano/keyboard with weighted keys
- adequate lighting and comfortable temperature

Structure and Workflow

With all your best practice tools assembled, let's get into the structure and workflow of practice. Good practice coordinates your goals with your learning preferences. Parts of your practice sessions will function differently—both how an activity helps you improve and how much mental effort it requires. In his book *The Musician's Way*, Gerald Klickstein shares five practice zones, or modes that help musicians feel less overwhelmed by what to do during practice.

The Five Practice Zones
- New Material
- Developing Material
- Performance Material
- Technique
- Musicianship

When starting a new piece, you are immediately thrust into the *new material* zone. You absorb basic music material, get an overview of a song/work, divide it into sections, and attempt hands separate and/or slow practice. In *developing material*, your focus can shift from basics to more expressive elements like interpretation, tempo, and potentially memorization. When the piece reaches its initial level of maturity – interpretation is solid and tempo at its peak—you enter *performance material*. This practice shifts from digesting new material to maintaining interpretative and technical skills, practicing performing, and maintaining memory.

Repertoire alone is insufficient for upgrading skills. In the *technique zone*, you drill scales, arpeggios, chord progressions, études, etc. to build facility and technical ease. In the *musicianship zone*, typical activities include sight-reading, structured improvisation, eurhythmics, singing (if not your primary instrument), and aural skills work.

These zones are also used to ensure well-rounded practice. All five zones are needed for sustainable progress. As you keep a practice journal, mark what kind of zones you used for a particular piece, exercise, or assignment. Ideally, each practice session includes all five zones.

While the zones may help you guide your practice from a zoomed-out lens, the ideas below help you navigate the work inside the zones.

Meet Yourself Where You Are

Music practice (and any skill acquisition) has an inherent tension between where you are (the skills you have in your current state) and where you want to be (your vision of what improving those skills sounds and feels like). Navigating that tension can often result in frustration if progress is not made the way you expected. In those instances, YOU should not be the subject of your criticism though, your structure, workflow, and activities should be. Refrain from judging, critiquing, or criticizing yourself for not being where you want to be. Meet yourself exactly as you are and acknowledge the discrepancies in your practicing that could cause less-than-ideal progress.

Mindful Repetition

Skill acquisition always involves drilling and plenty of repetition. However, the brain automatically tries to take repeated activities and turn them into mindless routines. Good practice is never mindless. Maintain your focus on specific elements of the current activity. If you're having trouble maintaining focus, take a break or plan on coming back to the session so you don't end up drilling something carelessly or incorrectly. It takes more effort to fix a bad habit or something learned incorrectly than it takes to learn it correctly the first time.

Personalization and Variety

No one person call tell you exactly how to practice. You must take ownership over what, where, when, and how you practice. Over time, you'll notice your practice activities evolving to become more personalized for your needs and learning preferences. Lean into this personalization now. Nobody should practice like you because they aren't you. Try variations of exercises or make up your own. You will learn quickly what works and what doesn't, which in turn, improves your practice skills.

The worksheet on the following page is a template you can use for planning and reflection.

Additional Resources:

Noa Kageyama, performance psychologist: www.bulletproofmusicianship.com

The Musician's Way by Gerald Klickstein: www.themusiciansway.com

The Perfect Wrong Note: Learning to Trust Your Musical Self by William Westney

PRACTICE STRATEGY WORKSHEET

Date:　　　　　　　Duration:

BEFORE

What I need to focus on during this practice:

What strategies will help me make the most progress?

- -

AFTER

What did I make progress on?

What needs more work?

What does my next practice need to look like?

What do I need to ask my instructor?

Progress over perfection. Process over product.

Advanced Topics I

Notes:

Unit Two

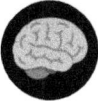     

- ❏ **Building Major and Minor Scales**
- ❏ **Practicing Scales: Essential Patterns and Variations**
- ❏ **Scalar Melodies and Basslines**
- ❏ **Music for Reading**
- ❏ **Lead Sheet Reading**
- ❏ **Rhythm Training**
- ❏ **Diatonic Triads and Nashville Numbers**
- ❏ **Chord Charts**
- ❏ **Chord Functions and Harmonization**
- ❏ **Reharmonization Using Simple Substitution**
- ❏ **Unit Two Diatonic Triads Playback**
- ❏ **Unit Two Melodies for Playback**

Notes:

Building Major and Minor Scales

At its most fundamental, a scale is a pattern of intervals that divides the octave. That means there are thousands (if not millions) of possible scales. However, most music you will hear and play uses only a handful. This text focuses on the major and minor scales along with their respective modes, giving you the ability to build, play, and create with fluency.

The Major Scale

The major scale is an extension of the major five-finger pattern discussed in Unit 1. As a review, the major five-finger pattern uses the intervallic pattern of half and whole steps below:

Tonic (first note) – Whole Step (W) – Whole Step – Half Step (H) – Whole Step

A major scale uses the same intervallic pattern with an additional three intervals:

*Tonic – Whole – Whole – Half – Whole – **Whole – Whole – Half***

The C Major Scale

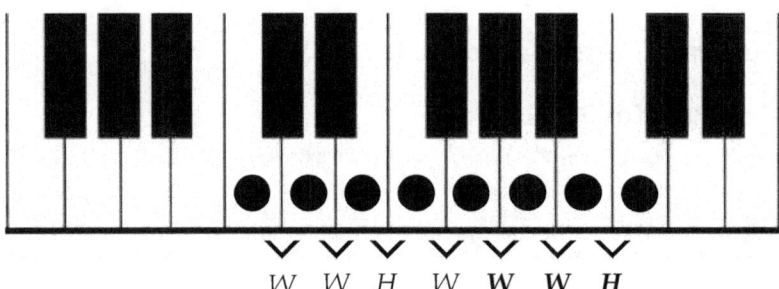

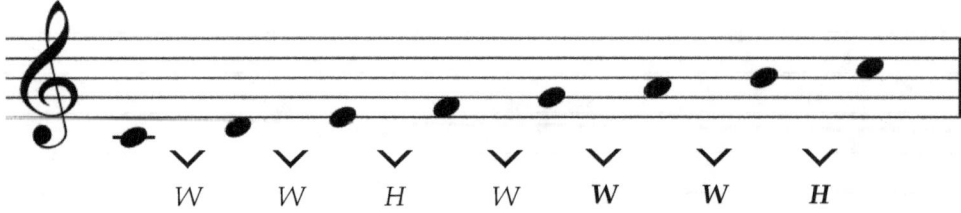

The Minor Scale

An easy way to convert a major scale into its corresponding minor scale involves lowering the 3rd, 6th, and 7th notes by a half step. This new set of notes will give you the **parallel natural minor**, or the minor key with the same tonic note as the major. This also results in a different combination of half steps and whole steps:

*Tonic – Whole – Whole – Half – Whole – **Whole – Whole – Half***

Parallel Natural Minor Formula:

$$1 - 2 - {}^\flat 3 - 4 - 5 - {}^\flat 6 - {}^\flat 7 - 1$$

An important note: the flat signs in the formulas throughout this text indicate a note should be lowered a half step. They do not mean that the change will result in a note needing a flat sign. For example, an F-sharp lowered a half step results in an F, not an F-flat.

The C Minor Scale

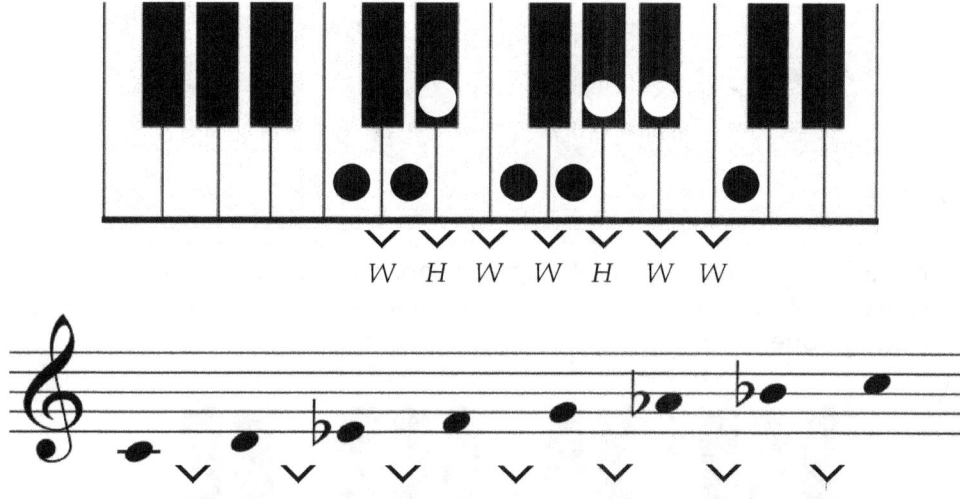

> ### Why do we need to learn scales?
> This is a common and important question. One of the keys to understanding music on a deeper level is being able to identifying patterns; music is filled with them. Understanding and internalizing scales is a foundational step to being able to understand other musical building blocks like chords and melodies.

FAQs

Unit 2   39

Building Minor Scale Alterations

The minor scale is divided into two primary alterations: harmonic and melodic. They serve different purposes in different scenarios. The examples below demonstrate these two alterations based on the C natural minor scale.

Harmonic Minor

The harmonic minor scale raises the seventh degree in order to have only a half step separate the 7th and 1st scale degrees. This creates a **leading tone** that provides essential tonal structure to a scale clarifying what note is tonic.

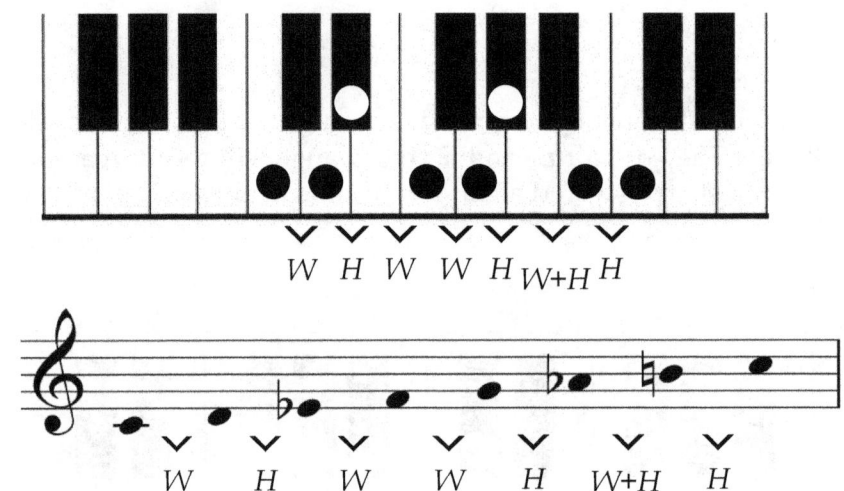

Melodic Minor

In order to avoid having the 6th and 7th degrees separated by three half steps, the melodic minor scale raises the 6th *and* 7th degrees. This creates a smoother-sounding scale while also keeping the leading tone.

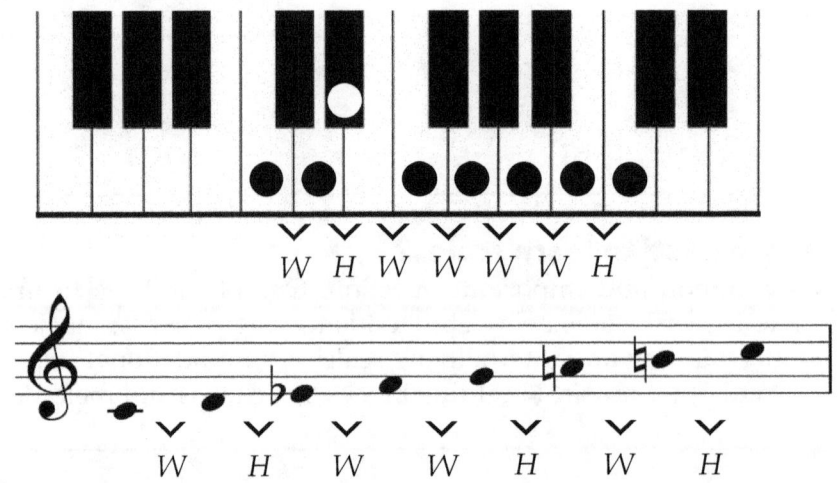

The Foundations of Scale Practice

Two gestures form the foundation for playing scales: the thumb under and the 3rd/4th finger crossing over. Use the exercises below to get more comfortable moving the thumb under the hand and crossing fingers over.

3 - 1 and 1 - 3

4 - 1 and 1 - 4

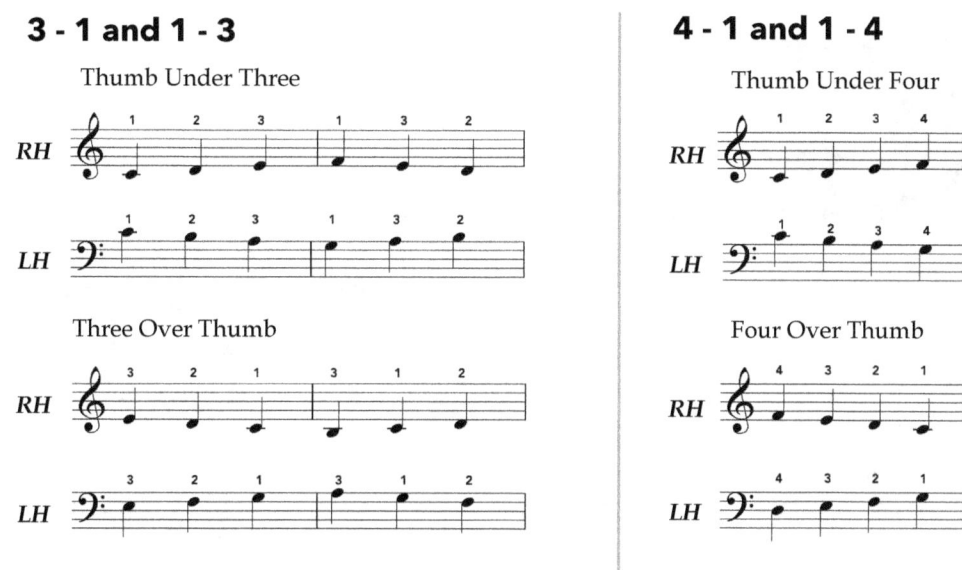

Practice Hack

To build new skills as quickly as possible, professionals will often practice in groups, or chunks, based on the gestures required for an exercise or passage of music. Since scales are primarily two gestures, the exercises below show you how to chunk scale preparation exercises so you can learn fingering and coordination quickly.

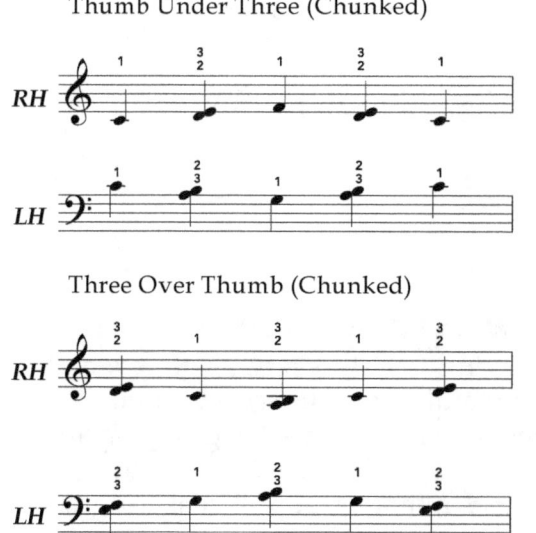

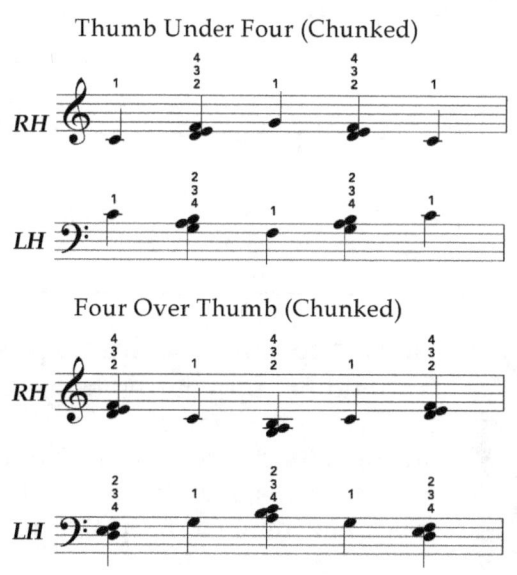

Scale Groupings

Scales are grouped together based on the fingering used to play them most efficiently. Groups 1 and 2 contain all scales that start on a white key. The keys of C, G, D, A, and E have the same fingering patterns while the keys of F and B are slightly different. Group 3 keys will be introduced in Unit 4.

Group 1	C, G, D, A, and E
Group 2	F and B
Group 3	B♭, E♭, A♭, D♭(C#), and G♭(F#)

C Major

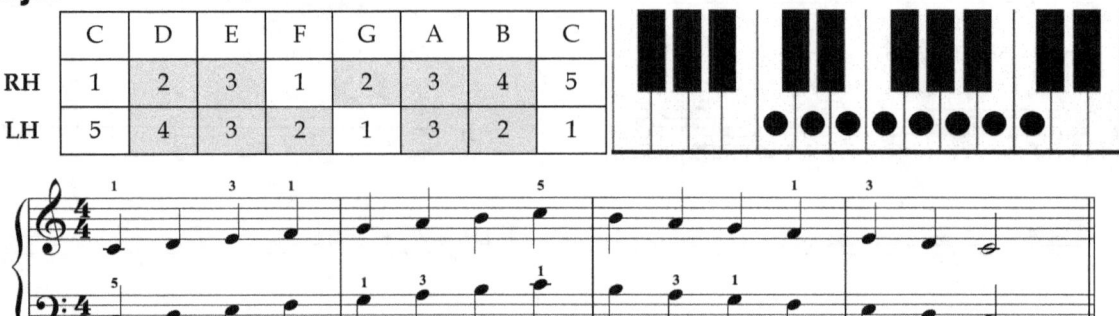

C Minor

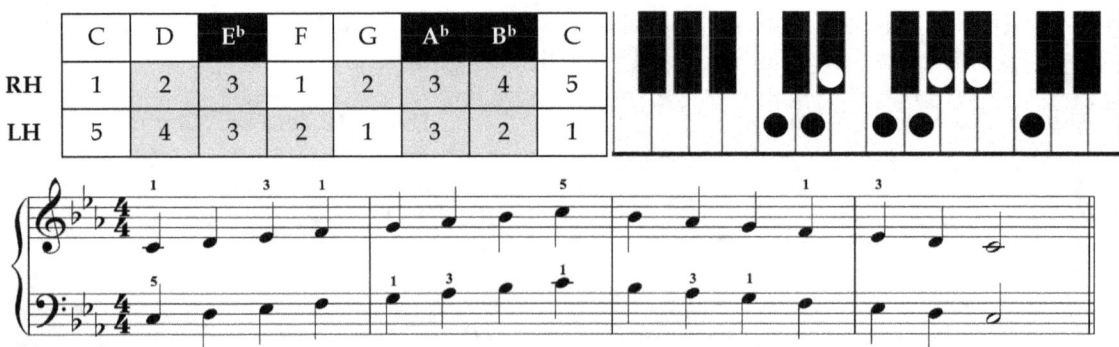

FAQs

There's so many scales to practice. How do I practice all of them?
It would eat up your entire practice time trying to drill every single scale. A good way to organize your scale practice is to think about the scale groupings at the top of this page. For daily practice, choose one note from each grouping and practice its major and minor scales. For example, G major and minor (group 1), B major and minor (group 2), and E♭ major and minor (group 3) make a great combination.

G Major

G Minor

D Major

D Minor

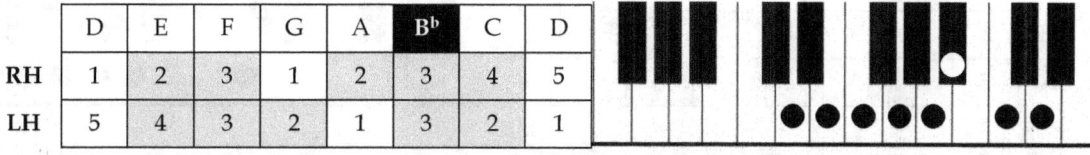

A Major

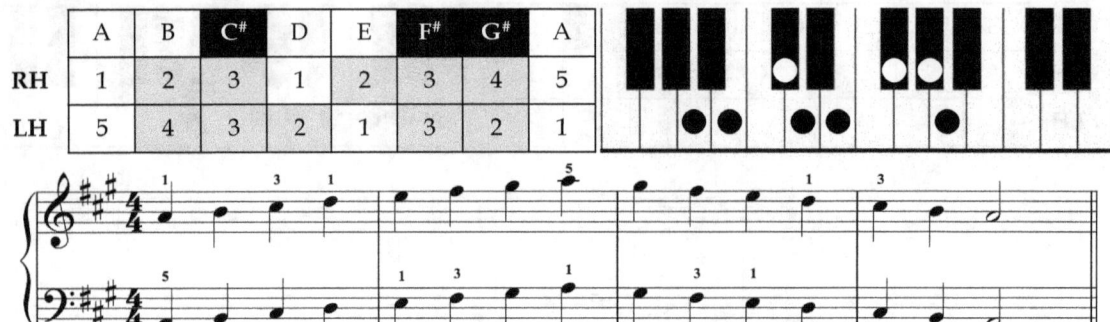

A Minor

E Major

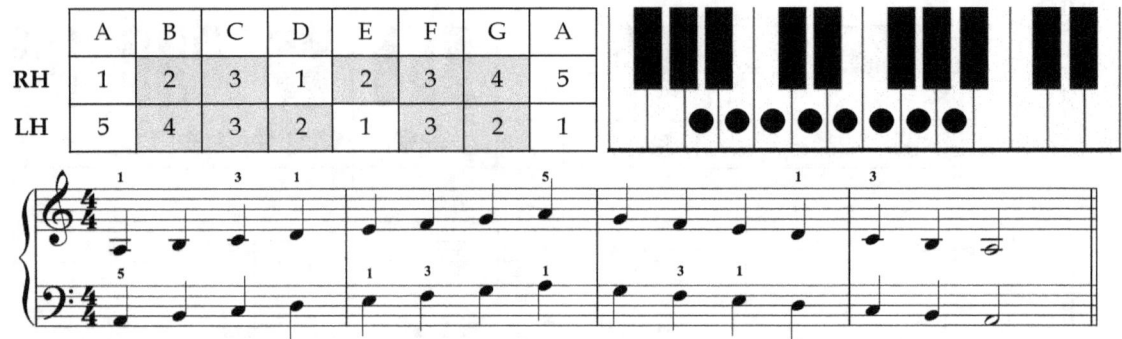

E Minor

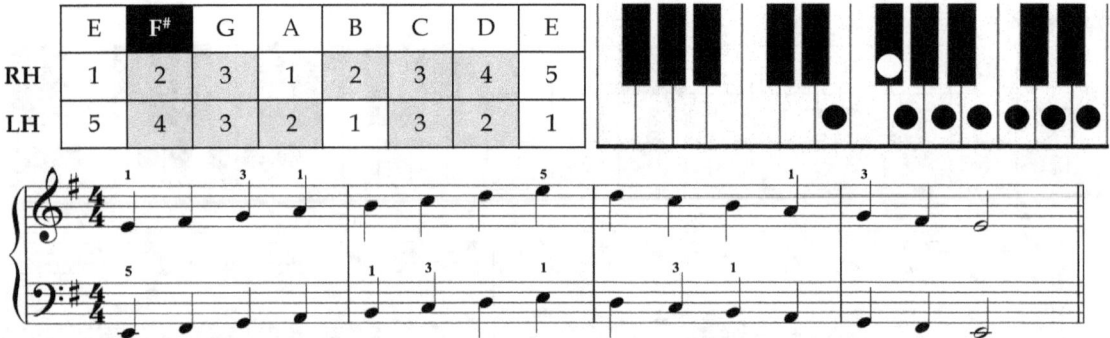

B Major

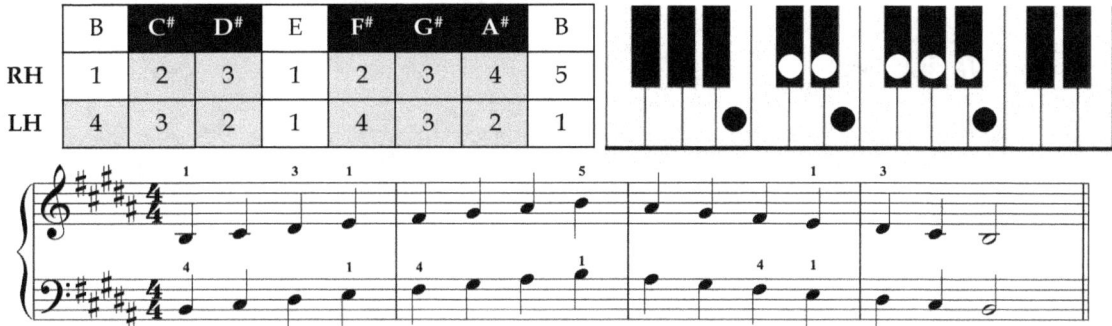

B Minor

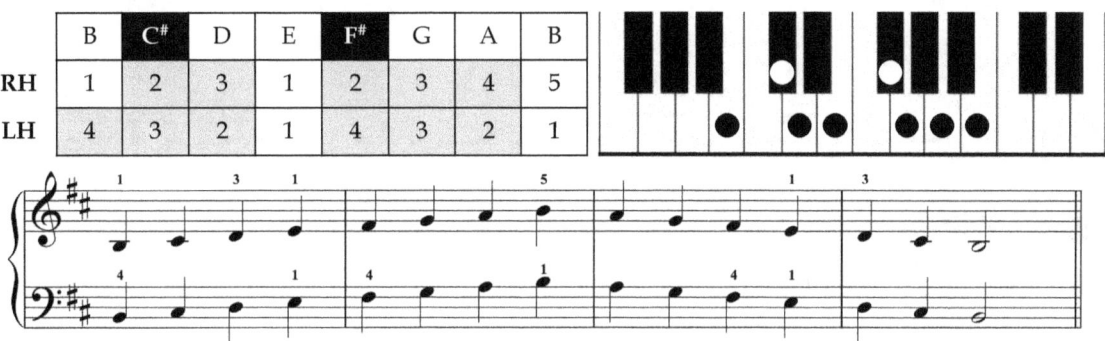

F Major

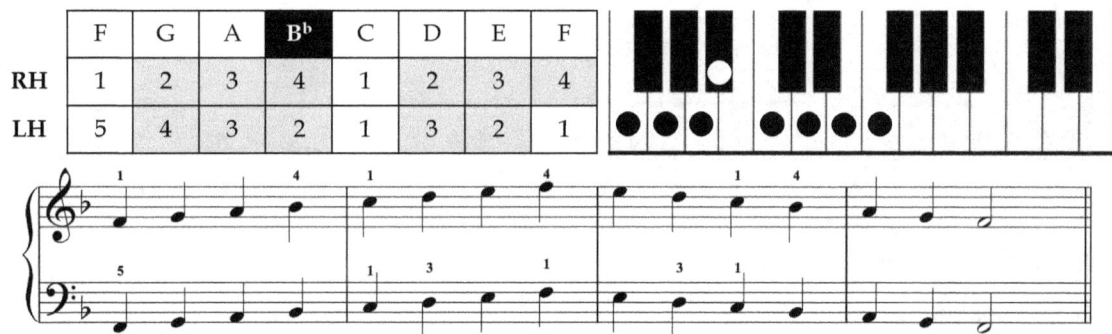

F Minor

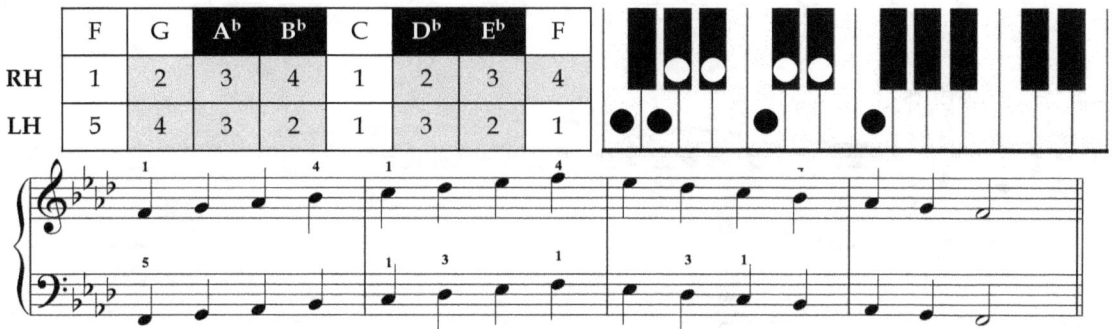

Practicing Scales: Essential Patterns and Variations

Rhythmic Variations

1a. 1b.

2a. 2b.

3a. 3b.

4a. 4b.

Melodic Patterns

Add-one-note Sequence

Articulation Patterns

Strong-beat Accents

Offbeat Accents

Accents in Groups of 3

Scalar Melodies and Basslines

As you study and play the single-hand melodies and bass lines below, focus on the thumb-under and 3-over gestures. These excerpts are designed to be played hands separately. Listen for evenness of tone and rhythm.

For each example:
1. Identify the major or minor scale pattern being used.
2. Scan the example for rhythms and intervals.
3. Practice with a steady pulse.
4. Transpose to another Group 1 or Group 2 key.

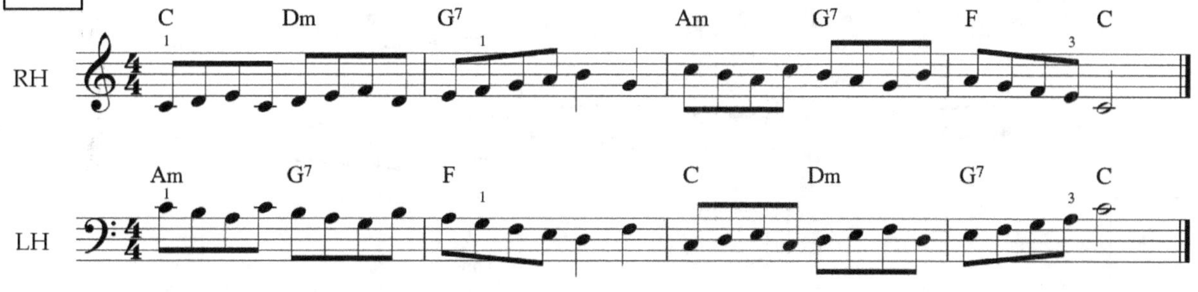

Music for Reading

How to practice each example:
- Identify the starting hand position in each hand.
- Scan the example for intervals, articulation, and dynamics.
- Play with a steady pulse.
- Identify smaller sections that need repetitive practice.

1

2

> **PRO TIP** — A successful music reader (on any instrument) prioritizes rhythm and pulse over notes.

Unit 2

TIP: Before playing #3 as written, practice chunking each measure (i.e., playing all the notes of the measure at once). Notice what chord(s) each hand plays when moving to a new measure.

TIP: Before playing #4 as written, practice tapping the rhythm for the RH and feeling each measure in one or two big beats.

Lead Sheet Reading

Practice the following lead sheets with the RH playing the notated melody and the LH playing the chord symbols. Before diving in with both hands, make sure you can do the following:
1. Find and play the given chords with the LH in the "Golden Chord Area."
2. Play the RH melody by itself without breaking the pulse. (Write in fingerings if needed.)

Quick Tip: SLASH CHORDS

In the example below, you will see one chord spelled in a new way—with a slash followed by another letter name (D/A). This kind of chord notation is called a slash chord. It gives musicians a little more information on how to interpret a chord symbol. The first letter is the primary chord that should be played. The letter name *after* the slash indicates what note should be the lowest note, or bass note.

EXAMPLE:

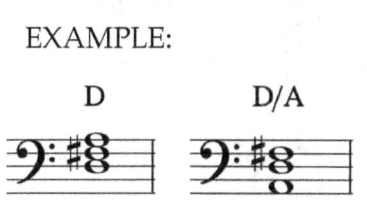

Unit Two Rhythm Training

Part One: Micro Beats

The following rhythm drills prepare you to play simple and repetitive beat patterns for performance or production. Instruments are notated so that you can use drum pads or a percussion patch on a keyboard. Focus on the overall feel of these patterns and your relationship to the pulse. **Don't let mistakes derail the groove.**

The patterns for Unit 2 are notated in three parts: kick drum, snare, and high hat. However, feel free to replace those parts with other sounds that still function as low, mid, and high.

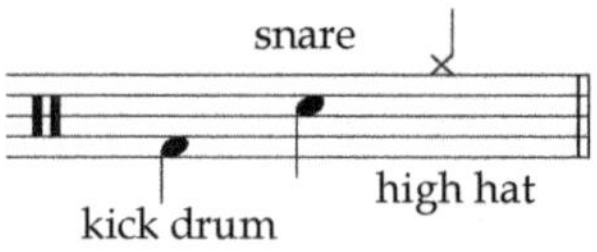

Practice at a variety of tempos.
(♩ = 56–140)

1

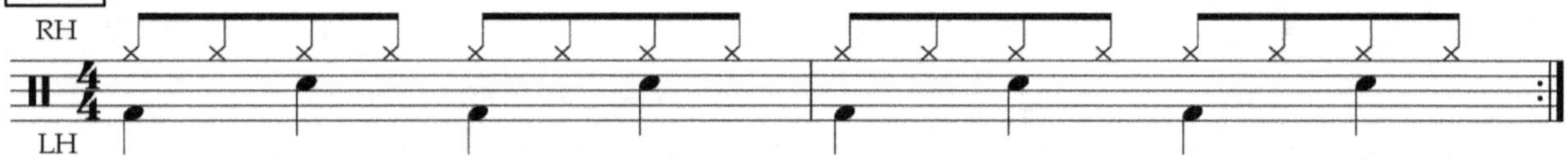

2

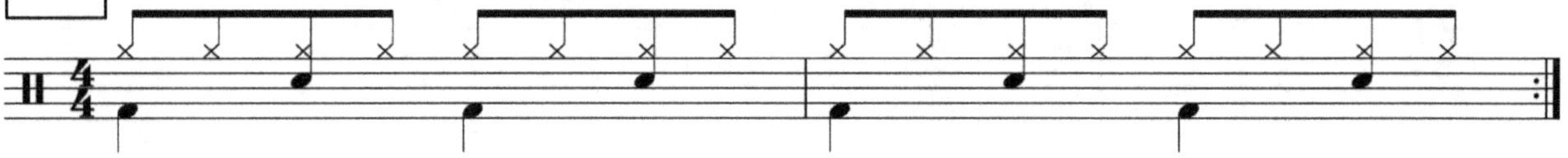

3

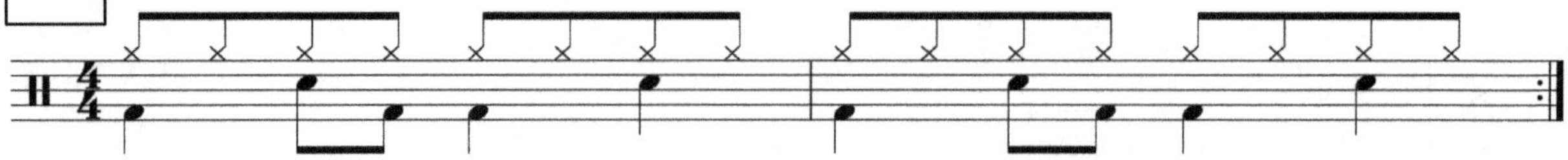

4

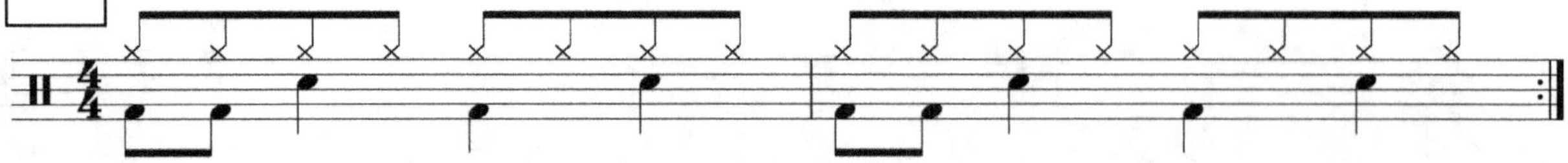

Add kick drum and snare parts to the high-hat patterns below. Use a combination of quarter and 8th notes/rests.

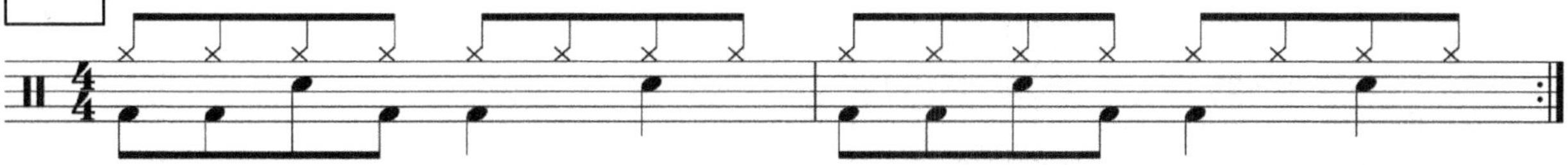

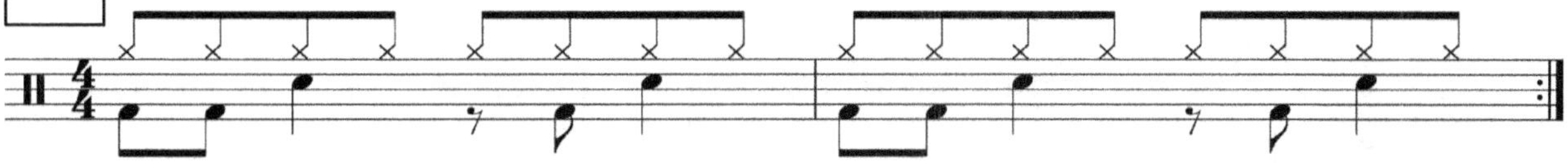

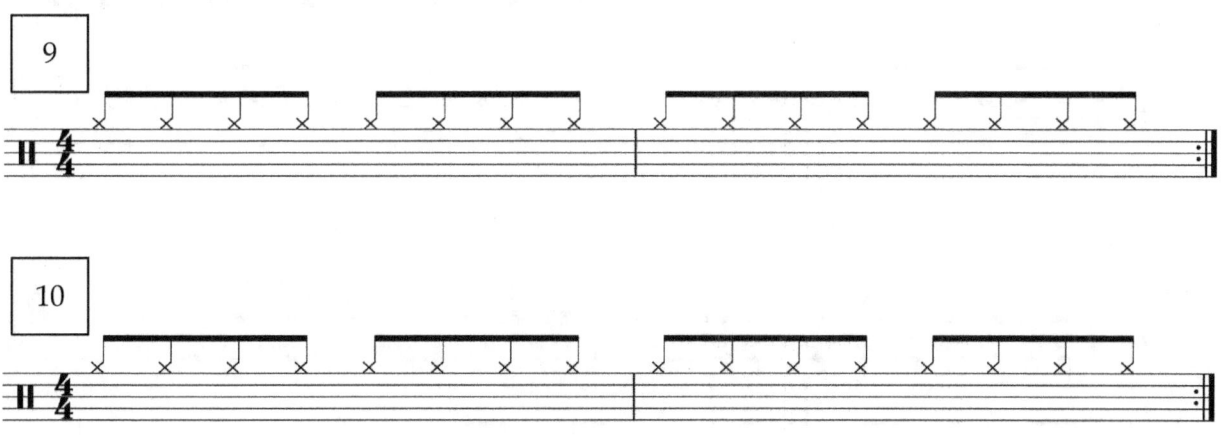

Unit 2 55

Part Two: Rhythm Reading

For all rhythm reading exercises:
1. Your primary is goal is fluency, not perfection.
2. Prioritize the pulse.
3. Don't stop.

Practice at a variety of tempos.

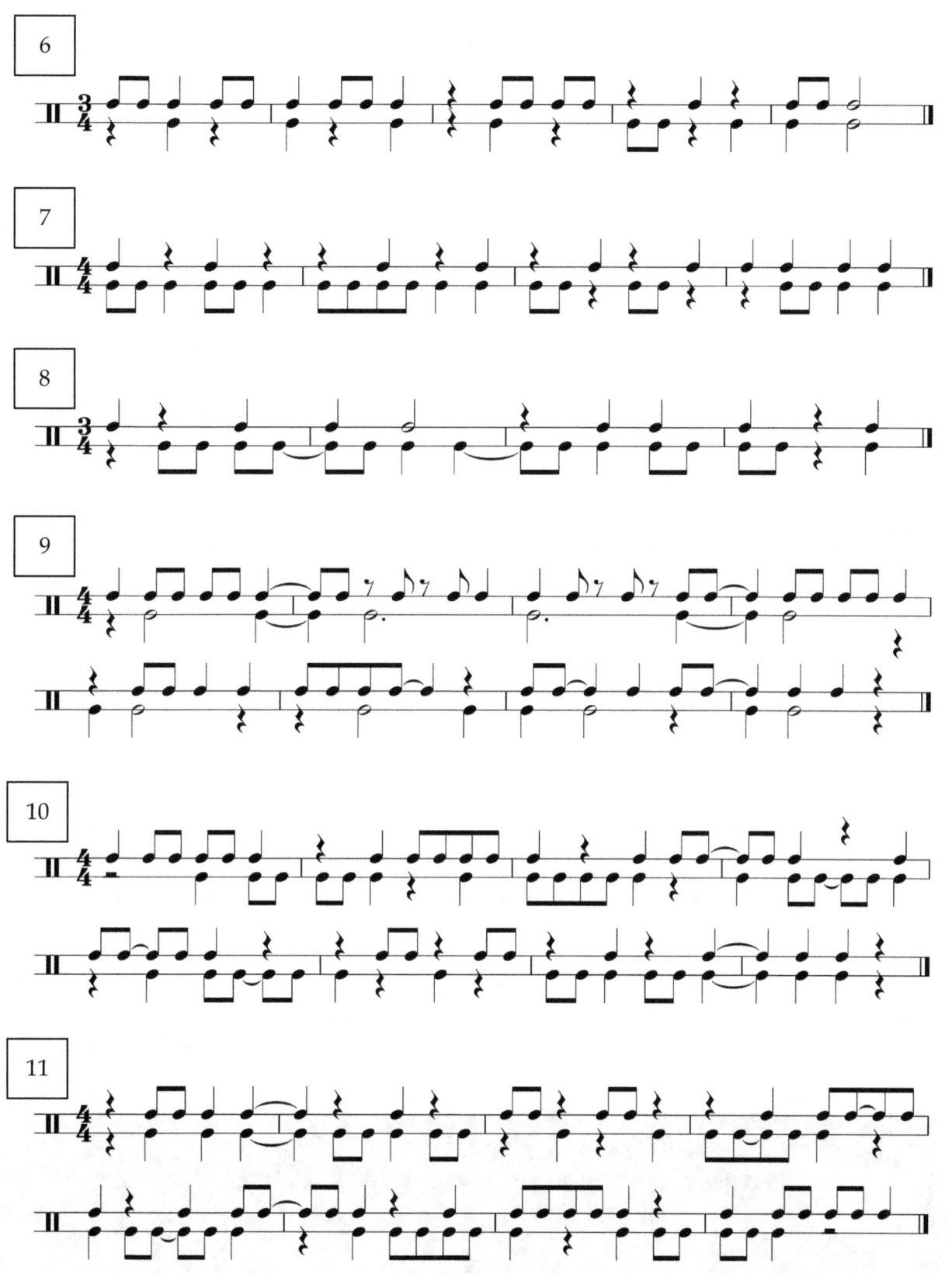

Unit 2

Rhythm Ensemble

> **Practice Variations and Challenges:**
> 1. For individual work, practice different two-part combinations.
> 2. For paired or group work, assign alternating measures.

Diatonic Triads and Nashville Numbers

The word **diatonic** means a group of notes that are associated with a given key. For example, notes that are diatonic within the key of G Major are all the notes of that scale (i.e., *g – a – b – c – d – e – f#*). The "opposite" of diatonic would be **chromatic** — notes that are *not* associated with a given key.

Building chords based on each note of a scale results in **diatonic triads**. A third and fifth is added to each note of the scale making sure to use notes found only in the given key. (As a reminder, all triads use the interval of a 3rd as their building block.)

When you stack thirds on top of each note of the scale, you'll get all seven diatonic triads. The quality of each diatonic triad is the same for each scale degree in every major key.

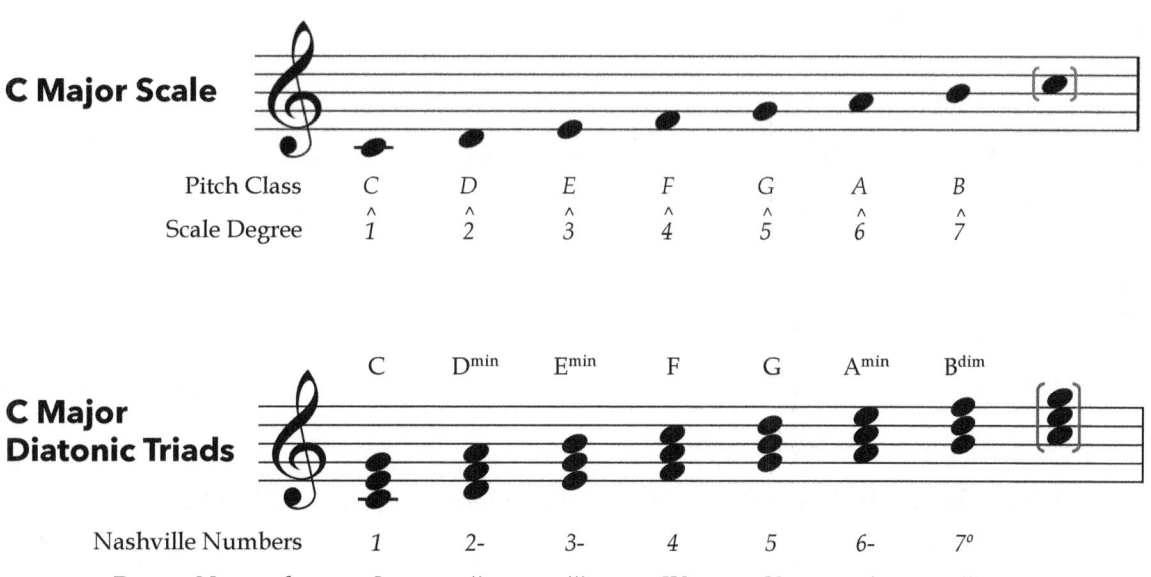

Nashville Numbers

The Nashville Number System (NNS) is a method of analyzing and performing music that uses numbers to represent chords based on their scale degree rather than their chord name. Nashville numbers will always refer to a scale degree for a major scale. When a flat or sharp is preceding a scale degree, that indicates the lowering or raising of the scale degree by a half step. It does not necessarily mean the note will have a sharp or flat. The remainder of the text incorporates Nashville numbers into its exercises so you can start to identify harmonic patterns and practice transposing songs into different keys.

Diatonic Triads and Nashville Number Exercises

PART ONE: Find and play each chord.

1	2- in the key of F	6	3- in the key of F	11	2- in the key of B
2	5 in the key of D	7	4 in the key of A	12	5 in the key of G
3	3- in the key of G	8	5 in the key of B	13	7° in the key of F
4	6- in the key of E	9	2- in the key of D	14	2- in the key of E
5	7° in the key of C	10	2- in the key of E	15	6- in the key of D

PART TWO: Play each chord progression and convert to Nashville Numbers.

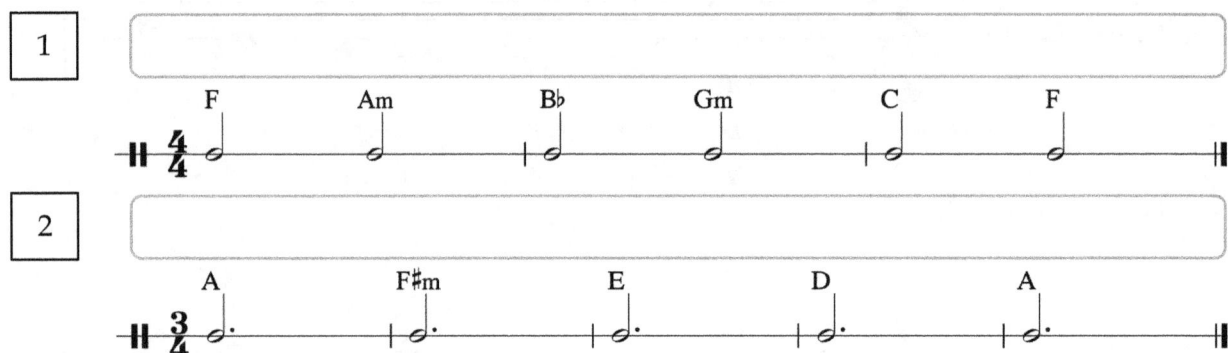

PART THREE: Play each chord progression and convert to Nashville Numbers.

Unit 2

 **Chord Charts**

The following charts are examples of common chord progressions in various styles. Play chord tones in the RH and root/bass notes in the LH using the notated accompaniment patterns as a guide.

1 You can hear a chord progression like exercise 1 in the song "Love Like This" as performed by Ben Rector.

KEY: D   Pop Ballad ($\rule{0pt}{0pt}$ = 70)

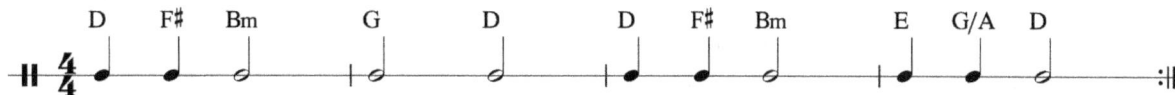

Blocked Chord Accompaniment Pattern:

2 You can hear a chord progression like exercise 2 in the song "Get Lucky" as performed by Daft Punk.

KEY: A   Dance Pop ($\rule{0pt}{0pt}$ = 85)

Accompaniment Pattern(s):

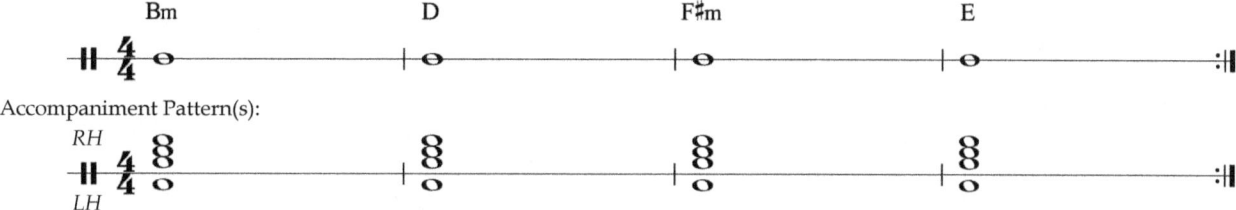

3 You can hear a chord progression like exercise 3 in the song "Mr. Blue Sky" as performed by Electric Light Orchestra.

KEY: F   Symphonic Rock ($\rule{0pt}{0pt}$ = 89)

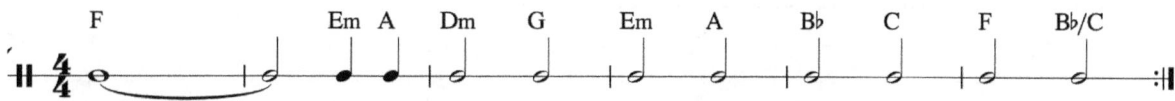

Accompaniment Pattern(s):

Unit 2

4 You can hear a chord progression like exercise 4 in the song "In My Life" as performed by the Beatles.

KEY: A 60s Medium Ballad (♩ = 102)

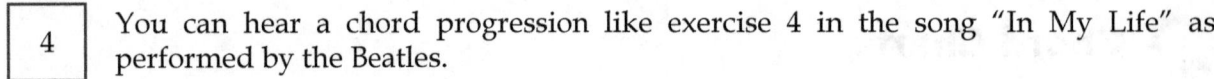

Blocked Chord Accompaniment Pattern:

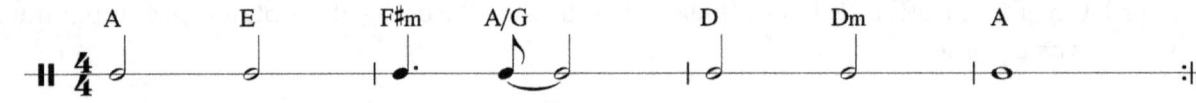

Practice the same exercise in a different key.

4b
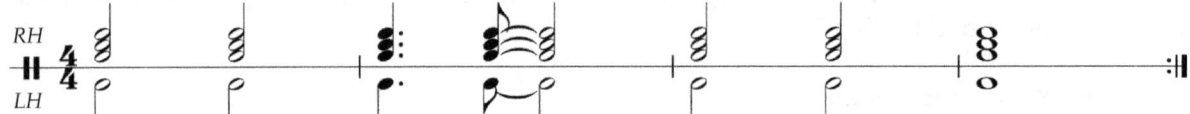

5 You can hear a chord progression like exercise 5 in the song "Edelweiss" from the musical, *The Sound of Music*.

KEY: G Medium Waltz (♩ = 110)

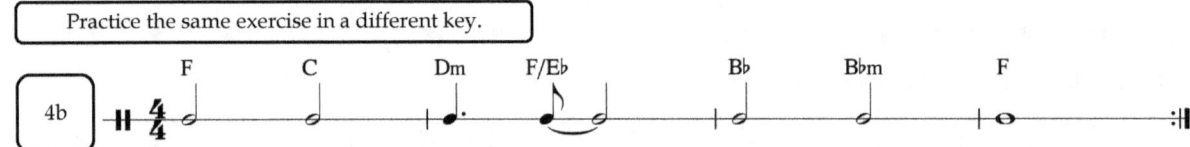

Accompaniment Pattern(s):

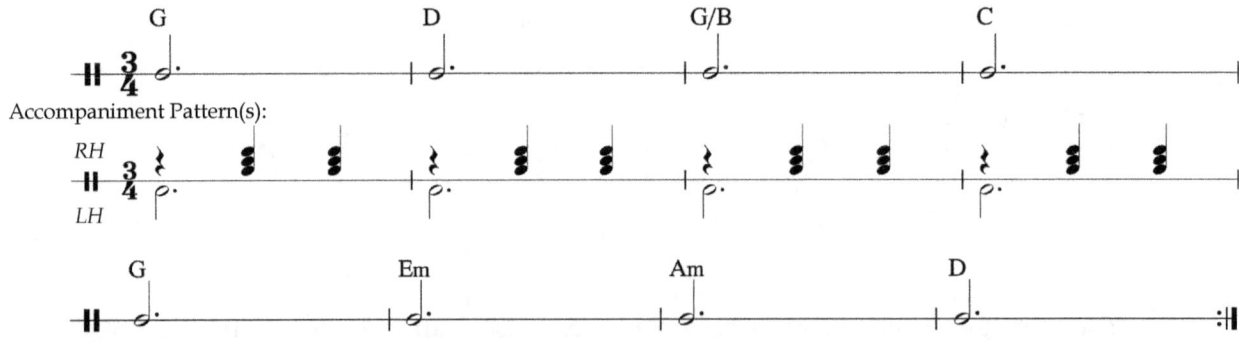

Continue the same accompaniment pattern.

Practice the same exercise in a different key.

5b
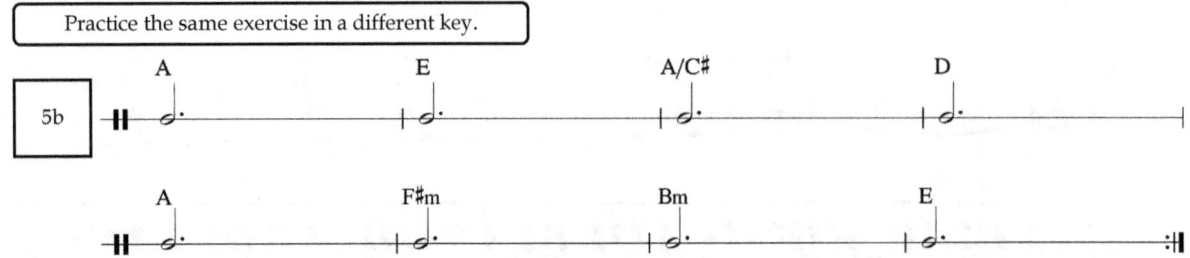

6 You can hear a chord progression like exercise 6 in the song "Chandelier" as performed by Sia.

KEY: D♭   Pop Power Ballad (♩ = 87)

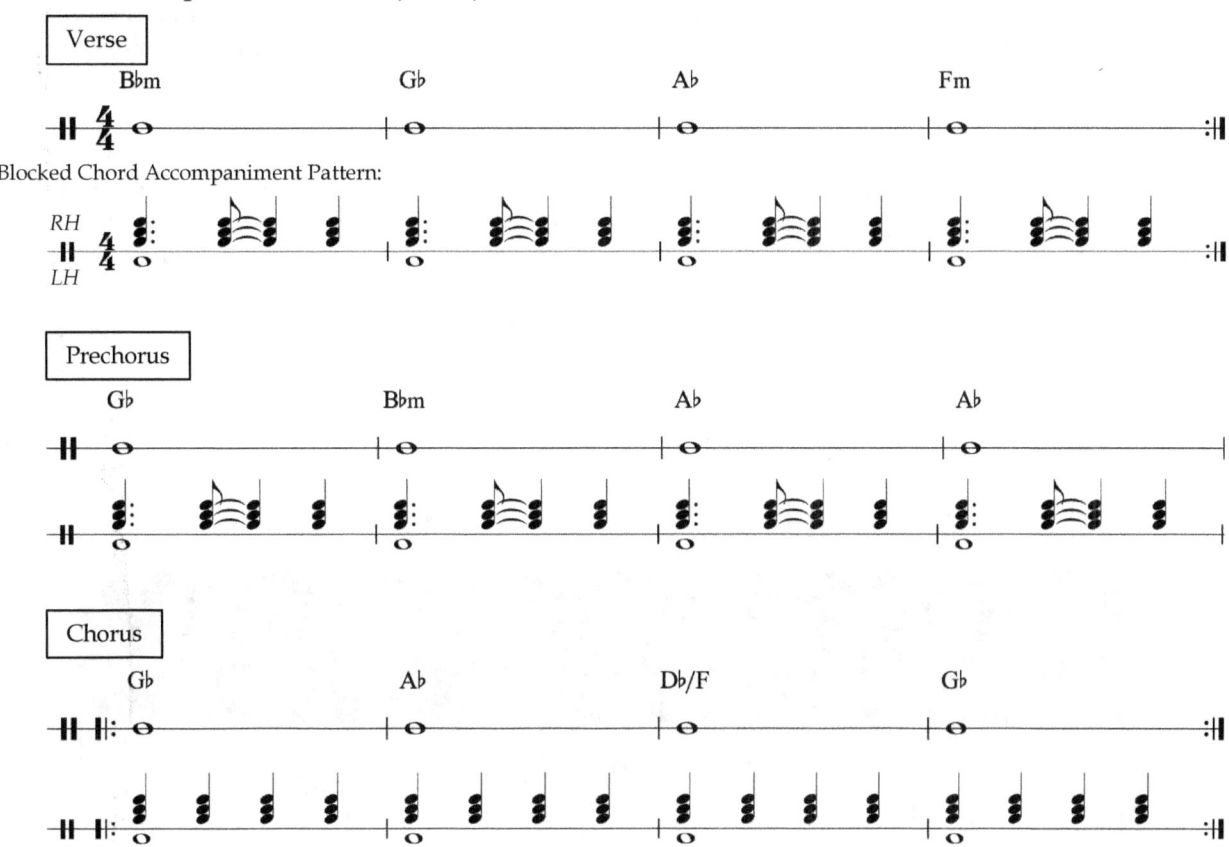

Use the template below to add your own **chord substitutions** in the verse, prechorus, and chorus of this song. To see how your chord choices will sound, practice singing the melody while playing the chord progression. Experiment with lots of different options to find a unique-sounding progression that works with the melody.

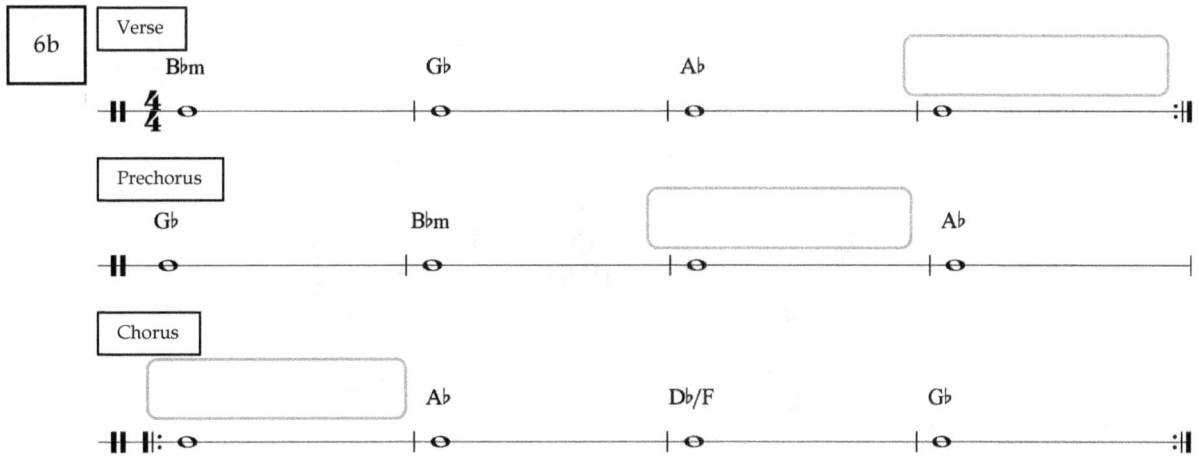

Unit 2   63

Chord Functions and Harmonization

Music is a cyclical pattern of increased and decreased energy, or tension and resolution. Understanding how chords affect energy will help you make thoughtful choices when harmonizing a melody. Chords fall into three basic functions: **tonic** (T), **predominant** (P), and **dominant** (D).

The **tonic** chord and those that behave like it are resolutions or points of rest. They feel like an exhale or release, large or small, in the context of a harmonic progression. **Predominant** chords are bridge chords between tonic and dominant. They are used to build energy to the dominant, and they can also be used to decrease tension more slowly than going directly back to tonic from dominant. **Dominant** chords contain the most energy and feel like they need resolution or release.

For any given set of diatonic triads, we can identify which triads behave in similar ways through the Circle of Thirds chart below. Different chords behave similarly when they share multiple scale degrees.

HARMONIC FUNCTION	TONIC	PREDOMINANT	DOMINANT
COMMON TRAITS	• Points of Rest • Resolutions	• Maintain or slight increase/decrease in energy	• Highest energy • leads to resolution
DIATONIC TRIADS	1, 3-, and 6-	2-, 4, and 6-	5, 7°, and 3-

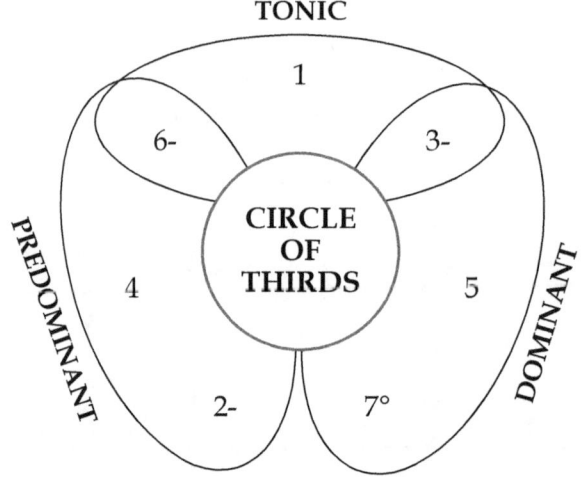

Example Melody:

Key: C Major

As you play and listen to the three harmonizations below, reflect on the following questions.

1. How do the different harmonizations affect how we hear the melody?
2. Which chords support melody notes that are non-chord tones?
3. Where do chords add, suspend, or take away energy? Where are there points of rest?

Example Harmonizations:

Your Harmonization:

Melodies to Harmonize

After playing each melody, identify where tonic (T), predominant (PD), and dominant chords (D) could be placed. Then, harmonize the melody with the appropriate diatonic chords based on the functions you identified.

Example 1:
   Step 1: Identify Functions

| Function | T | PD | D | T | T or PD | D | T |

   Step 2: Add chords to the melody using diatonic triads that correspond to the functions labeled in step 1.

| Chord | C | Dm | G | Am | C | G | C |

| NNS | 1 | 2- | 5 | 6- | 1 | 5 | 1 |

1 Key: A Major

Chord

NNS
Function

2 Key: F Major

Chord

NNS
Function

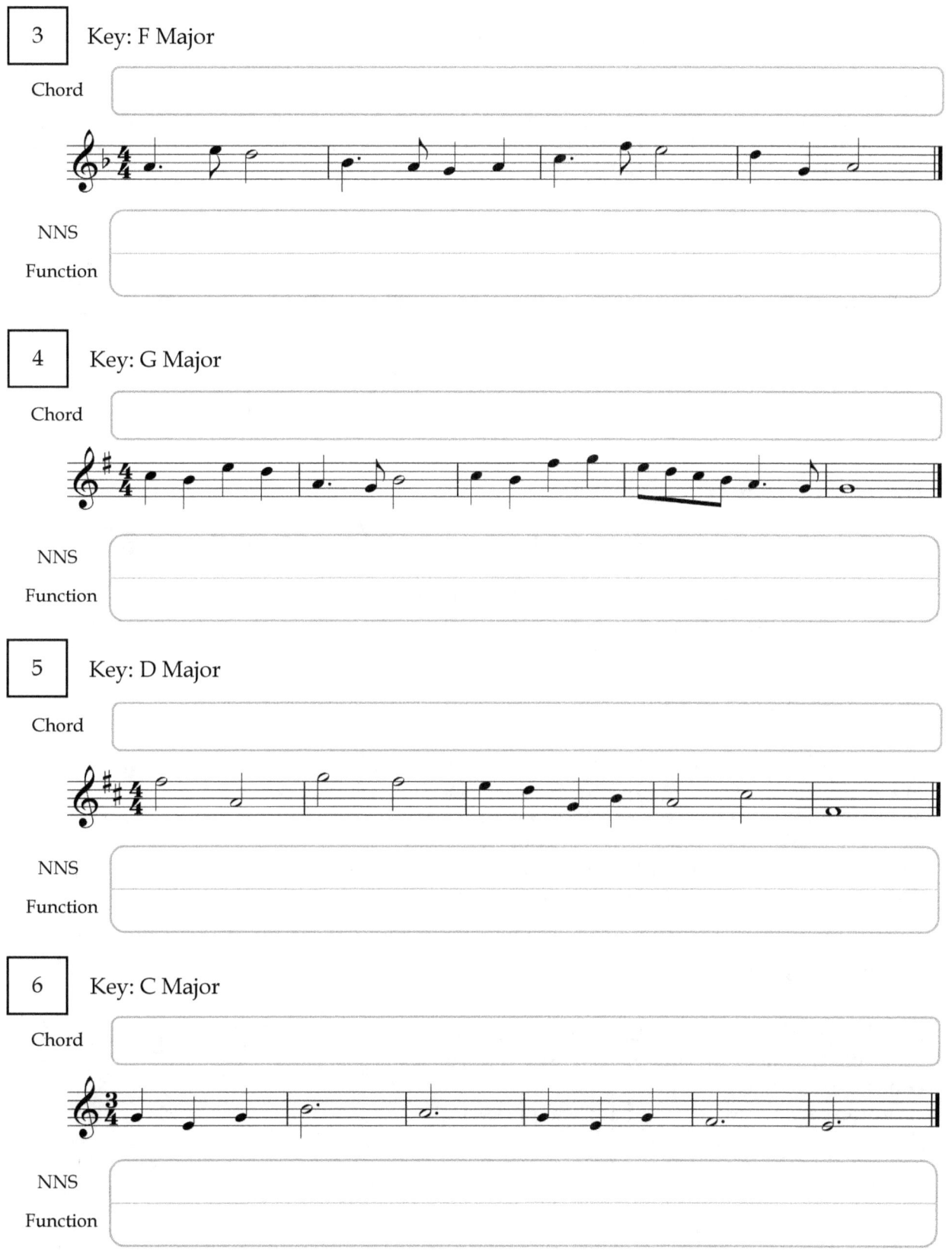

Reharmonization Using Simple Substitution

Harmonization is often described as "coloring a melody." Using simple substitution is like replacing one color with a different shade of the same. The harmonic function of a chord gives it its unique shade or color. With this tool, you are simply substituting a chord for one with a similar harmonic function.

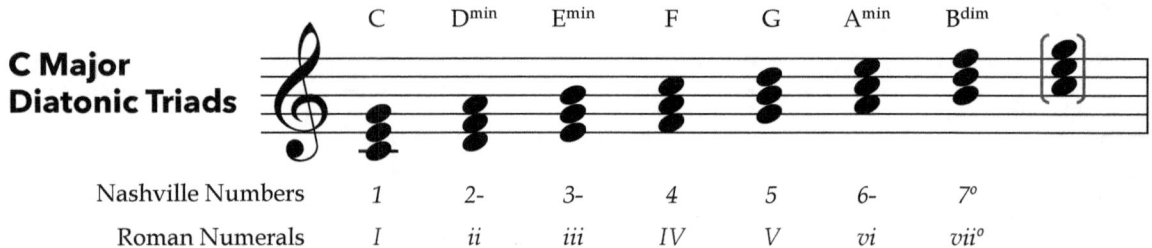

The Tonic Family (T)

Members of the tonic family of chords are stable and usually serve as resolutions or points of rest. Since their forward energy is low, this allows them to be placed at the beginning or ends of phrases.

The Predominant Family (PD)

Members of the predominant family of chords have moderate energy, which allows them to be placed in the middle of phrases especially as a connection between tonic and dominant function chords. Additionally, the 5^{sus} could be included because it does not contain the seventh scale degree.

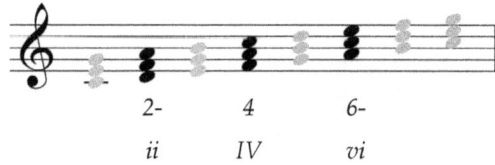

The Dominant Family (D)

Members of the dominant family of chords have a high energy and an unresolved sound. These chords usually appear immediately before tonic chords especially at the end of musical phrases.

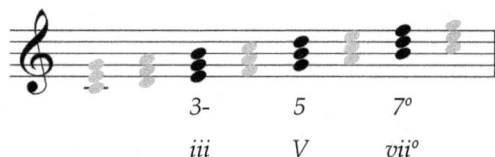

Simple Substitution Example:

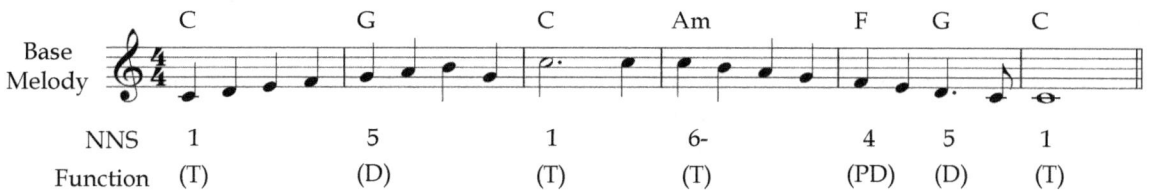

In the variation below, all harmonic functions are kept the same except for measure two. In this measure, the dominant was delayed by two beats using a sus chord.

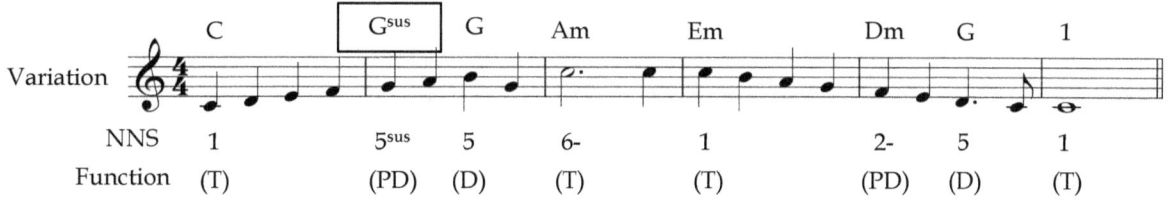

Below are the same melodies found on page 67. Use simple substitution to reharmonize your original chord choices.

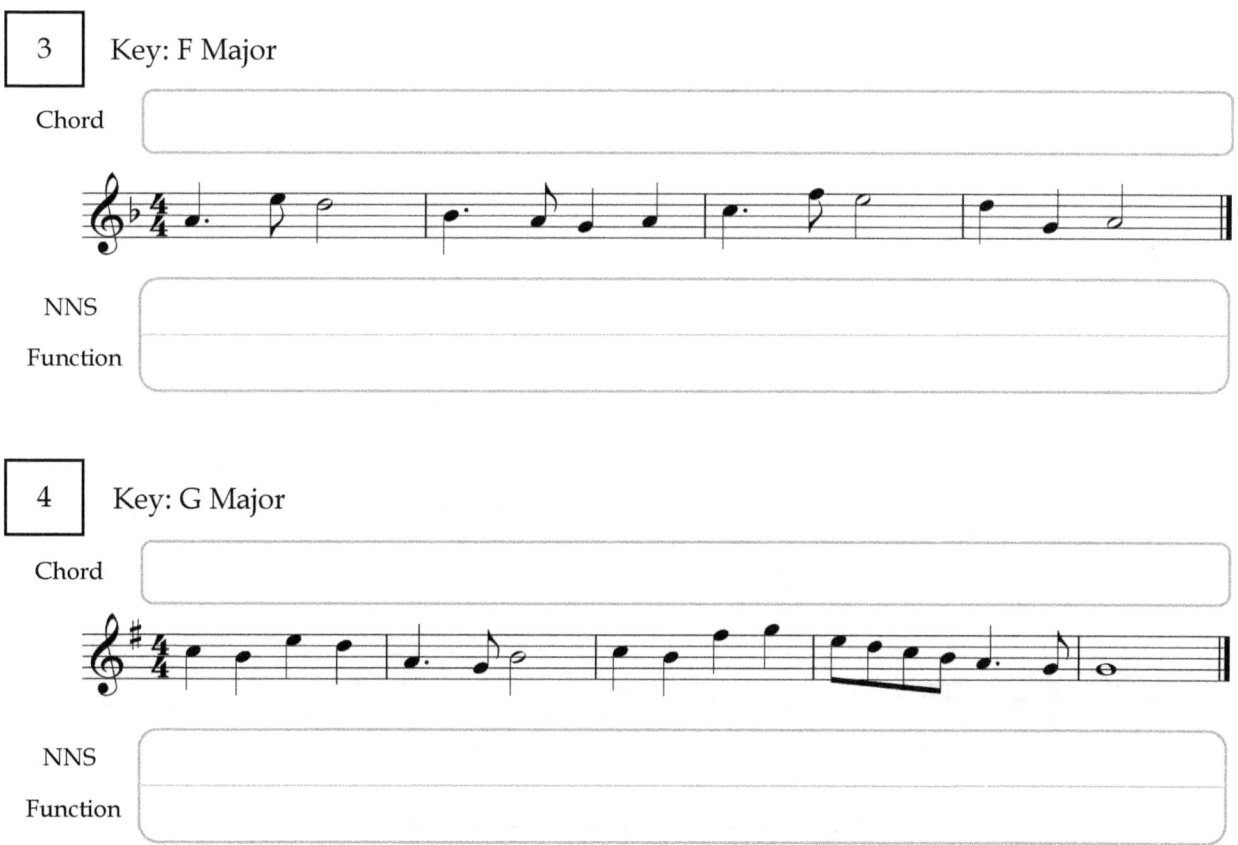

Melodies to Harmonize (and Reharmonize)

Use the activities in this section to create three different harmonizations of the same melody. Each harmonization has a different set of guidelines or area of focus.

Key: A Major

1. Use only diatonic triads in the boxes provided.

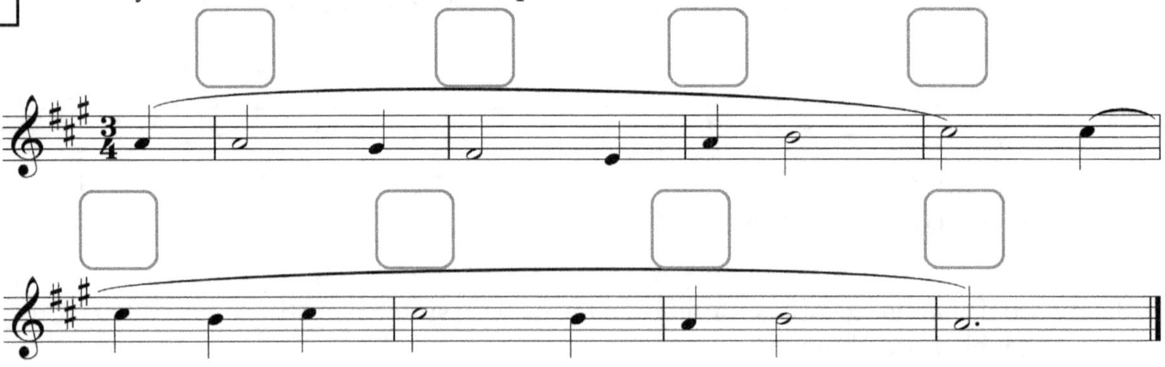

2. Use reharmonization techniques to create a variation of the harmonization in #1. Chords may be diatonic or chromatic.

3. Explore unknown combinations of melody and harmony. Chords may be diatonic or chromatic. (Make it weird. Go wild.)

Key: E Major

| 1 | Use only diatonic triads in the boxes provided. |

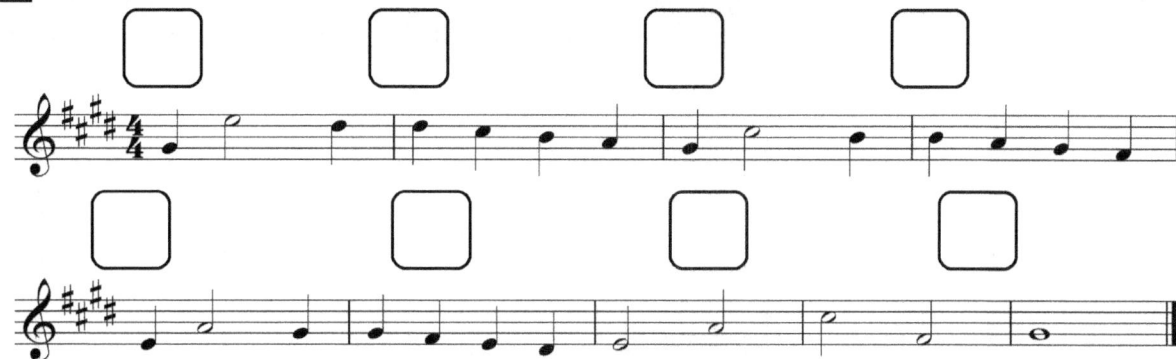

| 2 | Use reharmonization techniques to create a variation of the harmonization in #1. Chords may be diatonic or chromatic. |

| 3 | Explore unknown combinations of melody and harmony. Chords may be diatonic or chromatic. (Make it weird. Go wild.) |

Unit Two Diatonic Triads Playback   INSTRUCTOR PAGE

Guidelines for drilling playback:
1. Play the following chord progression before each set of exercises in different keys.
2. Before playing, students should say the Nashville Number of each chord in the exercise. (EX: "1 – minor 3 – 1")
3. Play all triads in root position and keyboard style.

Unit Two Melodies for Playback   **INSTRUCTOR PAGE**

Guidelines for drilling playback:
1. Give the hand position (but not major/minor) of the example along with playing the tonic chord.
2. Count in one measure before playing.

Notes:

Unit Three

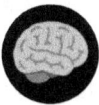     

- ❏ Chord Inversions
- ❏ Expanded Scale Practice (Group 1 and 2)
- ❏ Intro to Keyboard Style
- ❏ Lead Sheets
- ❏ Keyboard Style with Chord Charts
- ❏ Common Chord Progressions with Triads
- ❏ Harmonization with Target Chords and Types of Cadences
- ❏ Unit Three Diatonic Triads Playback
- ❏ Unit Three Melodies for Playback
- ❏ Unit Three Rhythm Training
- ❏ Twinkle Twinkle Challenge
- ❏ Solo Repertoire
- ❏ Composing with Chord Inversions

Notes:

Chord Inversions

Triads (and all chords) can be arranged in different ways called **inversions**. Chord inversions explore using each note of a triad as its lowest note. For example, a C major triad is spelled *C - E - G*. It can be arranged in three different inversions:

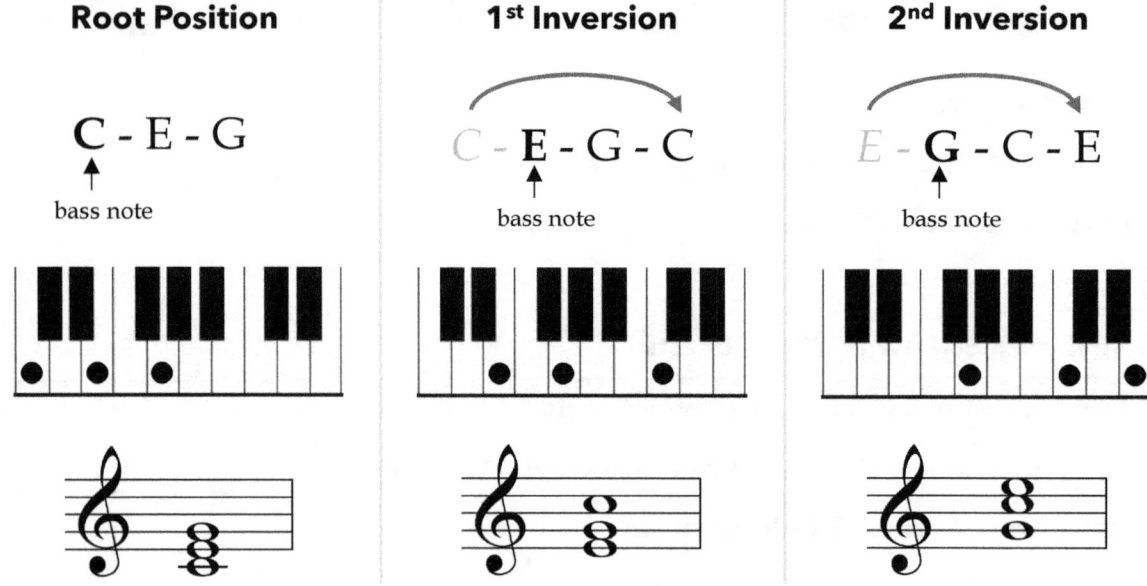

Building Inversions

Notate (with accidentals) and play the following chords with their inversions.

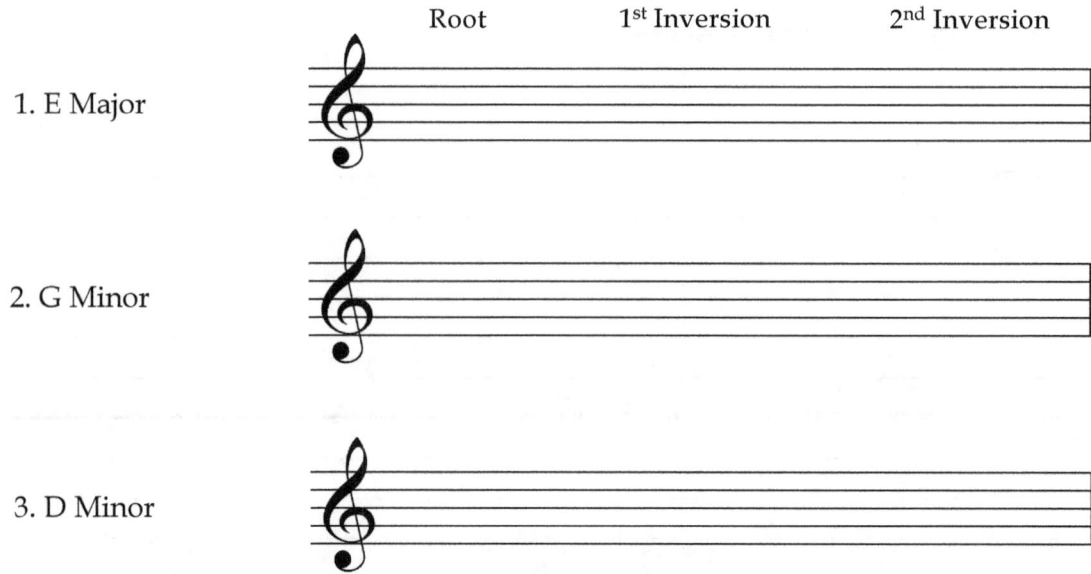

Practicing Chord Inversions

In each hand, inversions for all triads, regardless of quality or root, use the same fingering. The table and exercises below use C major as an example.

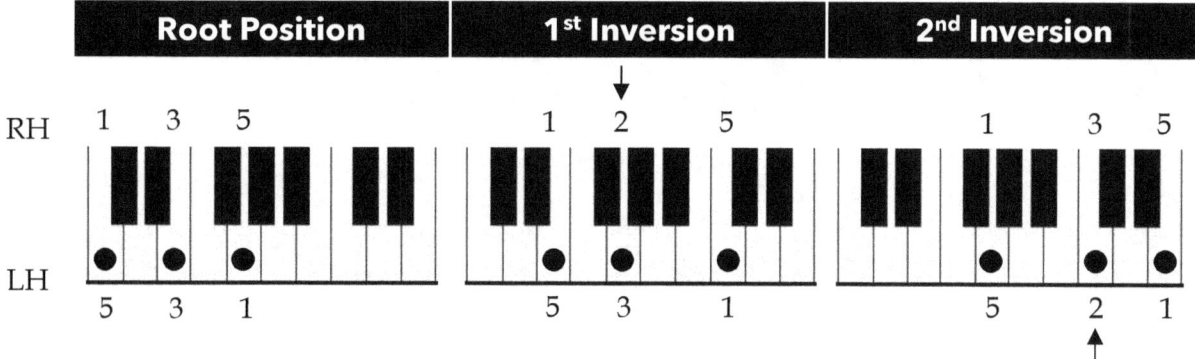

Primary Exercises

Blocked

Half Blocked

Broken

Essential Variations

Practice exercises are like tools in a tool belt. Choosing the right ones for the goals you have will help you progress more quickly.

There is an endless variety of practice variations for chord inversions, and you do not need to limit yourself to the variations above. There are simply examples of how base exercises can be varied with different rhythms, textures, and arrangement of notes. Next practice session, get creative and invent a new variation.

Expanded Scale Practice (Groups 1 and 2)

Playing Beyond the Octave

A crucial step in practicing and internalizing scales is working "beyond the octave." This means understanding the best fingering for each scale so you can play more than one octave and easily change direction at any point in the scale.

Scale Practice Review

There's a lot of scales to practice, and that can be overwhelming. As a reminder from last unit, choose one key from each grouping and practice its major and minor scales. For example, G major and minor (group 1) and B major and minor (group 2) make a great combination. Since group 3 scales won't be covered until Unit 4, you don't need to worry about adding those to your daily practice yet.

Along with starting two-octave scale practice hands separately, review the essential practice variations for scales on page 46.

C Major

	C	D	E	F	G	A	B	C	D	E	F	G	A	B	C
RH	1	2	3	1	2	3	4	1	2	3	1	2	3	4	5
LH	5	4	3	2	1	3	2	1	4	3	2	1	3	2	1

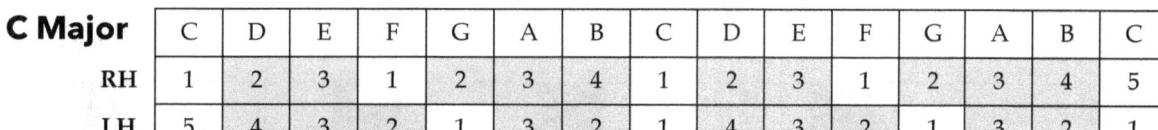

C Minor

	C	D	E♭	F	G	A♭	B♭	C	D	E♭	F	G	A♭	B♭	C
RH	1	2	3	1	2	3	4	1	2	3	1	2	3	4	5
LH	5	4	3	2	1	3	2	1	4	3	2	1	3	2	1

G Major

	G	A	B	C	D	E	F#	G	A	B	C	D	E	F#	G
RH	1	2	3	1	2	3	4	1	2	3	1	2	3	4	5
LH	5	4	3	2	1	3	2	1	4	3	2	1	3	2	1

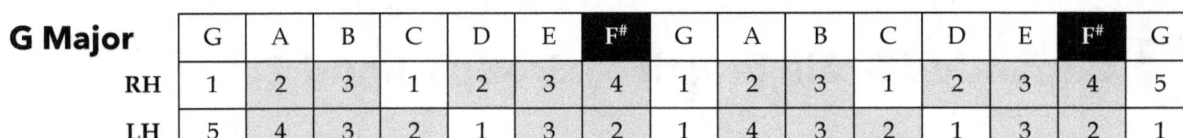

G Minor

	G	A	B♭	C	D	E♭	F	G	A	B♭	C	D	E♭	F	G
RH	1	2	3	1	2	3	4	5	2	3	1	2	3	4	5
LH	5	4	3	2	1	3	2	1	4	3	2	1	3	2	1

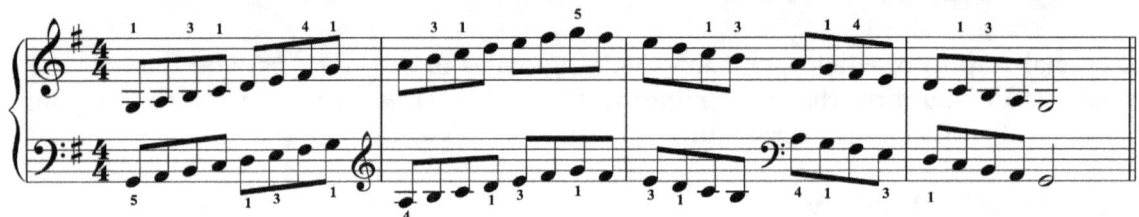

D Major

	D	E	F#	G	A	B	C#	D	E	F#	G	A	B	C#	D
RH	1	2	3	1	2	3	4	1	2	3	1	2	3	4	5
LH	5	4	3	2	1	3	2	1	4	3	2	1	3	2	1

D Minor

	D	E	F	G	A	B♭	C	D	E	F	G	A	B♭	C	D
RH	1	2	3	1	2	3	4	5	2	3	1	2	3	4	5
LH	5	4	3	2	1	3	2	1	4	3	2	1	3	2	1

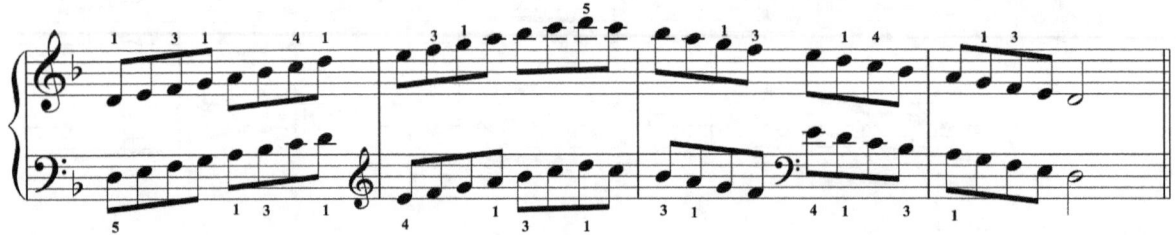

A Major

	A	B	C#	D	E	F#	G#	A	B	C#	D	E	F#	G#	A
RH	1	2	3	1	2	3	4	1	2	3	1	2	3	4	5
LH	5	4	3	2	1	3	2	1	4	3	2	1	3	2	1

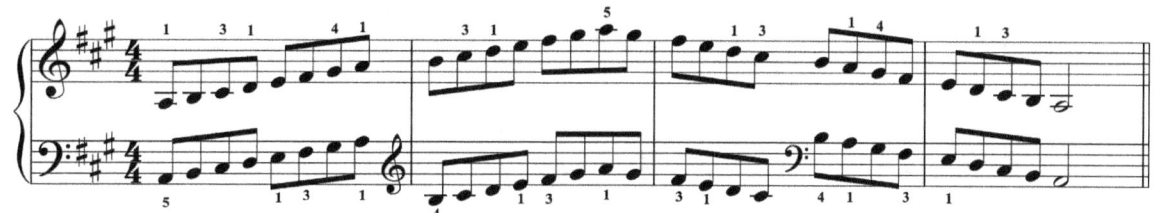

A Minor

	A	B	C	D	E	F	G	A	B	C	D	E	F	G	A
RH	1	2	3	1	2	3	4	5	2	3	1	2	3	4	5
LH	5	4	3	2	1	3	2	1	4	3	2	1	3	2	1

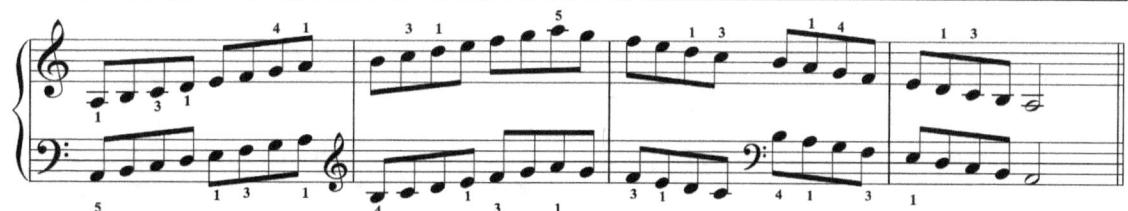

E Major

	E	F#	G#	A	B	C#	D#	E	F#	G#	A	B	C#	D#	E
RH	1	2	3	1	2	3	4	1	2	3	1	2	3	4	5
LH	5	4	3	2	1	3	2	1	4	3	2	1	3	2	1

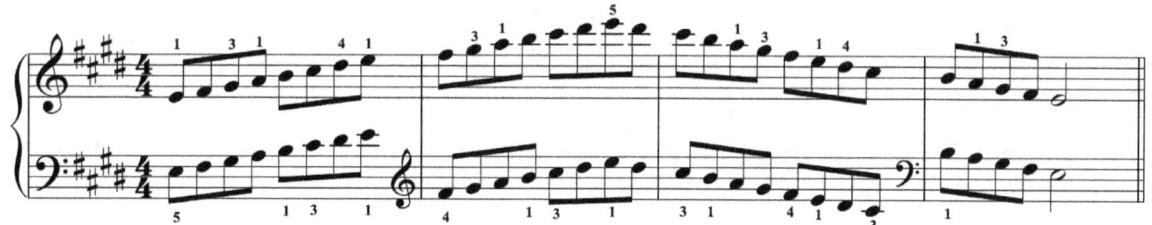

E Minor

	E	F#	G	A	B	C	D	E	F#	G	A	B	C	D	E
RH	1	2	3	1	2	3	4	5	2	3	1	2	3	4	5
LH	5	4	3	2	1	3	2	1	4	3	2	1	3	2	1

Unit 3

B Major

	B	C#	D#	E	F#	G#	A#	B	C#	D#	E	F#	G#	A#	B
RH	1	2	3	1	2	3	4	1	2	3	1	2	3	4	5
LH	4	3	2	1	4	3	2	1	3	2	1	4	3	2	1

B Minor

	B	C#	D	E	F#	G	A	B	C#	D	E	F#	G	A	B
RH	1	2	3	1	2	3	4	5	2	3	1	2	3	4	5
LH	4	3	2	1	4	3	2	1	3	2	1	4	3	2	1

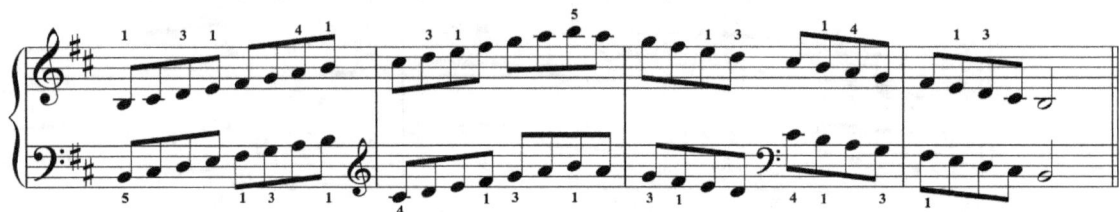

F Major

	F	G	A	B♭	C	D	E	F	G	A	B♭	C	D	E	F
RH	1	2	3	4	1	2	3	1	2	3	4	1	2	3	4
LH	5	4	3	2	1	3	2	1	4	3	2	1	3	2	1

F Minor

	F	G	A♭	B♭	C	D♭	E♭	F	G	A♭	B♭	C	D♭	E♭	F
RH	1	2	3	4	1	2	3	1	2	3	4	1	2	3	4
LH	5	4	3	2	1	3	2	1	4	3	2	1	3	2	1

Intro to Keyboard Style

In lead sheet notation and chord charts, it is the keyboardist's job to add chord tones in an appropriate voicing and register. Depending on the size of the band/ensemble, instrument patch, style, etc., the keyboardist's choices might change. However, this set of exercises serves as a starting point for any situation.

Keyboard Style is a term used to describe how keyboardists interpret notation in lead sheets and chord charts. Basic keyboard style puts the root or bass note in the LH, the melodic note on the top of the RH, and other chord tones falling underneath the melodic note in the RH. Take a look at the examples below.

Example 1

What You See

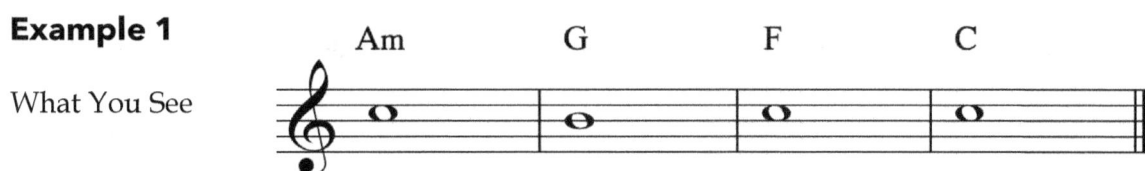

What You Play

melody →
additional chord tones →

bass note →

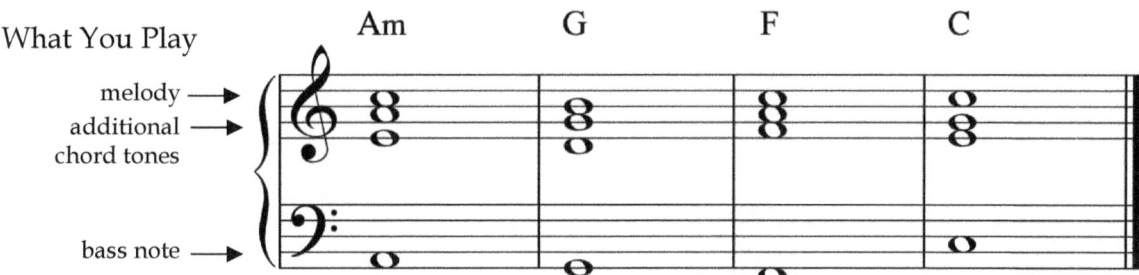

Example 2

What You See

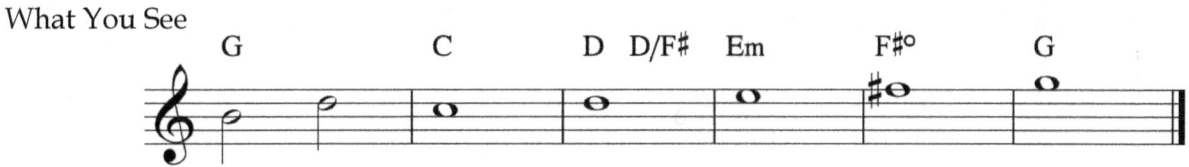

What You Play

Keyboard Style Reading

Use the following exercises to practice playing in a keyboard style texture. The melodic note should be the highest note in the RH with the chord tones underneath, and the LH plays the bass note of the indicated chord.

Practice Guide:
1. RH only: play the given melody with only the RH pinky.
2. RH only: play the melody with the supporting chord tones underneath.
3. RH only: drill hand position and chord changes in small segments (2–4 chords at a time).
4. LH only: play indicated root/bass note parts. Find a starting hand position that doesn't require you to move your hand a lot.
5. Both hands: drill hands together in small segments (2–4 chords at a time).

Practice at a variety of tempos.

($\quad$ = 56–140)

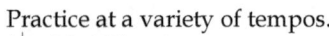

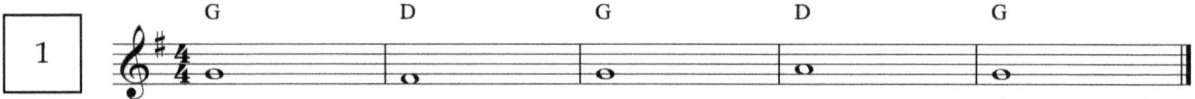

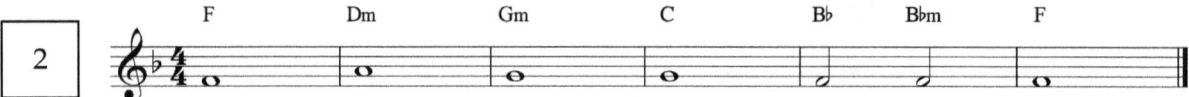

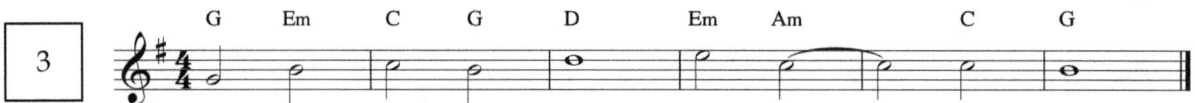

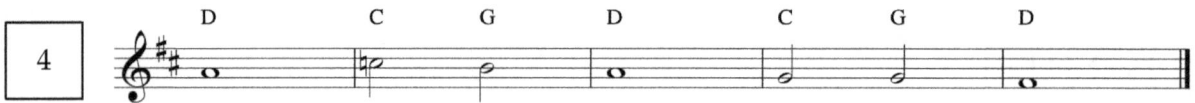

Chord tones underneath a melody are needed only when the harmony changes.

Unit 3

Lead Sheets

Practice the following lead sheet two ways—as a solo and a duet. As a solo, the RH plays the melody and LH plays broken chord accompaniment. As a duet, the soloist plays the melody while the accompanist plays the chords using one of the notated accompaniment patterns.

Accompaniment Patterns

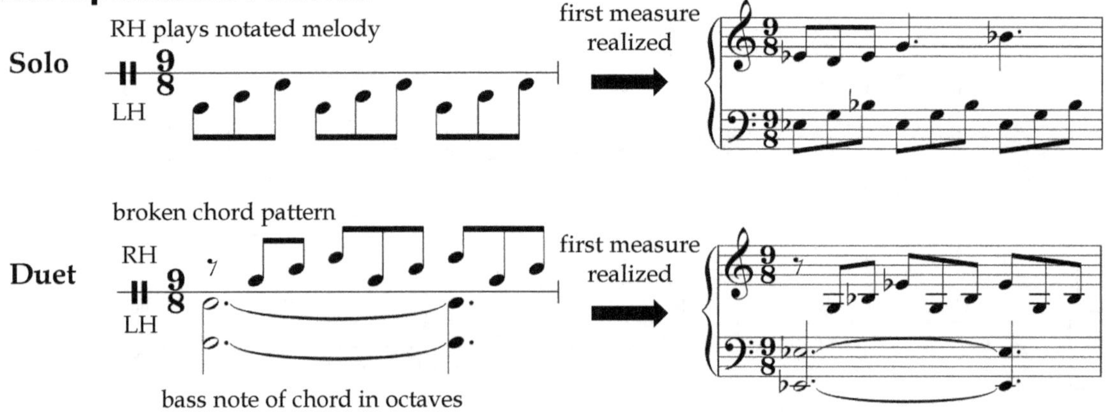

Dreamer

Medium Ballad (♩. = 48–60)

Andy Villemez

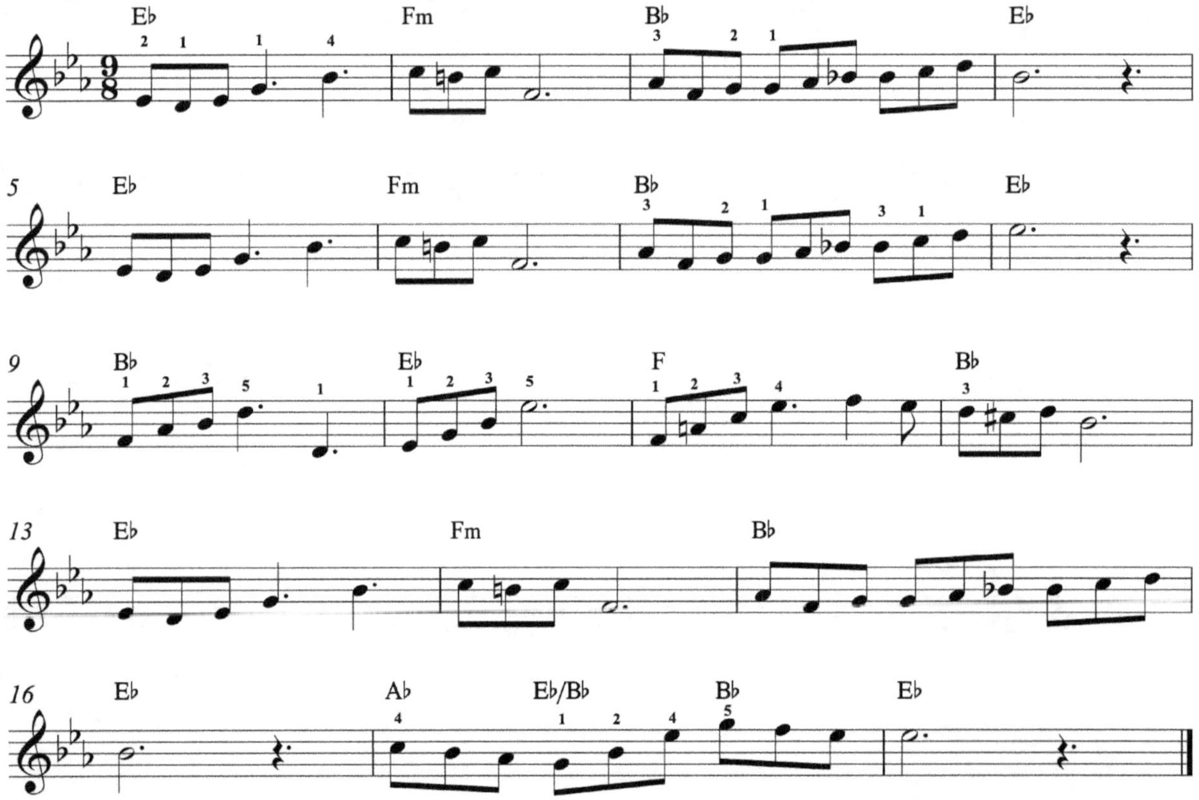

Play the lead sheet below in keyboard style. Use the same practice steps on page 79 to guide your practice.

Practice the following lead sheet two ways as a solo and a duet. As a solo, the RH plays the melody and LH plays broken chord accompaniment. As a duet, the soloist plays the melody while the accompanist plays the chords using one of the notated accompaniment patterns.

Accompaniment Patterns

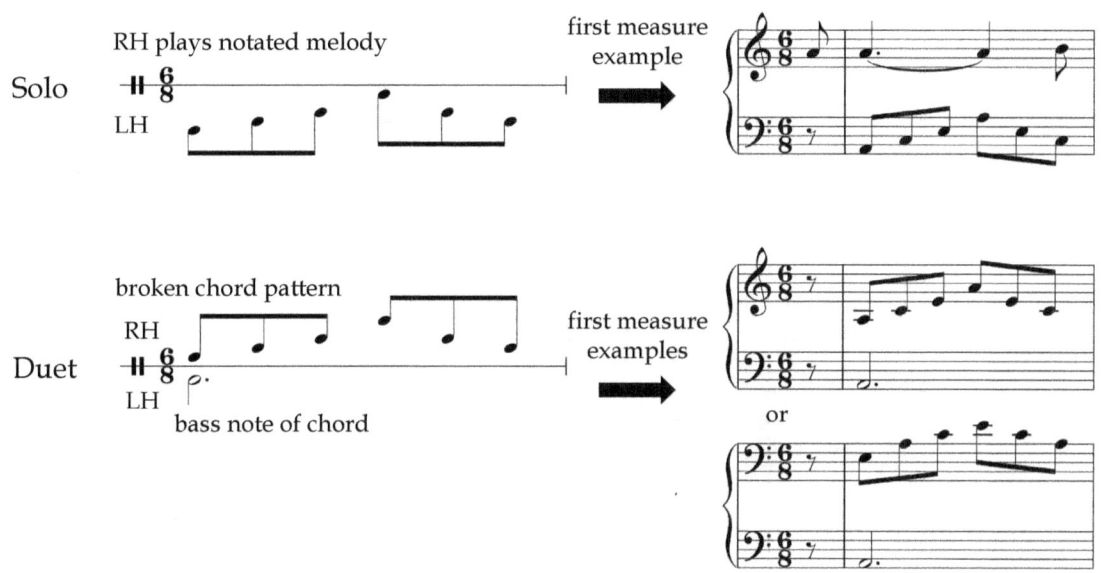

House of the Rising Sun

Slow (♩.= 60)

Traditional Folk Song

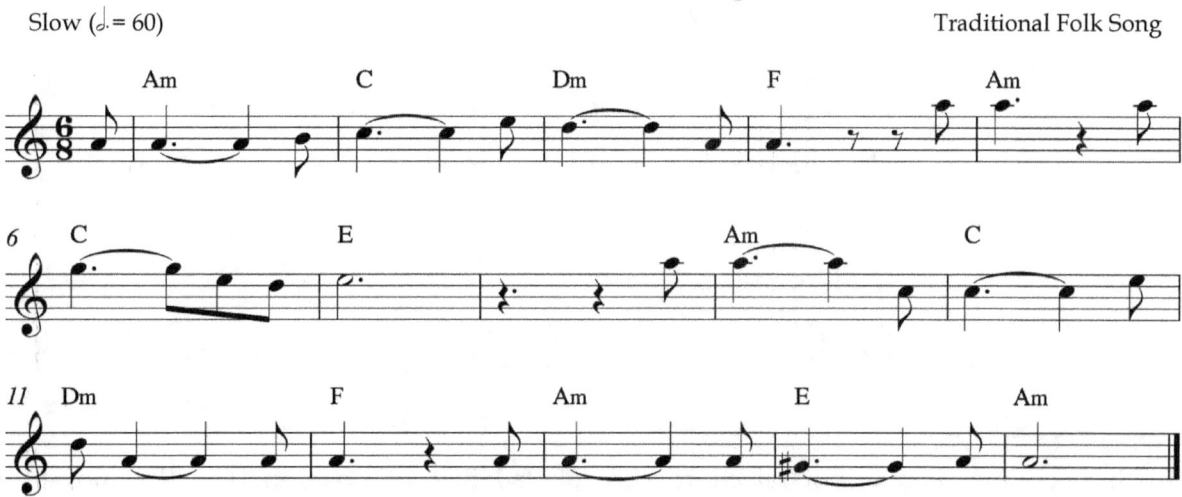

Keyboard Style with Chord Charts

In chord charts, there will not be a notated melody. Most often, it will not be the keyboardist's job to play the melody either. It will be the keyboardist's job to play the given chords in an appropriate register with *smooth voice leading*. That means that chords need to move as efficiently as possible from one to another. The examples below show you what you might see in a chord chart and how you should approach chord voicing when playing keyboard style in chord charts.

Example 1

What you *SEE*

What you *could PLAY*
a.
b.

Example 2

a.
b.

In the examples above, not all chords are played in root position. The RH moves as smoothly as possible from one chord to the next. Any chord tones that are shared from one to the next are kept.

The following charts are examples of common chord progressions in various styles. Play the following exercises in **keyboard style** with the notated accompaniment patterns.

1. You can hear a chord progression like exercise 1 in the song "When I Was Your Man" as performed by Bruno Mars.

Accompaniment Pattern: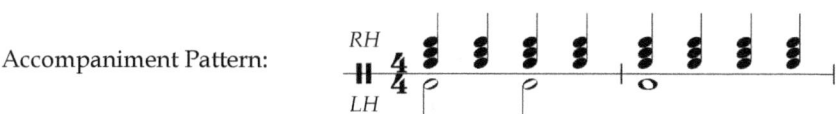

KEY: C   Pop Ballad (♩ = 110)

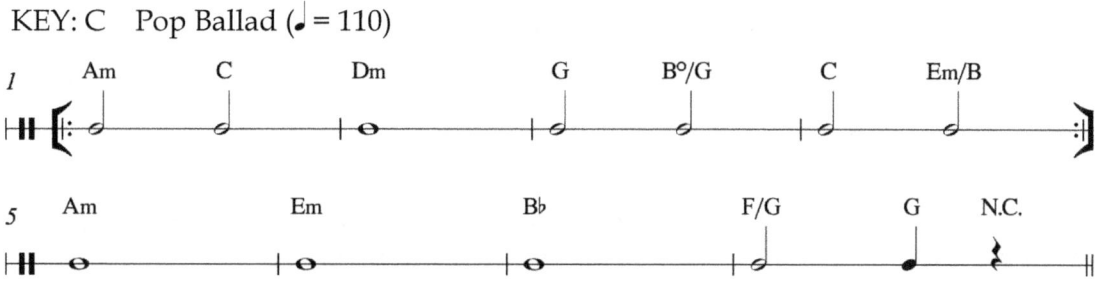

2. You can hear a chord progression like exercise 2 in the song "Liability" as performed by Lorde.

Accompaniment Pattern: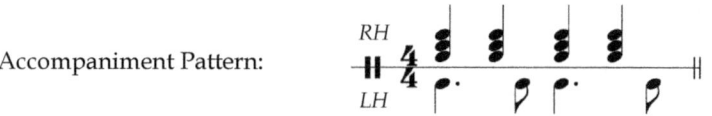

KEY: D   Pop Piano Ballad (♩ = 85)

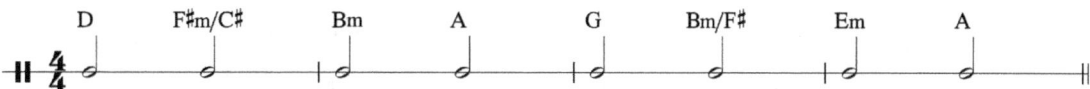

Try the same progression transposed down a half step.

KEY: D♭   Pop Piano Ballad (♩ = 85)

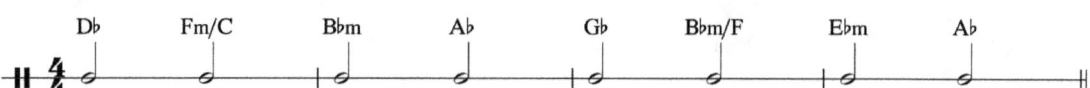

3 You can hear a chord progression like exercise 1 in the song "Lovely Day" as performed by Bill Withers.

Accompaniment Pattern:

KEY: E   R&B/Soul (♩ = 110)

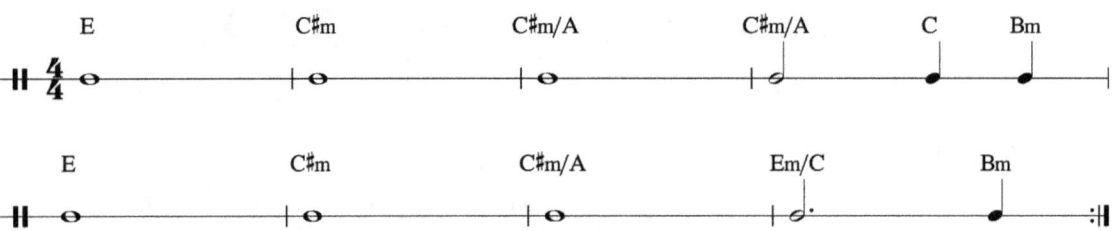

4 You can hear a chord progression like exercise 2 in the song "Everybody Needs Somebody to Love" as performed by the Blues Brothers.

Accompaniment Pattern:

KEY: C   Blues Rock (♩ = 194)

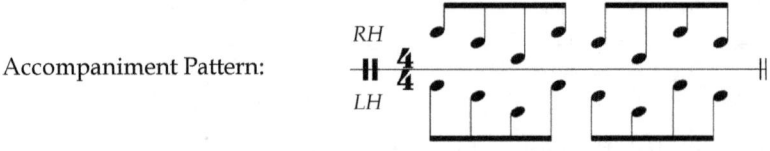

5 You can hear a chord progression like exercise 2 in the song "Clocks" as performed by Coldplay.

Accompaniment Pattern:

KEY: E♭   Alternative Rock (♩ = 85)

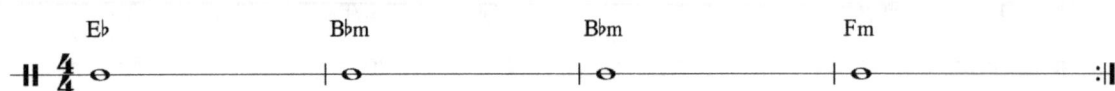

Common Chord Progressions with Triads

It is common to find the same harmonic progression in multiple songs. Below are common chord progressions notated in the Nashville Number System. Practice these exercises in group 1 and group 2 keys using keyboard style with smooth voice leading. Use the sustain pedal to make transitions between chords sound smooth.

Example 1

What you SEE 4/4 1 | 6- | 4 | 5 :||

What you could PLAY

KEY: F

a.

b.

1 4/4 1 | 5 | 6- | 4 :||

Write in chord names and practice in the following keys:

A:

D:

B:

2 4/4 4 | 5 | 6- | 1/3 :||

Write in chord names and practice in the following keys:

C:

E:

F:

Unit 3

☐ 3   **4/4** 1 | 5/7 | 6- | 5   :||

Write in chord names and practice in the following keys:

G: [ ]

A: [ ]

B: [ ]

☐ 4   **4/4** 1 | 2- | 1/3 | 4   :||

Write in chord names and practice in the following keys:

C: [ ]

D: [ ]

E: [ ]

☐ 5   **4/4** 1 | 3 | 4 | 4-   :||

Write in chord names and practice in the following keys:

C: [ ]

E: [ ]

F: [ ]

Harmonization with Target Chords and Types of Cadences

If a complete song or musical work is thought of as a short story, then musical phrases are sentences in that story. Just like each word in a sentence functions differently, so does the harmony in a musical phrase. Read the following sentences out loud like a narrator and notice your natural inflection.

Next time, let's try to stop at the stop sign.

I didn't ever think I was going to make it this far.

When you read those out loud, which words did you naturally emphasize? Was there a tendency to raise energy toward a word then release that energy? In musical phrases, a **target chord** functions the same as those words we naturally emphasize in speech. It is the harmonic destination of a musical phrase. Any chord in a musical phrase can be treated as a target chord, but the most common are the last or next-to-last chords. How you approach a target chord has a significant effect on the musical phrase.

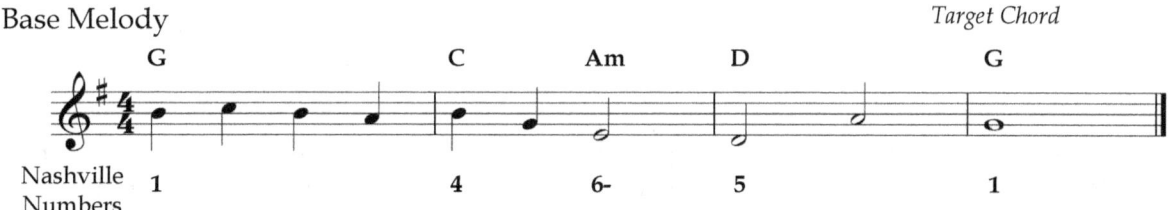

Like sentences have punctation, musical phrases contain **cadences**. A cadence serves as important junction between the end of one musical phrase and usually the beginning of another. While the field of music theory has categorized specific types of cadences, this text categorizes them into three broad categories: **strong, weak,** and **deceptive.** Their names come from the amount and type of resolution one hears in a musical phrase. Strong cadences produce a marked resolution to a target chord, and they are characterized by significant contrast between **approach chord** (the chord immediately before the target) and target chord. As a general guide, strong cadences occur when the approach chord and target chord have less notes in common. When using triads, only one note in common creates a strong cadence.

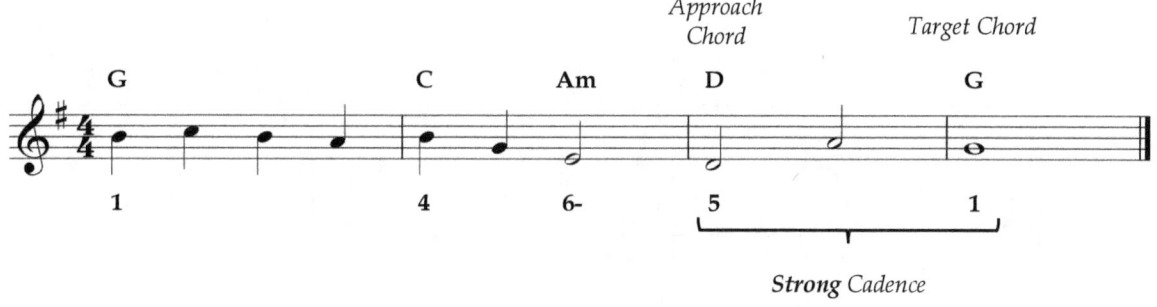

Weak cadences have a gentler effect. They occur when the approach chord and target chord have three or more notes in common. Weaker cadences often occur toward the beginning of a musical phrase since the effect is subtle.

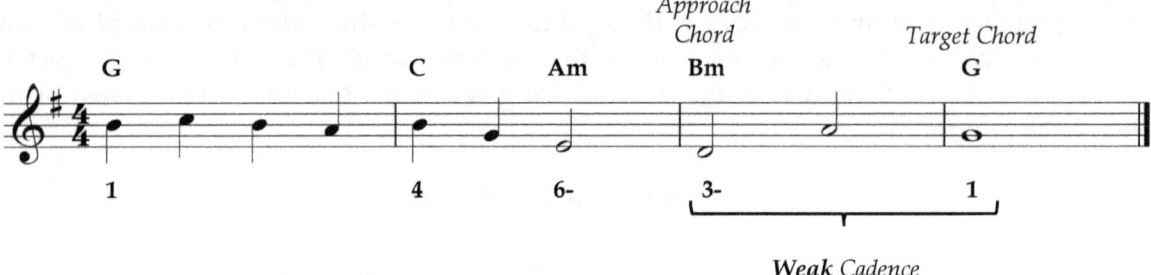

Deceptive cadences occur when a strong cadence is resolved in an unexpected way. The most common example of a deceptive cadence is shown below: a *V (5)* chord resolving to a *vi (6-)* or *bVI (b6)*.

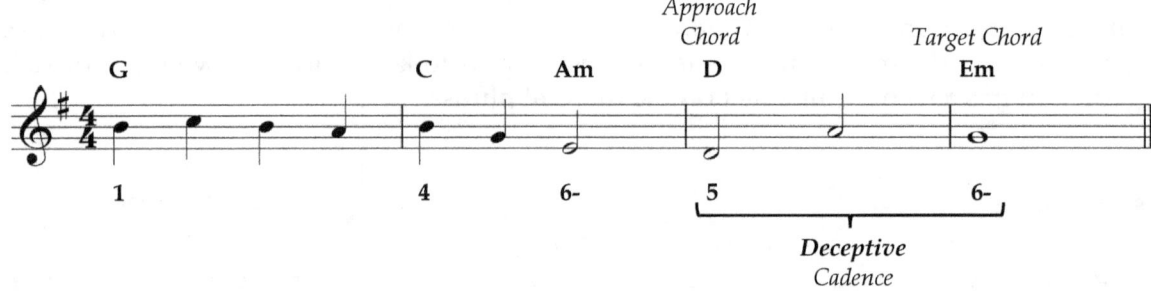

In each melody below, identify a target chord and harmonize the melody with the indicated cadence. Use lead sheet chord names (i.e., Gm, F, etc.) above the melody and Nashville numbers below.

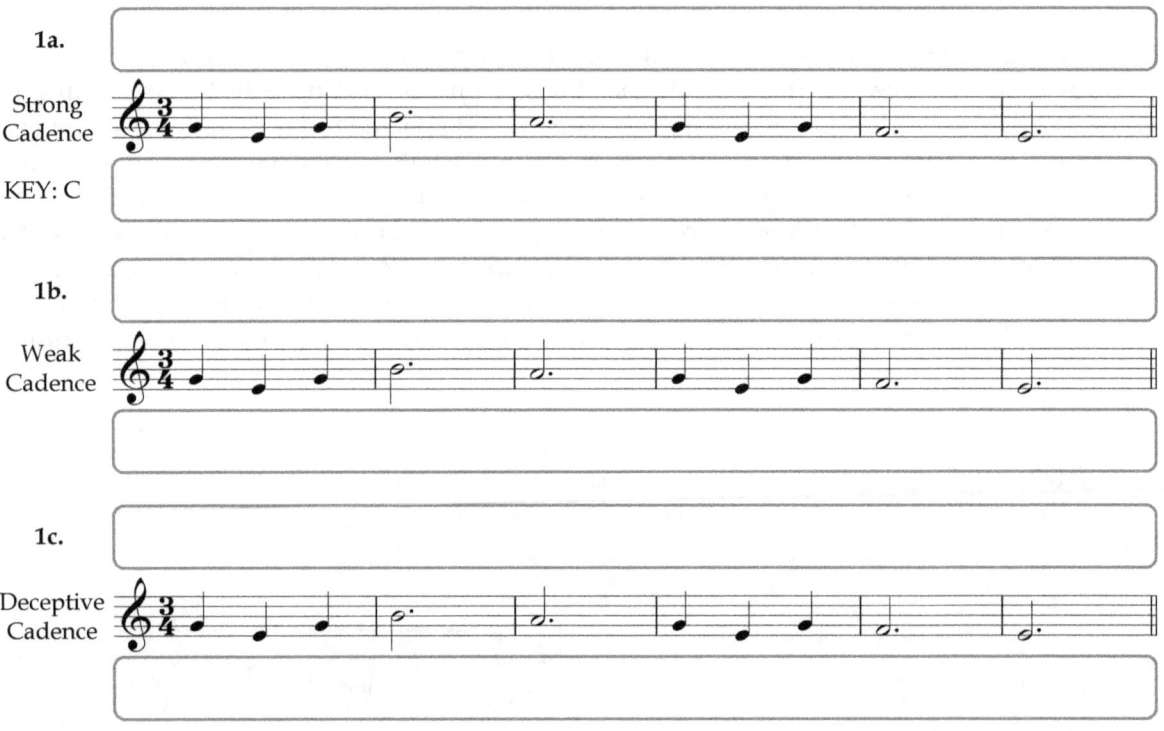

Harmonize the first melody in each exercise using lead sheet chord names (i.e., Gm, F, etc.). Use the second melody in each exercise to Identify a target chord and reharmonize the melody with different kinds of cadences.

Unit Three Diatonic Triads Playback   INSTRUCTOR PAGE

Guidelines for drilling playback:
1. Play the following chord progression in the key of the exercise before each row of examples.
2. Before playing, students should say the Nashville Number of each chord in the exercise. (EX: "1 – minor 3 – 1")
3. Play all triads in root position and keyboard style with smooth voice leading in the RH.

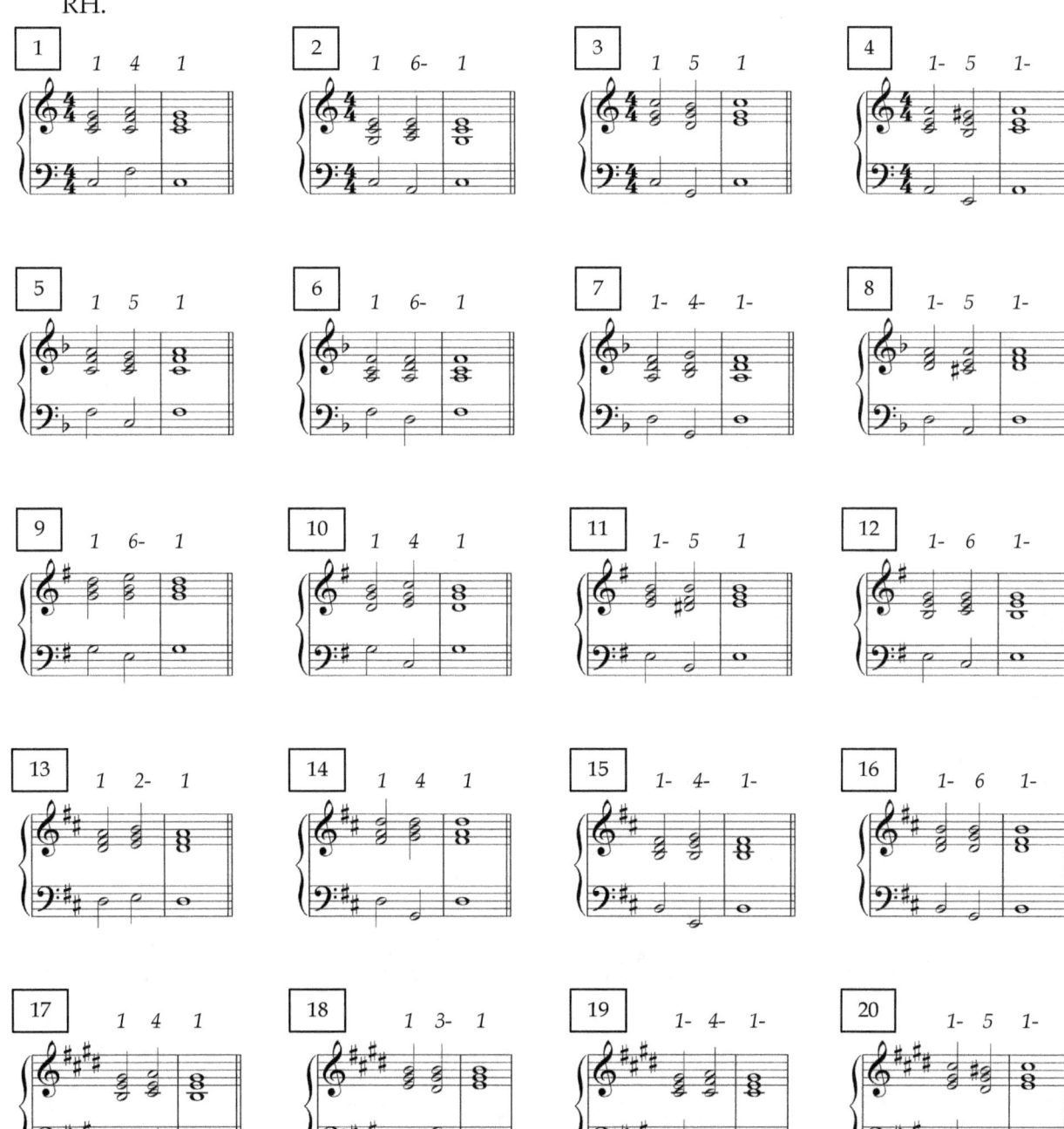

Unit Three Melodies for Playback

INSTRUCTOR PAGE

Guidelines for drilling playback:
1. Give the hand position (but not major/minor) of the example along with playing the tonic chord.
2. Count in one measure before playing.

👁 Unit Three Rhythm Training

The following rhythm drills prepare you to play simple and repetitive beat patterns for performance or production. Instruments are notated so that you can use drum pads or a percussion patch on a keyboard. Focus on the overall feel of these patterns and your relationship to the pulse. Don't let mistakes derail the groove.

The patterns for Unit 3 are notated in four parts: kick drum, snare, high hat, and open high hat. However, feel free to replace those parts with other sounds that still function similarly.

5

6

7

8

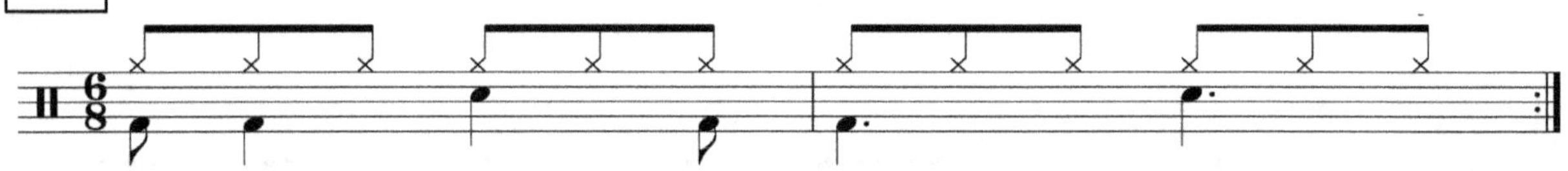

Add kick drum and snare parts to the high-hat patterns below. Use a combination of quarter and 8th notes/rests.

9

10

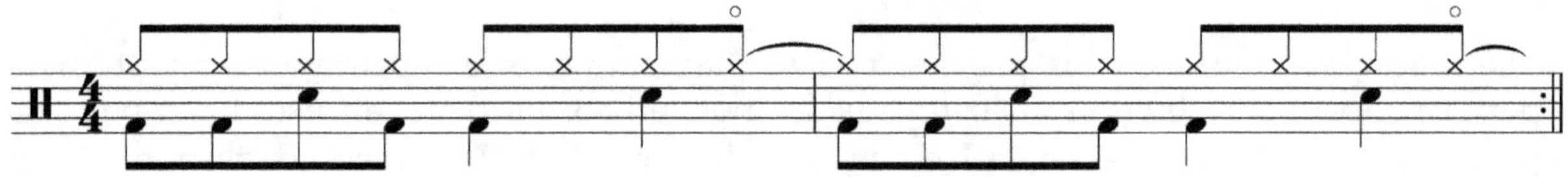

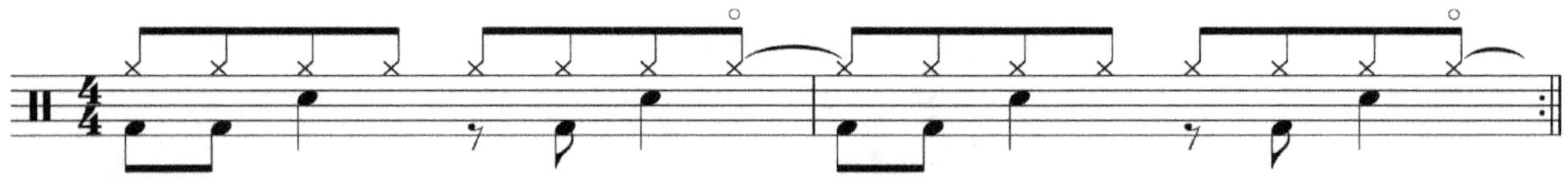

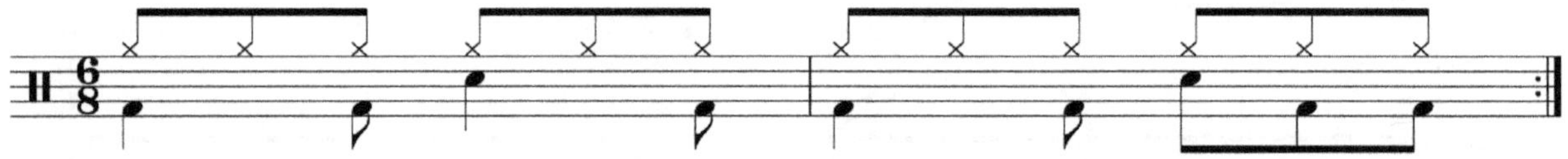

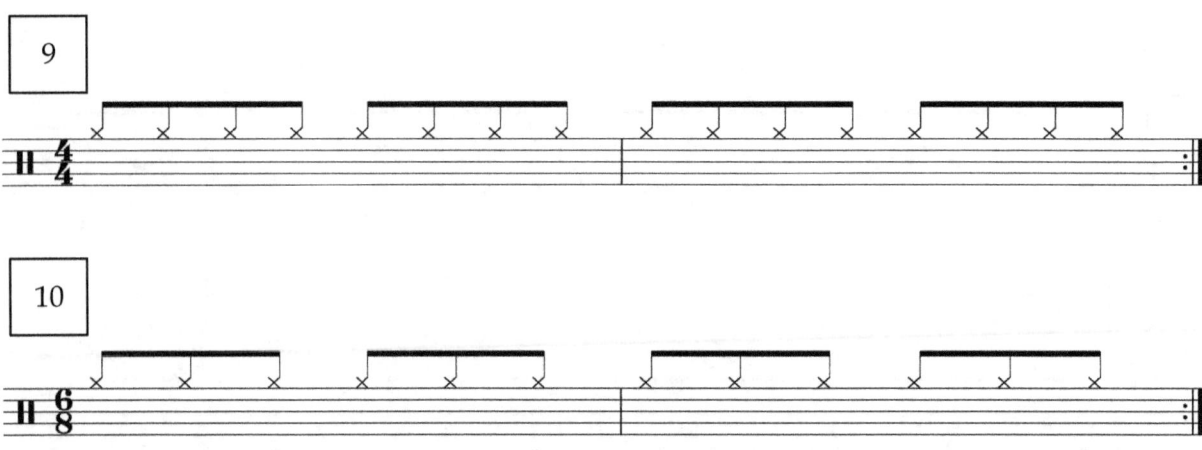

Part Two: Rhythm Reading

For all rhythm reading exercises:
1. Your primary goal is fluency, not perfection.
2. Prioritize the pulse.
3. Don't stop.

Practice at a variety of tempos.

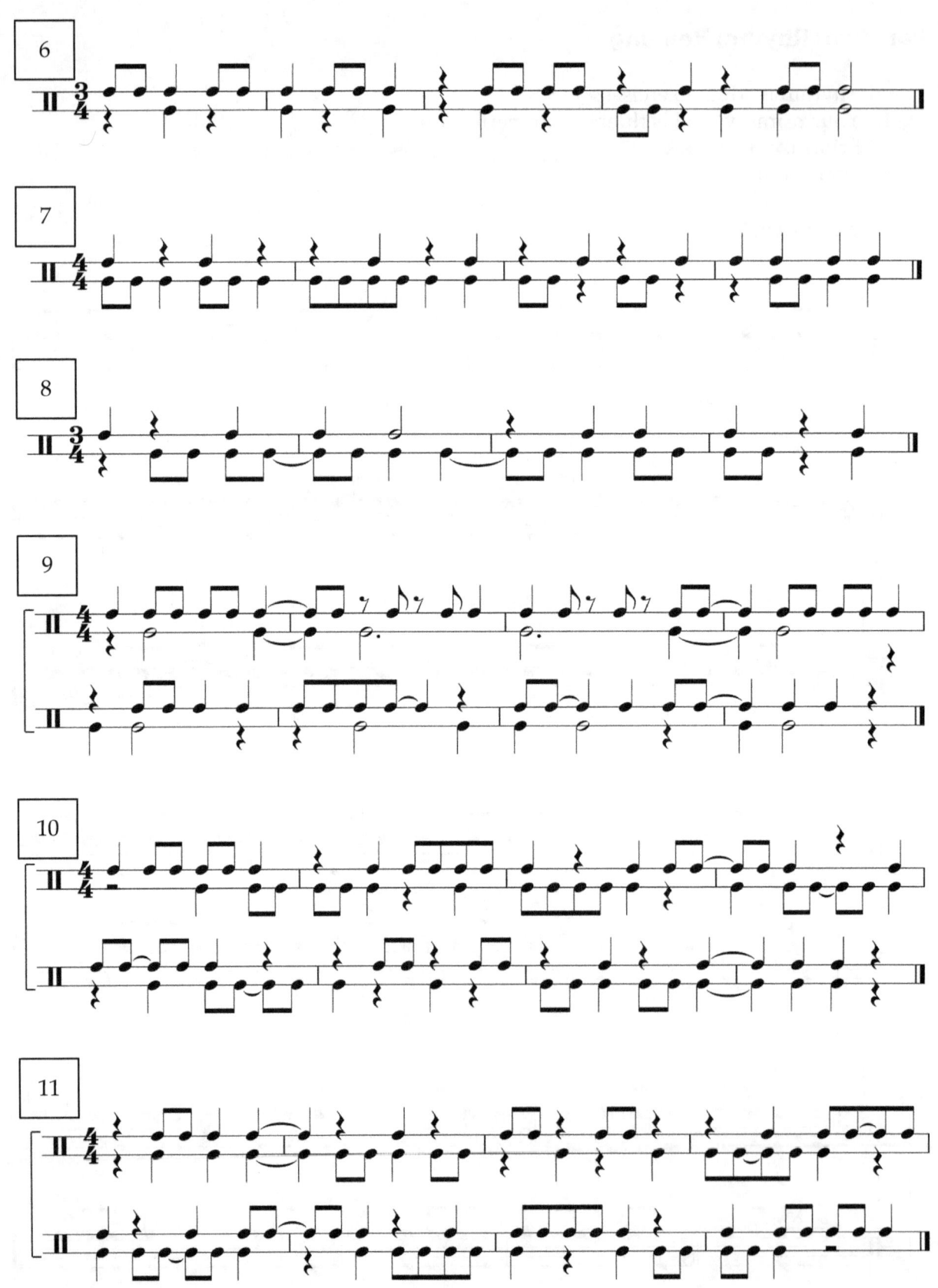

Rhythm Ensemble

Practice Variations and Challenges:
1. For individual work, practice different two-part combinations.
2. For paired or group work, assign alternating measures.

The Twinkle Twinkle Challenge

After learning a standard harmonization of "Twinkle Twinkle" in #1, reharmonize this popular melody to create your own version.

1. Practice in keyboard style. Convert the chord names to Nashville numbers below the staff.

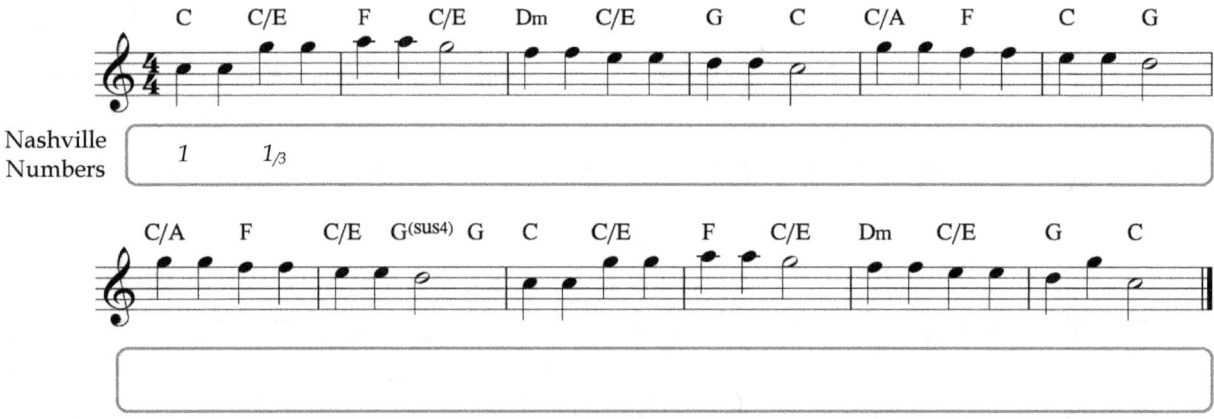

2. Reharmonize exercise 1 using a combination of simple substitution and chord borrowing. Write chord names above the melody and Nashville numbers below. Practice in keyboard style.

3. Use the Nashville numbers from exercise 2 to transpose it to another group 1 or group 2 key.

Solo Repertoire

While practicing the piece below, fill in each box above and below the staff with the appropriate chord names, Nashville numbers, and harmonic function (*T, PD,* or *D*) for each broken chord.

Smooth and flowing (♩ = 102–120)

Petite Prelude

Ludwig Schytte

Chord Names: Am

NNS: 1-

Function: T

Unit 3

Composing with Chord Inversions

Using the same texture and pattern as "Petite Prelude" on page 105, compose your own piece using descending broken chords. Use the completed first measure as a starting point to choose a different chord progression. Use simple substitution and chord borrowing as tools for reharmonization.

Title: _____

Composer: _____

Smooth and flowing (♩ = 102–120)

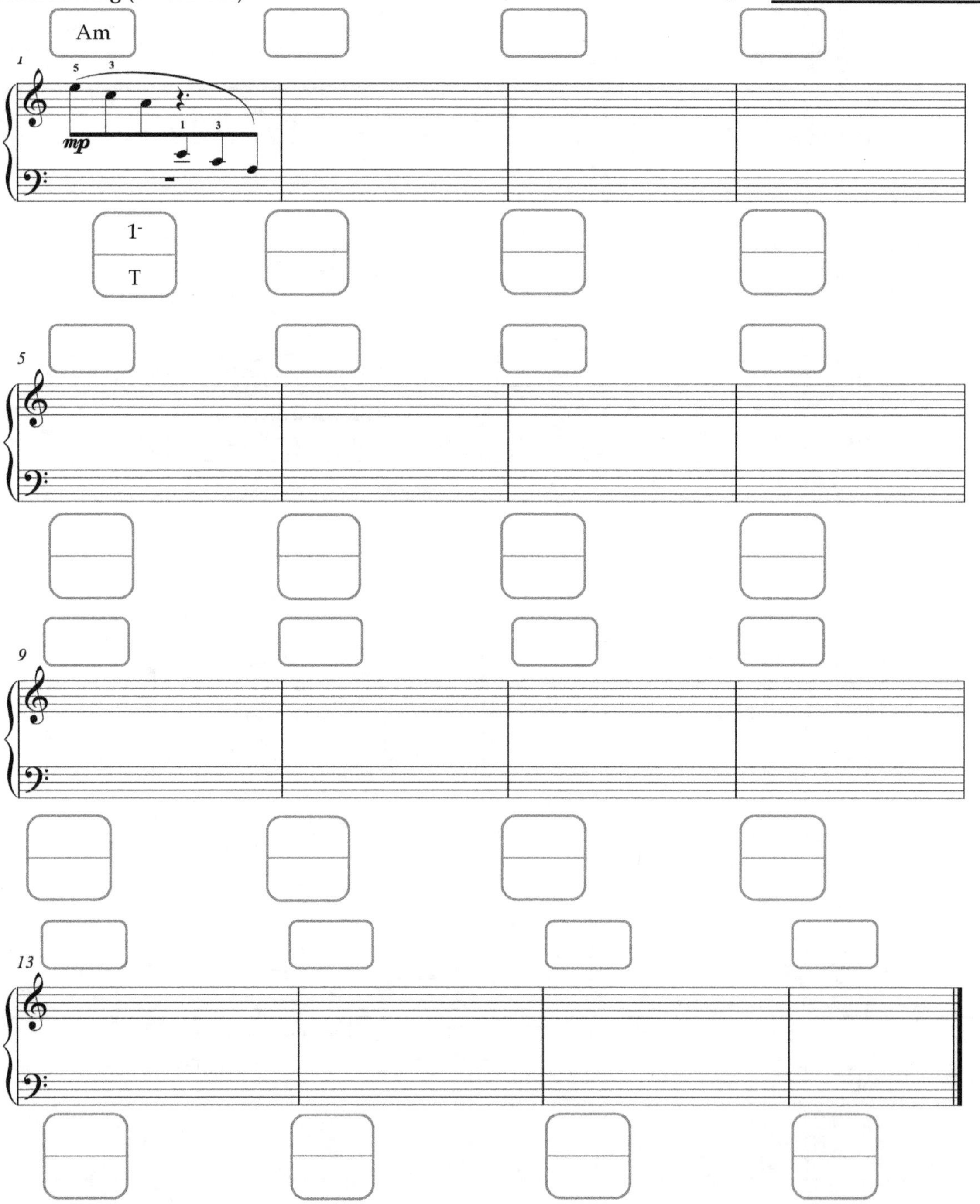

ADVANCED TOPICS II:
UNDERSTANDING PERFORMANCE MISTAKES

"Perfectionism is not as much the desire for excellence, as it is the fear of failure couched in procrastination." – Dan Miller

Learning any new skill brings with it a need to understand more about yourself – how your brain works, your learning preferences, strengths, weaknesses, biases, etc. In practicing a new skill, how you respond to and reflect on errors is crucial. Mistakes are some of the best data you can use to understand more about your own learning and cognition. While they may be frustrating, performance mistakes are a necessary and useful phenomenon. Perfection is an impossible standard, and it often distracts us from the information that helps us improve. Using the work of internationally recognized music cognition and musicianship expert, Marianne Ploger, this advanced topic discusses the three main causes of performance mistakes, why they happen, how to identify them, and how to prevent them.[1]

Why Some Mistakes Happen

Practice is often a repetitive task, built from a desire for comfort and routine. When our learning becomes too routine, it is easily susceptible to disruption. Established behaviors in practice create well-worn neural pathways, and our brain sees routine behaviors as an opportunity to implement energy-saving procedures that decrease our attentiveness. Your brain will shut down some of its processing power in areas it doesn't think it needs. These quick timeouts are often predictable, as well. As much as thirty seconds before a mental lapse, scientists can see how blood flow decreases to parts of the brain responsible for maintaining focus.[2] Since this is a normal procedure for our brain, mistakes are impossible to eliminate completely. However, in musical performance, we can engage in mindful practice while also studying behaviors that lead us to destructive outcomes.

The Three Main Types of Mistakes

Reaction

During performance or practice, we are not immune from outside stimuli. Whether it's a sneeze from an audience member, a friend that bangs on your practice room door, or your own stomach growling, there are infinite possibilities for how we can be surprised during moments of heightened focus. A mistake caused by reaction is a primitive part of brain being activated from a sudden change in the status quo. Reaction is a mistake caused by a fight, flight, or freeze response, and that response causes a jarring change of focus in our brain, derailing us from our previous area of attention.

You can prepare for surprises and prevent reactionary mistakes by expanding your awareness during practice to include everything you might encounter during a performance. This includes your own emotional, physical, and mental stimuli, but also those that come from the environment. While we might want to control every aspect of a performance, we must accept that as impossible. To the mature performer, surprises are reminders to "zoom out" their mental perspective so they can easily follow and accept all elements of a performance.

Anticipation

Imagine you're on a hike. The trail is mostly flat but littered with small obstacles—rocks and tree roots protruding from the ground. You've been on this hike many times. You know it intimately. At a few points of the hike, you start daydreaming—maybe about family, friends, food, or something else. Your pleasant daydream prevents you from seeing the detail of changing terrain below your feet. You're "awoken" from the daydream by a tree root that trips you. You catch yourself, bring your focus back to the trail in front of you, and keep moving forward. After a few minutes, you see a steep change in elevation in the distance. You know this part of the hike was coming, but the difficulty of the steep ascent always makes you a bit anxious. In the past, you've had a few incidents on the way up that make you uneasy on subsequent attempts. While you're walking toward the ascent, you start thinking about a few things that could go wrong—maybe even seeing flashbacks of an incident from the past. Before you even reach the difficult portion of the hike, you've tripped again, and your focus is brought back to the trail in front of you.

These two "trips," illustrate the two types of anticipation mistakes. Errors of this variety are caused by disconnecting from reality. They take two forms: benevolent and malevolent. The benevolent anticipation mistake resembles daydreaming or thought wandering. The malevolent kind occurs from paranoia or arrogance. We disconnect from the present moment because we're worried (or overly confident) about something in the future. In a musical performance, how many times has your brain wandered off and starting thinking about what's for dinner? Or how often have you been so worried about a solo or difficult passage ahead that you make a mistake on something right in front of you? These are mistakes of anticipation.

Preventing this type of mistake requires you to direct the present activity with the best modality, or sense. If you're listening, allow the ears to lead. If you're watching, allow the eyes to lead. When our use of modalities doesn't match the task, we become susceptible to zooming out too far and losing a constructive sense of focus - i.e., we start thinking about other stuff.

Looking Back

Self-critique is an important skill, but there's a time and place for it. Mistakes that occur from looking back are a result of your inner judge trying to take control of the activities. Our brain takes on many roles as we practice and perform music. We can separate these roles into three sets of responsibilities—music director, band, and audience. Most of the large-scale ideas should come from the music director. The band is responsible for executing those ideas (the MD is not responsible for teaching you the mechanics of your instrument), and the audience serves as listener and critic. Our brain is doing all these things at once. What you will never see in a live performance is a member of the audience notice a band member make a small mistake and start shouting at them to fix their mistake. A real audience member would never do that, but we do that to ourselves. We will be playing, make a small mistake, and lose the ability to keep moving forward because our inner critic is obsessing about how one mistake means we're doing it all wrong. Ploger uses the analogy of an Olympic swimmer and her coach:

> *Imagine that the race has begun. The coach sees that the swimmer is doing something wrong, jumps into the pool and pulls on and screams at the swimmer who struggles to continue. The swimmer can neither keep swimming for long, nor can she hear what the coach is saying.*[3]

Preventing mistakes caused by looking back requires you to train your inner critic, or coach. First, prepare to the best of your ability. Don't withhold any strategy or advice for yourself when preparing. If you know you should be resting instead of practicing, do that. If you know you need to drill sections instead of running the piece, do that. You have an incredible amount of experience and skill in preparing for performance already. Use all of it. Second, plan time after a task for critique. Reflect on all elements of the task. Let your inner coach lead that whole session. Third, and most important, practice silencing your coach before they even open their mouth. Refrain from judging or even directing during a performance. Trust your inner performer to do the right thing. Trust the preparation you did to get to this moment.

Additional Resources:

The Ploger Method: Crafting a Fluent Musical Mind by Marianne Ploger
Musical Communication Podcast with Marianne Ploger and Karen Cubides

---

[1] Marianne Ploger, *The Ploger Method: Crafting a Fluent Musical Mind*, Self-published, CreateSpace, 2018.
[2] Tom Eichele, Stefan Debener, Vince D. Calhoun, Karsten Specht, Andreas K. Engel, Kenneth Hugdahl, D. Yves von Cramon, and Markus Ullsperger, 2008, "Prediction of Human Errors by Maladaptive Changes in Event-Related Brain Networks," *Proceedings of the National Academy of Sciences* vol 105, no. 16 (2008): 6173-78, accessed October 14, 2023, https://doi.org/10.1073/pnas.0708965105.
[3] Marianne Ploger, "The Three Causes of Error," The Ploger Method, accessed October 1, 2023. https://www.theplogermethod.com/articles.

Notes:

Unit Four

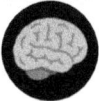     

- ❏ **Scale Fingering Review**
- ❏ **Expanded Scale Practice (Group 3)**
- ❏ **Technique: Introduction to Hanon**
- ❏ **Music for Reading (Riffs and Basslines)**
- ❏ **Solo Repertoire**
- ❏ **Samba (Duet)**
- ❏ **Lead Sheet Reading**
- ❏ **Creating Basic Accompaniment Patterns**
- ❏ **Common Chord Progressions with Triads**
- ❏ **Chord Charts with Accompaniment Patterns**
- ❏ **Harmonization with Mode Mixture**
- ❏ **Unit Four Diatonic Triads Playback**
- ❏ **Unit Four Melodies for Playback**
- ❏ **Unit Four Rhythm Training**

Notes:

 **Scale Fingering Review**

Fingering Pattern – (an absolute truth)

All 7-note scales use the same fingering pattern, but not all those scales start on the same finger. This unit reviews the basic fingering pattern for all scales.

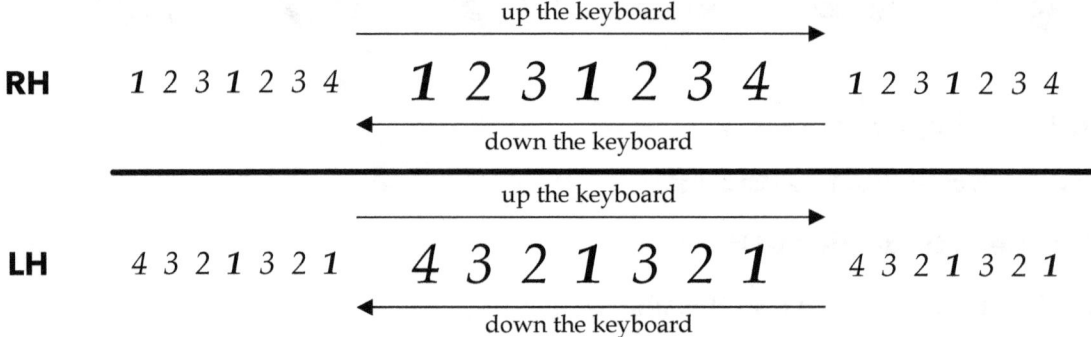

The only difference between scales is what finger you start on. If you are practicing multiple octaves, the pattern repeats.

Fingering Exercises

With both hands, choose any white key on the piano and play the following fingerings *up and down* without repeating the top note. (Using all white keys is recommended—just focus on the fingering.)

1.
RH	1	2	3	1	2	3	4	5
LH	5	4	3	2	1	3	2	1

2.
RH	2	3	1	2	3	4	1	2
LH	3	2	1	4	3	2	1	3

3.
RH	4	1	2	3	1	2	3	4
LH	3	2	1	4	3	2	1	3

4.
RH	2	3	4	1	2	3	1	2
LH	4	3	2	1	3	2	1	4

5.
RH	3	1	2	3	4	1	2	3
LH	2	1	4	3	2	1	3	2

Expanded Scale Practice (Group 3)

Scale Practice Review

I bet you did not forget that there's a lot of scales to practice, and that can be overwhelming. As a reminder from last unit, choose one key from each grouping and practice its major and minor scales. For example, G major and minor (group 1) and B major and minor (group 2) make a great combination.

Group 1	C, G, D, A, and E
Group 2	F and B
Group 3	B♭, E♭, A♭, D♭(C#), and G♭(F#)

Along with starting two-octave scale practice hands separately, review the essential practice variations for scales on page 46.

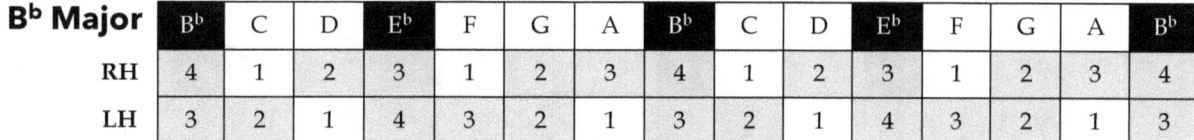

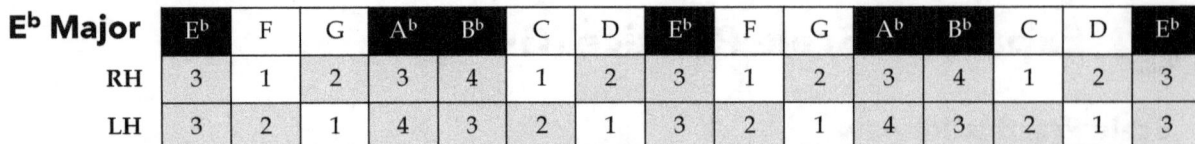

Technique: Introduction to Hanon

The exercise below comes from a famous (or sometimes infamous) book of technical exercises by Charles-Louis Hanon titled *The Virtuoso Pianist*. The first exercise in the text can be worked on in a variety of ways to help develop strength and coordination between arm and fingers.

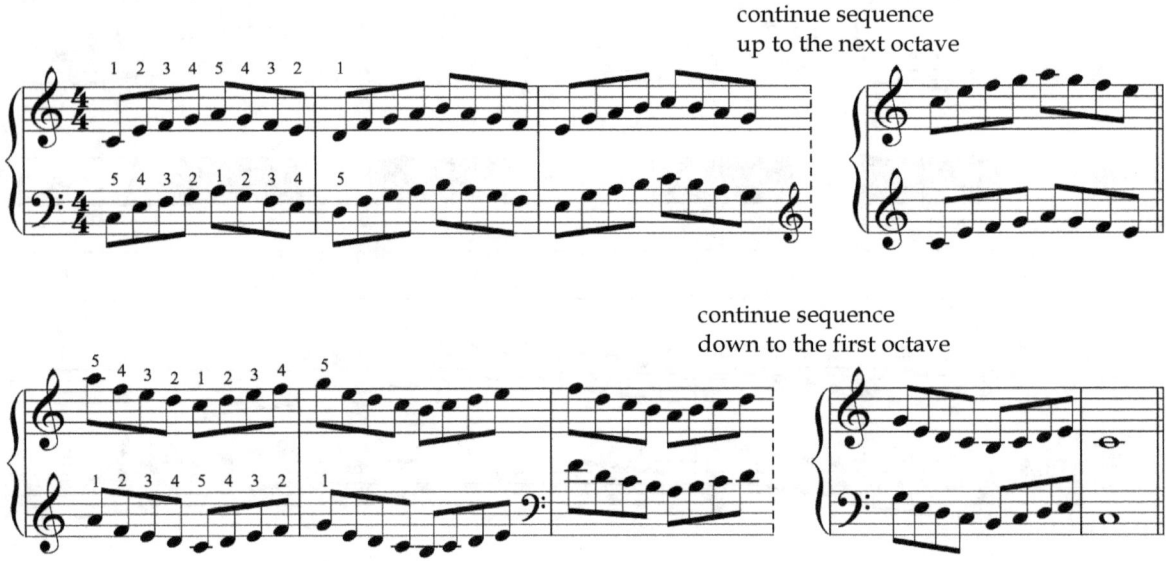

First Steps

Before you dive into drilled practice with this exercise, there's more to know besides the sequence above. The point of the exercise is not just playing the correct notes and rhythms; it is mean to work on a specific kind of movement coordinating fingers, wrist, and arm.

One of the primary movements is wrist circles. To practice this, start by placing your RH on the keys of the piano in a C major five-finger pattern. Without playing any keys and without lifting your fingers, move your wrist in a counterclockwise circle like the one indicated on page 117. Allow all the motion to be directed from the wrist (not the elbow). Do this same movement with the LH, but the circle will go clockwise as indicated on page 117. Now try the circles with both hands simultaneously. Their gestures should be going in opposite directions.

For both hands, the wrist will make a complete circle for each measure of the exercise. The RH wrist circle starts by scooping under from left to right as the notes go up. At the highest note, the RH starts to arch up and complete the other half of the circle as the notes go down. The LH circle starts by arching up from left to right as the notes go up. At the highest note, the LH begins scooping under from right to left as the notes go down.

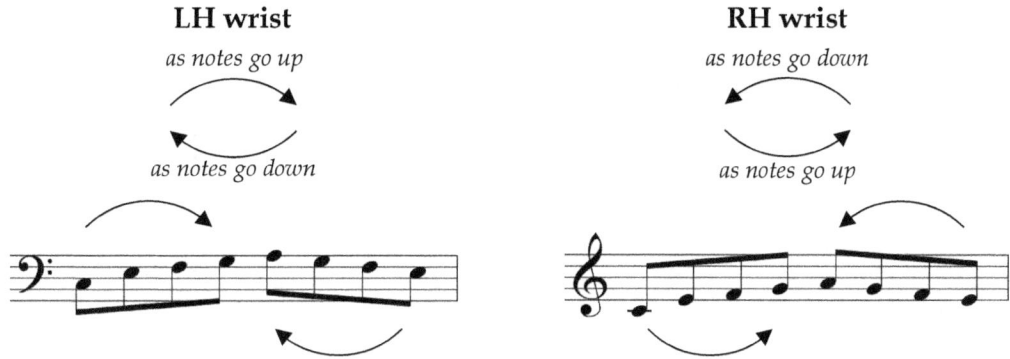

After gaining fluency with all white keys, practice Hanon #1 in F Major and G Major.

F Major

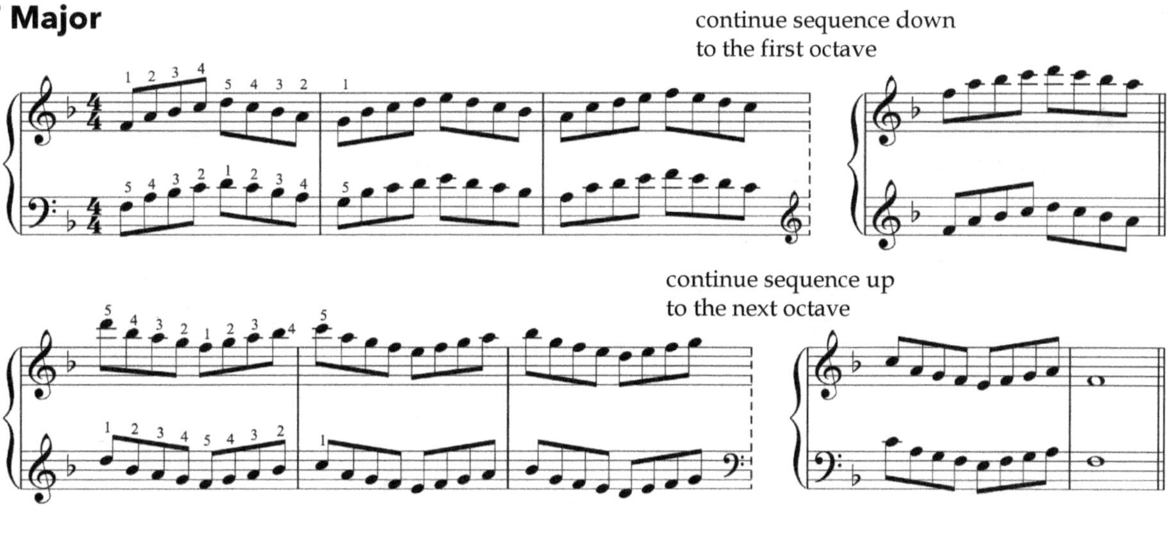

G Major

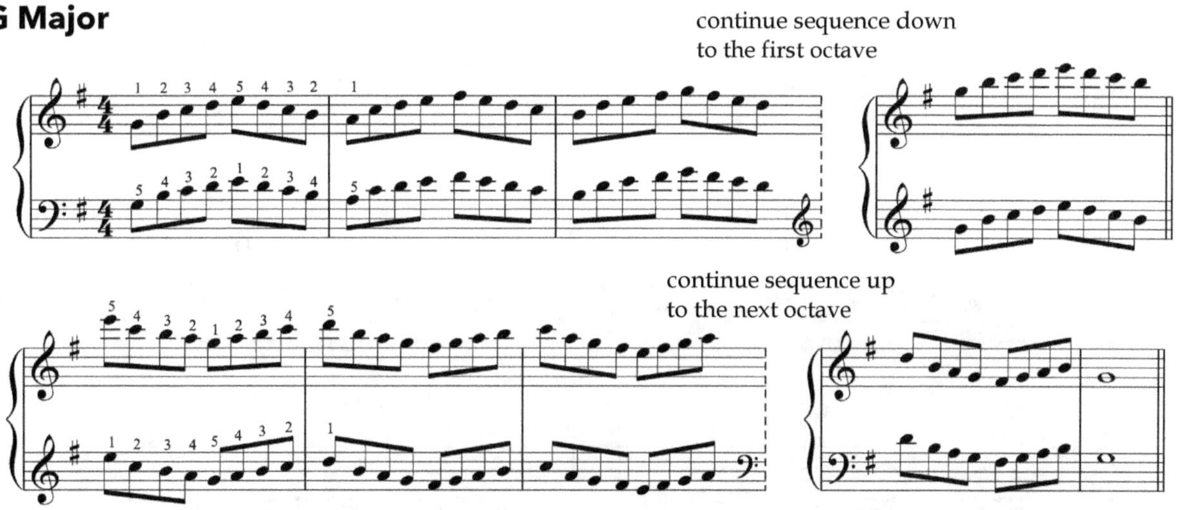

Unit 4

Music for Reading (Riffs and Basslines)

Each riff below is presented in two keys. Pay close attention to how fingering can differ from one key to the next.

1

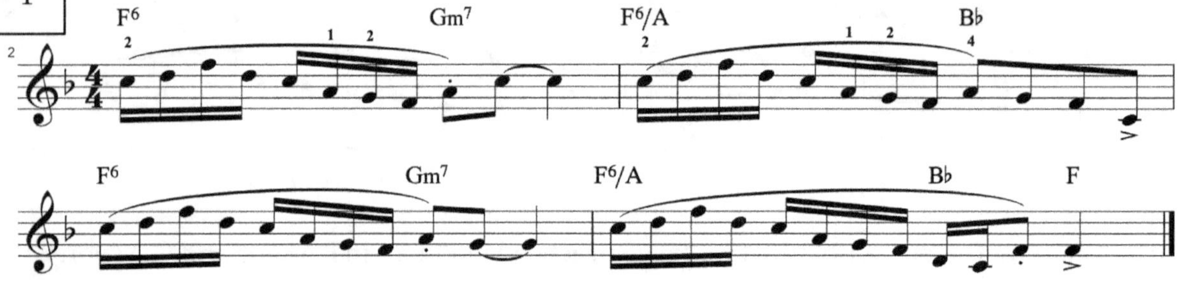

2

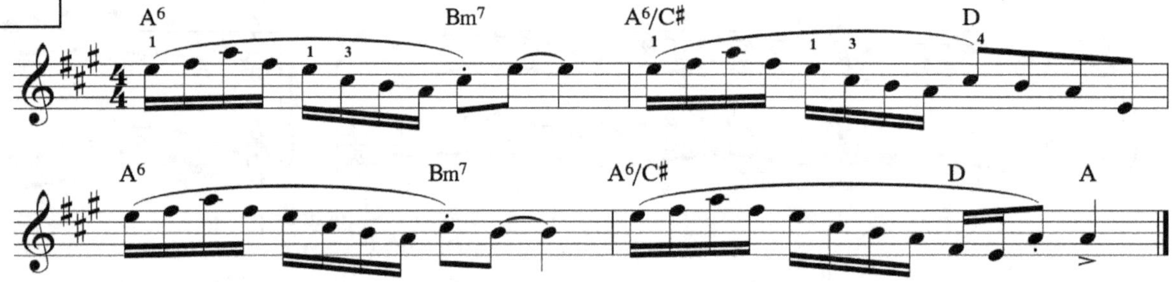

3

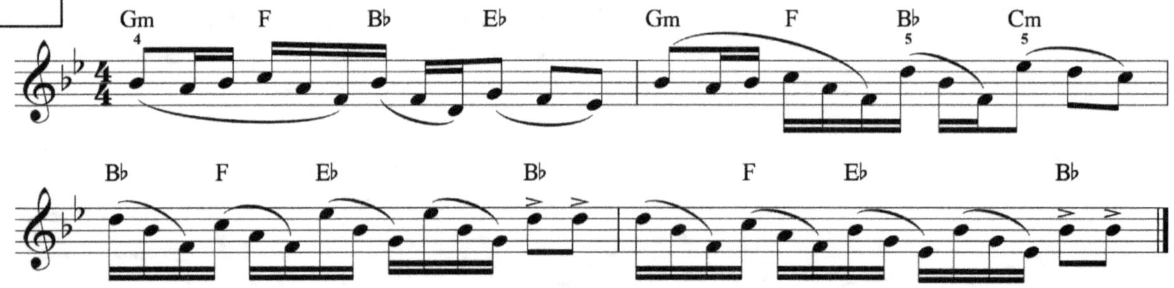

4

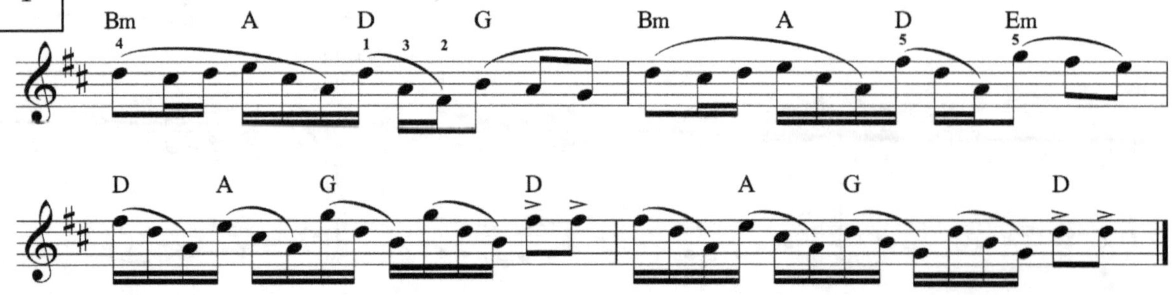

Two-Handed Basslines

Use both hands to play the basslines below. Distribute the notes in the most comfortable way for your hands. Exercise 5 shows one way notes could be redistributed between the hands. Write in fingerings as needed so you practice as consistently as possible.
WATCH OUT: playing in a different key may result in needing to use a different fingering.

5

6

7

8

Solo Repertoire

Song Without Words

Smooth and flowing (♩ = 102–120)

Andy Villemez

Forward

Steady but moving (♩ = 112)

Andy Villemez

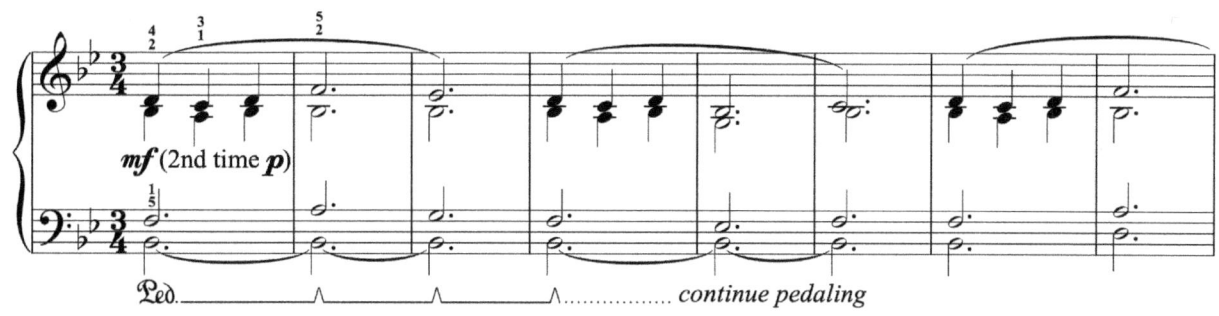

Practice the same repertoire piece transposed to the key of E♭.

Around the Corner

Smooth with energy (♩ = 80–90)

Andy Villemez

122　　　　　　　Unit 4

Samba

Andy Villemez

Samba (Duet)

Andy Villemez

(♩ = 96)

Lead Sheet Reading

Practice the following lead sheets in keyboard style making sure the melody is always the highest voice. Convert the chord names to Nashville Numbers under each melody.

1 A little slow (♩ = 70)

Eb Fm Cm Ab Eb Fm Cm Abm Eb

1

2 Medium pop (♩ = 116)

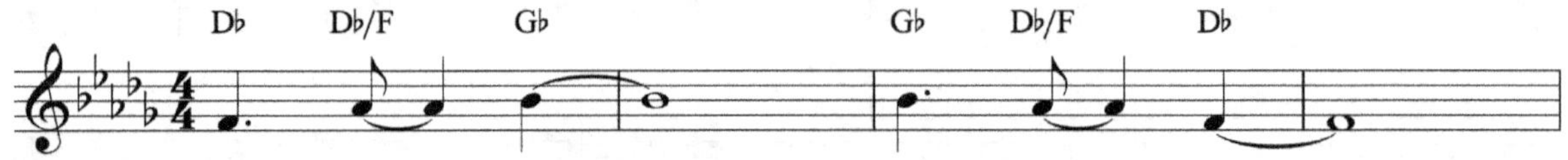

Db Db/F Gb Gb Db/F Db

1

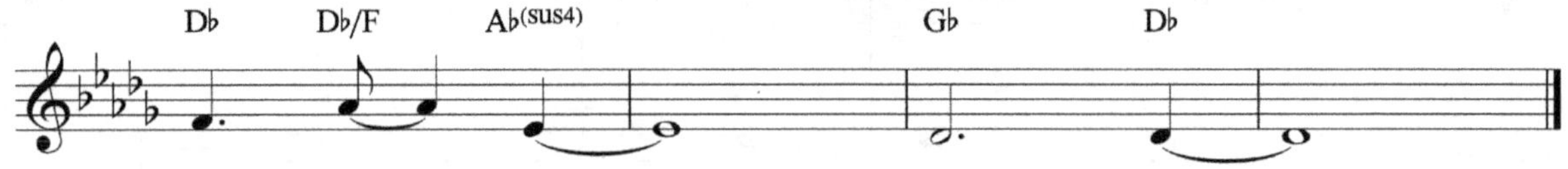

Db Db/F Ab(sus4) Gb Db

3 Dance pop (♩ = 125)

Ab Db/Bb E Gb Ab

1

Ab Db/Bb E Gb Ab

Creating Basic Accompaniment Patterns

Creating a unique accompaniment pattern that fits the style of the music you're working with is an essential skill. The exercises below will help you develop ideas based on common patterns found in popular music.

Qualities of effective accompaniment patterns:

1. They match the **energy** of the section/song/style.
2. They **support** the melody/soloist without getting in their way.
3. They utilize repeated **rhythmic patterns**.
4. They use efficient and purposeful **voice leading**.

The exercises below explore common pop accompaniment patterns from the same chord progression.

Pop Pattern 1

Simplified Notation

Pop Pattern 2

Pop Pattern 3

Pop Pattern 4

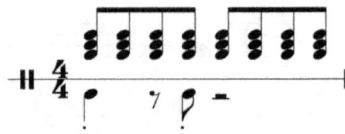

Use the accompaniment patterns on the previous page to practice the chord progressions below. Practice each progression in multiple accompaniment patterns.

1.
1	5	6-	4
G	D	Em	C

2.
6-	1/3	4	1/3	4/2	1
Fm	Ab/C	Db	Ab/C	Db/Bb	Ab

3.
1	5	7°/5	1	3°/1	4	4-
D	A	C#°/A	D	F#°/D	G	Gm

4.
1	5/7	6	4
Eb	Bb/D	Cm	Ab

5.
1	#5°/3	6	5	4
F	C#°/A	Dm	C	Bb

6.
1	1/3	4	4-/2
E	E/G#	A	Am/F#

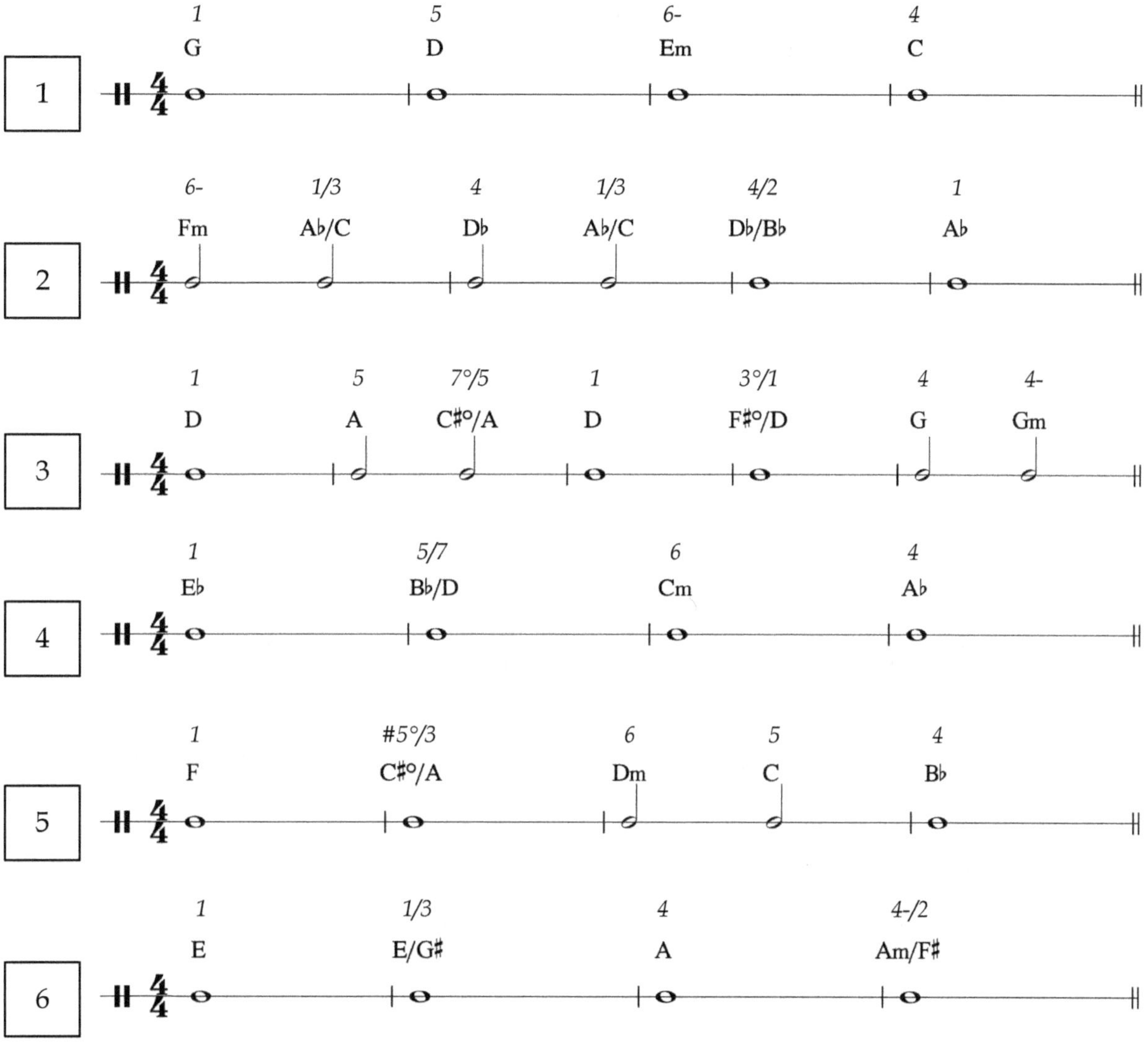

Using simplified notation like shown on the previous page, create your own accompaniment patterns that could be used for the chord progressions above.

Unit 4

Common Chord Progressions with Triads

Practice these exercises in group 3 keys using keyboard style with smooth voice leading. Use the sustain pedal to make transitions between chords sound smooth. Practice in a variety of accompaniment patterns and tempos.

1 | 4/4 1 | 5 | 6- | 4 :||

Write in chord names and practice in the following keys:

A♭:
D♭:
B♭:

2 | 4/4 1 | #1° | 2- | 4 :||

Write in chord names and practice in the following keys:

E♭:
A♭:
B♭:

3 | 4/4 6- | 2 | 4 | 1 :||

Write in chord names and practice in the following keys:

D♭:
E♭:
G♭:

Chord Charts with Accompaniment Patterns

The following charts are examples of common chord progressions in various styles that use accompaniment patterns similar to the basic patterns listed on page 128. Play the following exercises in **keyboard style** with the notated accompaniment patterns.

1 You can hear a chord progression like exercise 1 in the song "Someone Like You" as performed by Adele.

Accompaniment Pattern: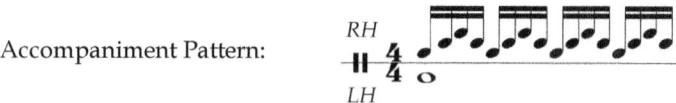

KEY: A   Pop Piano Ballad (♩ = 68)

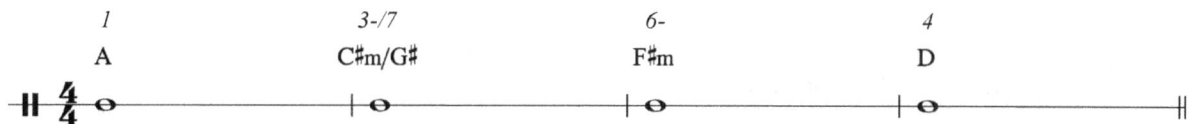

| 1 | 3-/7 | 6- | 4 |
| A | C#m/G# | F#m | D |

2 You can hear a chord progression like exercise 2 in the song "Make You Feel My Love" as performed by Adele.

Accompaniment Pattern: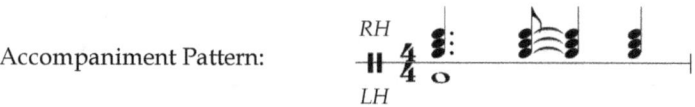

KEY: D   Pop Piano Ballad (♩ = 77)

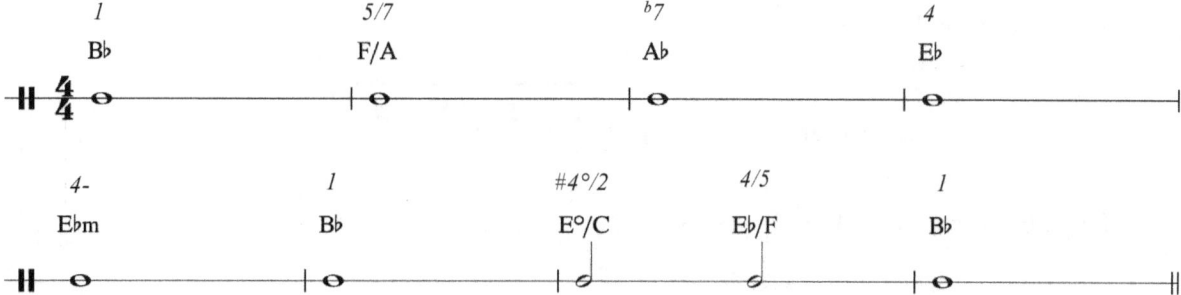

| 1 | 5/7 | ♭7 | 4 |
| B♭ | F/A | A♭ | E♭ |

| 4- | 1 | #4°/2 | 4/5 | 1 |
| E♭m | B♭ | E°/C | E♭/F | B♭ |

Unit 4   131

3. You can hear a chord progression like exercise 3 in the song "If I Ain't Got You" as performed by Alicia Keys.

Accompaniment Pattern:

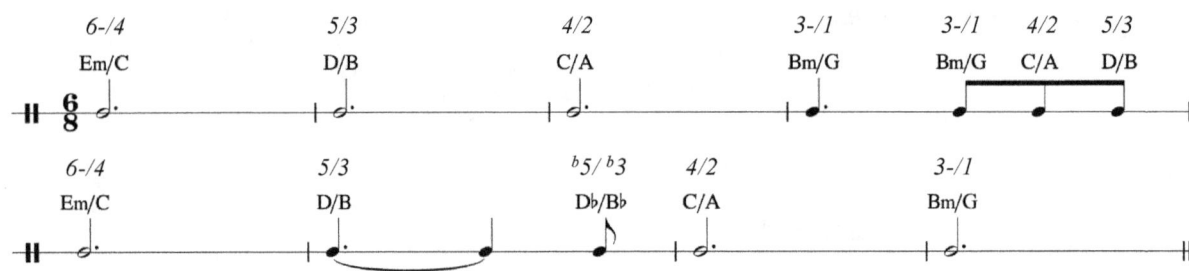

KEY: G   Pop Piano Ballad (♩. = 59)

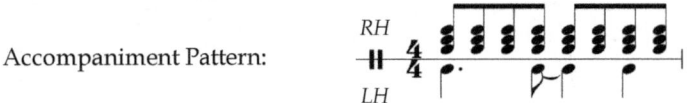

4. You can hear a chord progression like exercise 4 in the song "Groovin'" as performed by The Young Rascals.

Accompaniment Pattern:

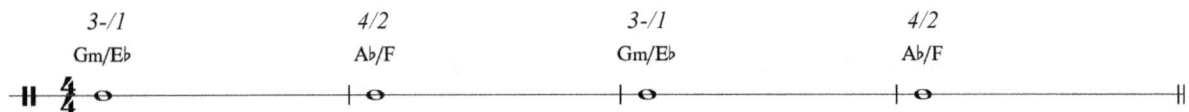

KEY: E♭   Pop R&B/Soul (♩ = 59)

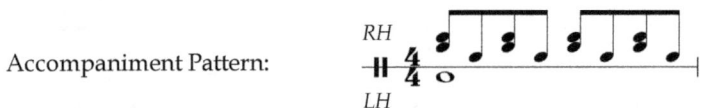

5. You can hear a chord progression like exercise 5 in the song "Talking to the Moon" as performed by Bruno Mars.

Accompaniment Pattern:

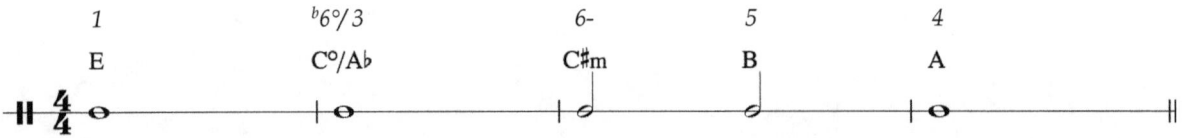

KEY: E   Pop/R&B Ballad (♩ = 73)

6 You can hear a chord progression like exercise 3 in the song "Best Part" as performed by Daniel Caesar.

Accompaniment Pattern:

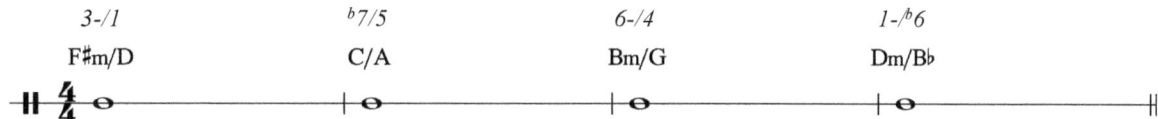

KEY: D   Contemporary R&B (♩ = 75)

3-/1	♭7/5	6-/4	1-/♭6
F#m/D	C/A	Bm/G	Dm/B♭

7 You can hear a chord progression like exercise 4 in the song "Movie'" as performed by Tom Misch.

Accompaniment Pattern:

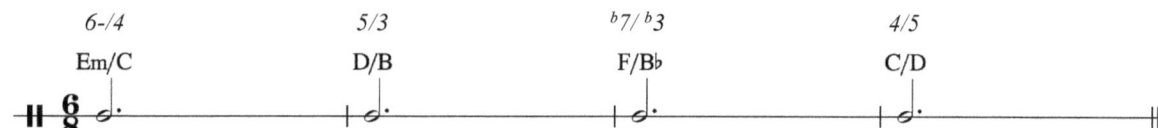

KEY: G   Contemporary R&B (♩. = 41)

6-/4	5/3	♭7/♭3	4/5
Em/C	D/B	F/B♭	C/D

8 You can hear a chord progression like exercise 5 in the song "A Sky Full of Stars" as performed by Coldplay.

KEY: G♭   Alternative Rock (♩ = 125)

6-	5	1/4	1	3-
E♭m	D♭	G♭/C♭	G♭	B♭m

Accompaniment Pattern:

Harmonization with Mode Mixture

Mode mixture, also known as modal borrowing or modal interchange, is a compositional technique where composers borrow chords from the parallel key. Using borrowed chords from another key allows you to add a variety of color to a musical phrase. While you can hear a variety of different "borrowing" in all styles of music, the most common type of mode mixture is a major-key song or phrase borrowing chords from its parallel minor. Adding color to a phrase in G major, for example, would involve reharmonizing with chords derived from the G natural, harmonic, or melodic minors. To understand how chords from these modes can be borrowed, try the exercise below.

1. Notate the minor scales of G indicated below. Use accidentals to notate sharps and flats (instead of a key signature).

G Natural Minor

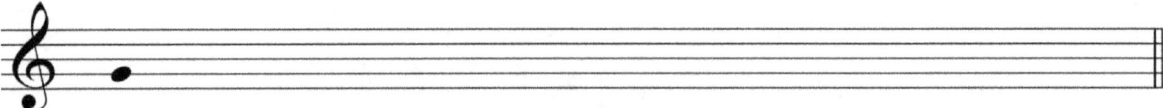

G Harmonic Minor

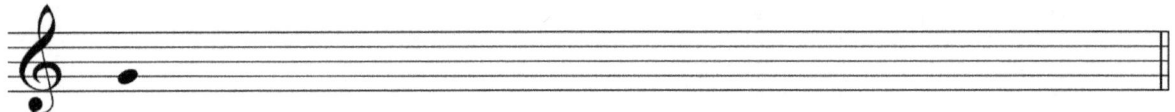

G Melodic Minor

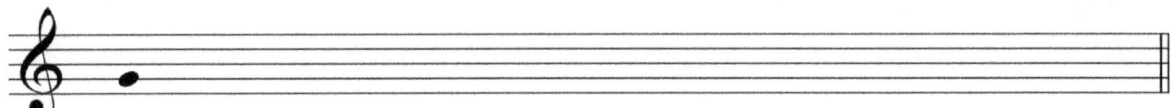

2. Build triads on each pitch of each minor scale. Write in the Nashville number and chord quality below each triad.

G Natural Minor

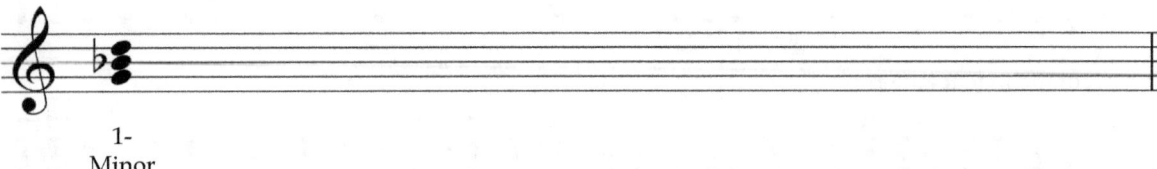

1-
Minor

G Harmonic Minor

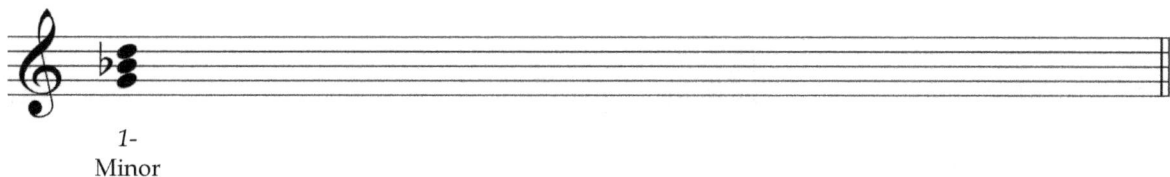

1-
Minor

G Melodic Minor

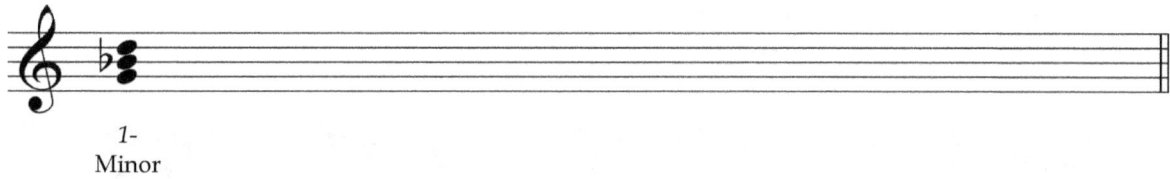

1-
Minor

3. Examine the chord qualities for each mode and note the significant differences.

Commonly borrowed chords are those built on the 3rd, 6th, and 7th scale degrees, as these are the notes that differ between the major and minor scales. In major keys, borrowing typically involves lowering these scale degrees to match their minor-key counterparts. For example, in G Major, a triad built on the sixth scale degree would be Em (6-). This chord is often replaced with E♭, or the lowered 6th scale degree. This is borrowed from the triad built on the sixth scale degree of the natural minor scale.

Compare the different effects of the chords in the harmonized melody below.

Diatonic Harmonization:

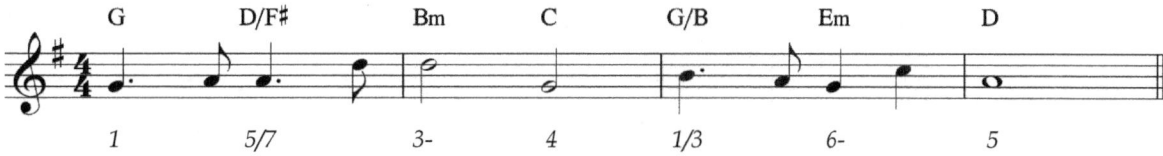

Harmonization with Mode Mixture:

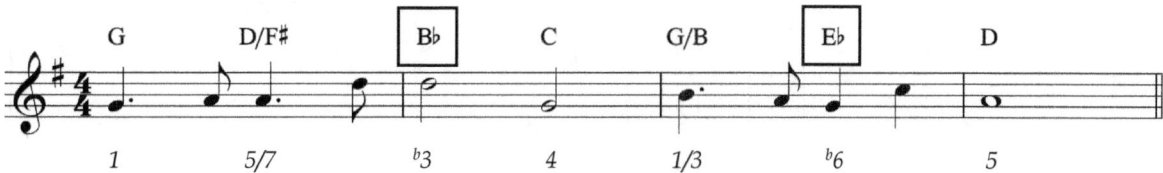

When borrowing occurs, the Roman numeral notation reflects the change with a flat sign (♭) for lowered roots. For instance, a chord like ♭6 in a major key indicates a major chord built on the lowered sixth scale degree.

Mode mixture enriches your harmonic palette and allows composers to express a wider range of emotions and colors. It's a subtle yet powerful tool that can significantly affect the mood and character of a piece.

The chart below summarizes common mode mixture chords. Since chord tones adjustments in mode mixture usually involve the lowering of scale degrees, borrowed chords are often described as "darkening" a melody.

Common Mode Mixture Chords		
Original Diatonic Chord	**Mode Mixture Chord**	**Example in G Major**
1	1-	G^{min}
2-	2°	A°
3-	♭3 or ♭3+	B♭ or B♭+
4	4-	C^{min}
5	5-	D^{min}
6-	♭6	E♭
7°	♭7	F

Harmonize the following melodies from the previous unit using only diatonic chords first. Then, reharmonize with mode mixture chords.

1 | Key: C Major

Diatonic Harmonization:

Chord Names: [   ]

[musical staff in 3/4, C major]

Nashville Numbers: [   ]

Harmonization with Mode Mixture:

Chord Names: [   ]

[musical staff in 3/4, C major]

Nashville Numbers: [   ]

2 | Key: D Major

Diatonic Harmonization:

Chord Names: [   ]

[musical staff in 4/4, D major]

Nashville Numbers: [   ]

Harmonization with Mode Mixture:

Chord Names: [   ]

[musical staff in 4/4, D major]

Nashville Numbers: [   ]

Melodies to Harmonize

Use the activities in this section to create three different harmonizations of the same melody. Each harmonization has a different set of guidelines or area of focus. Practice each harmonization by playing the melody in the RH and root position chords in the LH.

Key: E♭ Major

1. CONSERVATIVE: Use only diatonic triads in the boxes provided.

2. CLEVER: Use reharmonization techniques to create a variation of the harmonization in #1. Chords may be diatonic or chromatic.

3. CRAZY: Explore unknown combinations of melody and harmony. Chords may be diatonic or chromatic. (Make it weird. Go wild.)

Key: D♭ Major

1. CONSERVATIVE: Use only diatonic triads in the boxes provided.

2. CLEVER: Use reharmonization techniques to create a variation of the harmonization in #1. Chords may be diatonic or chromatic.

3. CRAZY: Explore unknown combinations of melody and harmony. Chords may be diatonic or chromatic. (Make it weird. Go wild.)

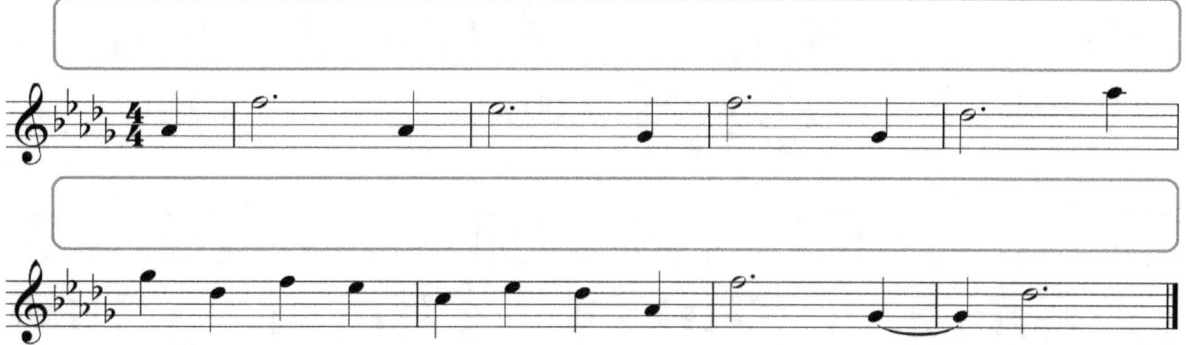

Unit Four Diatonic Triads Playback   INSTRUCTOR PAGE

Guidelines for drilling playback:
1. Play the following chord progression in the key of the exercise before each row of examples.
2. Before playing, students should say the Nashville Number of each chord in the exercise. (EX: "1 – minor 3 – 1")
3. Play all triads in root position and keyboard style **with smooth voice leading in the RH.**

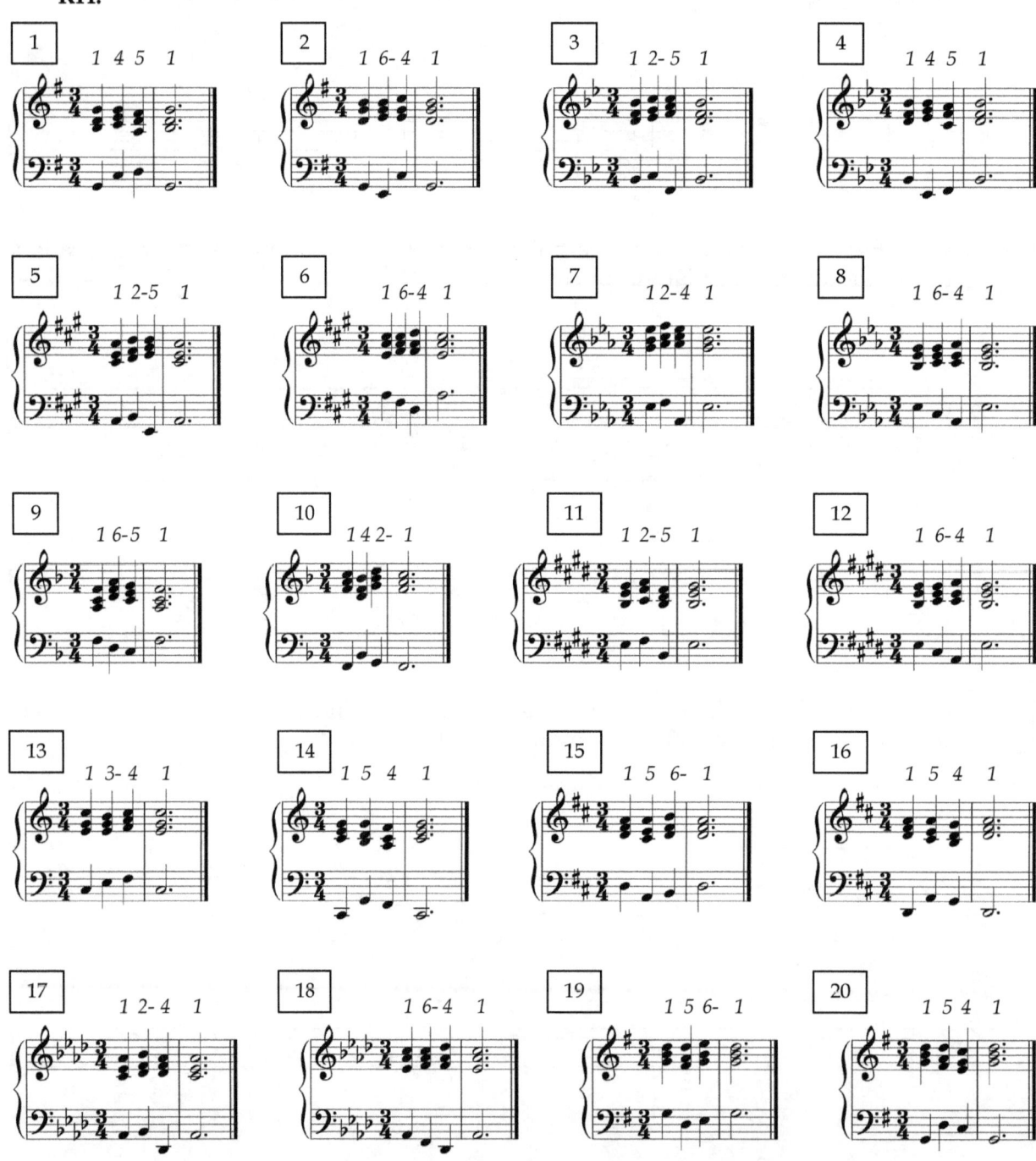

Unit Four Melodies for Playback INSTRUCTOR PAGE

Guidelines for drilling playback:
1. Give the hand position (but not major/minor) of the example along with playing the tonic chord.
2. Count in one measure before playing.

Unit 4 141

Unit Four Rhythm Training

The following rhythm drills prepare you to play simple and repetitive beat patterns for performance or production. Instruments are notated so that you can use drum pads or a percussion patch on a keyboard. Focus on the overall feel of these patterns and your relationship to the pulse. Don't let mistakes derail the groove.

The patterns for Unit 4 are notated in four parts: kick drum, snare, high hat, and open high hat. However, feel free to replace those parts with other sounds that still function similarly.

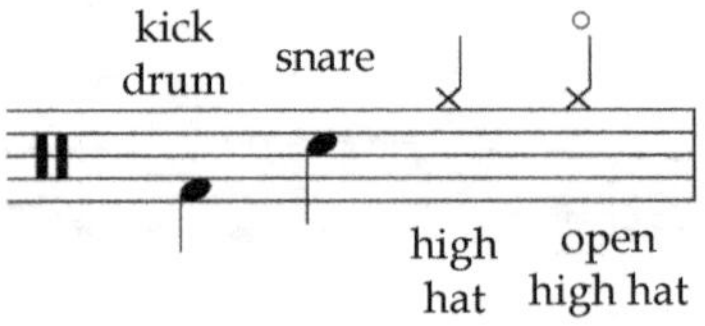

Practice at a variety of tempos.
(♩ = 56–140)

1

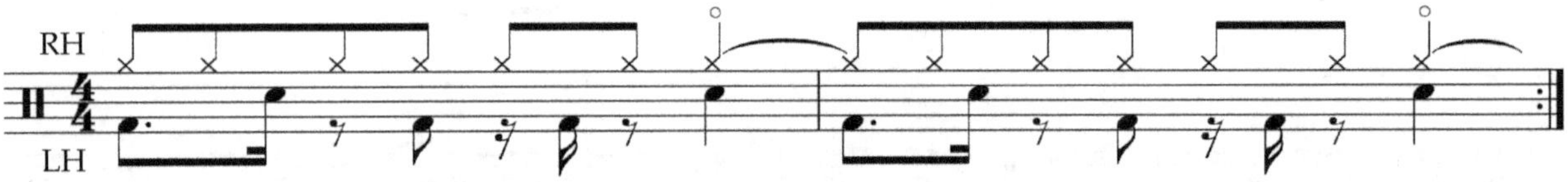

2

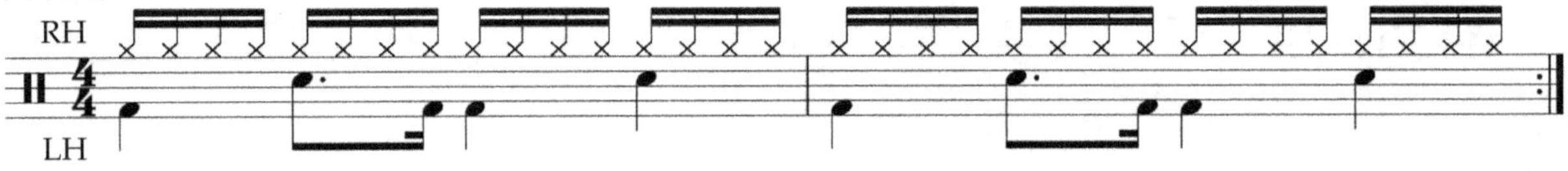

3

4

Add kick drum and snare parts to the high hat pattern below. Use a combination of quarter, 8th, and 16th notes/rests along with ties and syncopation.

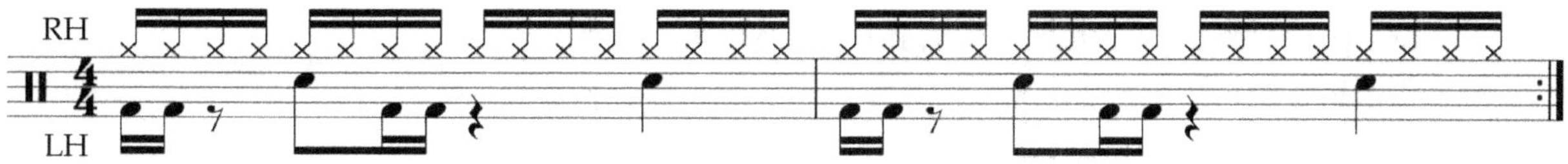

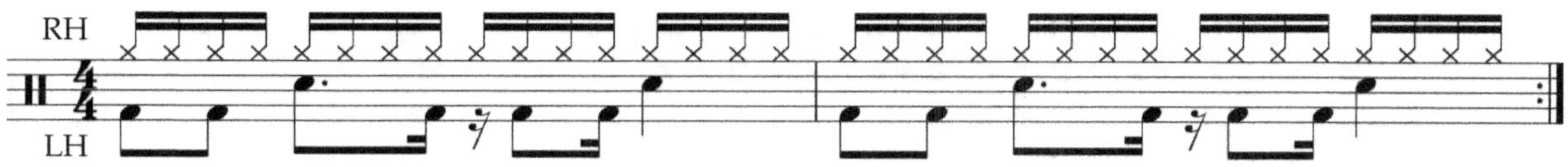

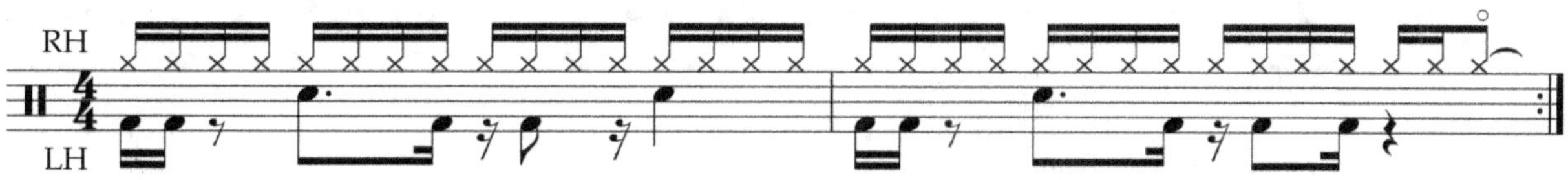

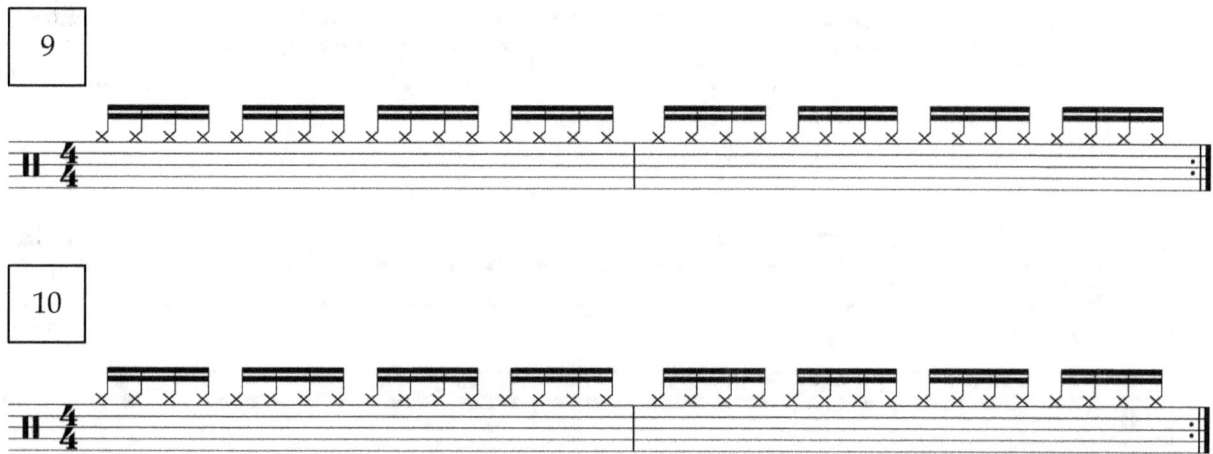

Unit 4 143

Part Two: Rhythm Reading

For all rhythm reading exercises:
1. Your primary is goal is fluency, not perfection.
2. Prioritize the pulse.
3. Don't stop.

Practice at a variety of tempos.

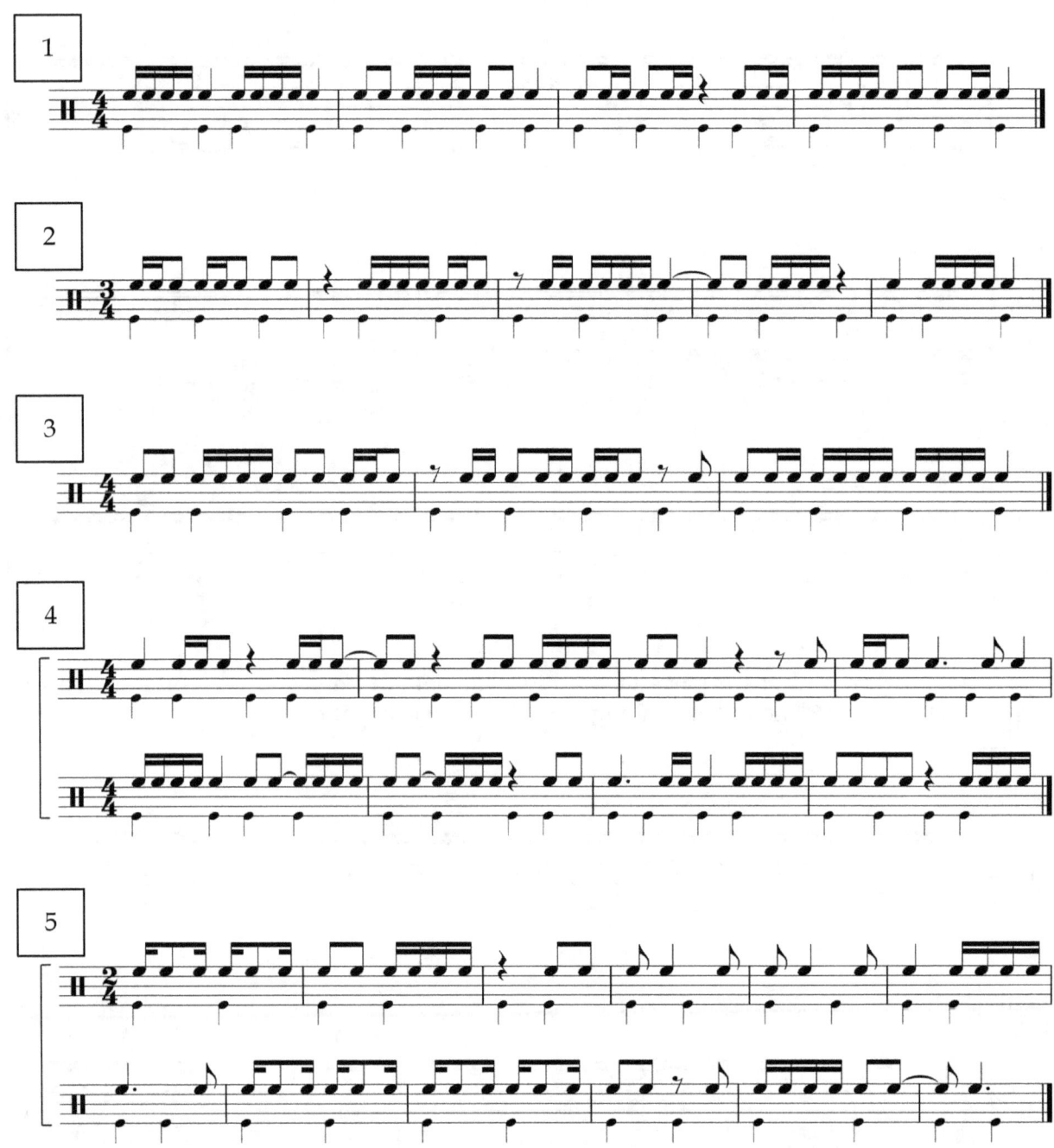

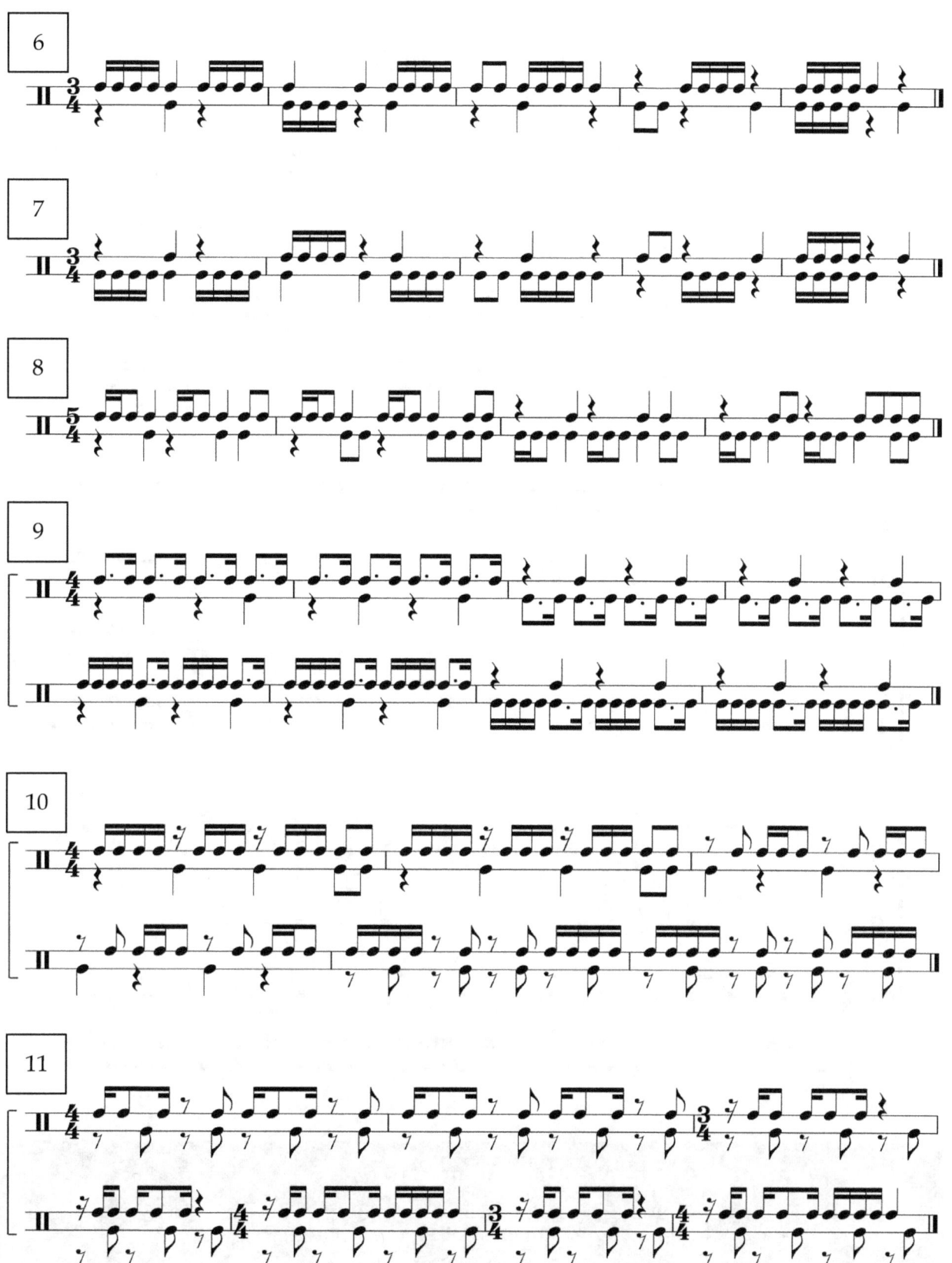

Rhythm Ensemble

Practice Variations and Challenges:
1. For individual work, practice different two-part combinations.
2. For paired or group work, assign alternating measures.

Unit Five

- ❏ **Introduction to 7th Chords**
- ❏ **Lead Sheets with 7th Chords**
- ❏ **Keyboard Style with 7th Chords**
- ❏ **Lead Sheet Reading with 7th Chords**
- ❏ **Chord Charts with 7th Chords**
- ❏ **Common Chord Progressions with 7th Chords**
- ❏ **Diatonic 7th Chords in Major Keys**
- ❏ **7th Chord Functions and Harmonization**
- ❏ **Unit Five Rhythm Training**
- ❏ **Solo Repertoire**
- ❏ **Unit Five Harmonic Playback**
- ❏ **Unit Five Melodies for Playback**

Notes:
_____
_____
_____
_____
_____
_____
_____
_____
_____
_____

Introduction to 7th Chords

If you know how to find major scales, you can find any 7th chord. All formulas in this book use the major scale as its reference point.

As a reminder, all triads and 7th chords (including other extended chords) are built using the interval of a 3rd. That means when you spell them in root position, you will always skip one (and only one) letter name for each note. For example, all triads and 7th chords with a root note of F will be spelled *F - A - C*. The only differences between the different types of chords (known as the "qualities" of chords) will be added sharps or flats that are used with the 3rd, 5th, or 7th of the chord.

One of the easiest ways to remember how to build 7th chords is by remembering the primary triad its based on combined with some interval of a 7th. For example, the Major 7 chord is a major triad combined with the interval of a maj7 on top. However you choose to internalize the chords below, its best to find patterns and connections among the chords instead of memorizing each of them in isolation.

Primary 7th Chords

MAJOR 7

Formula: *1 – 3 – 5 - 7*   D^{maj7}

 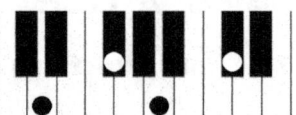

DOMINANT 7

Formula: *1 – 3 – 5 - ♭7*   D⁷

 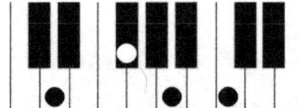

MINOR 7

Formula: *1 – ♭3 – 5 - ♭7*   D^{min7}

HALF-DIMINISHED 7

Formula: *1 – ♭3 – ♭5 - ♭7*   D^{ø7}

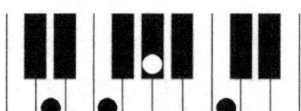

FULLY DIMINISHED 7

Formula: *1 – ♭3 – ♭5 - ♭♭7*   D^{o7}

7th Chord Cheat Sheet

Chord Quality	Formula	Example		Notations
Major 7	1 - 3 - 5 - 7	D^{maj7}	D F# A C#	$D^{maj7}, D^{\Delta 7}$
Dominant 7	1 - 3 - 5 - ♭7	D^7	D F# A C	D^7
Minor 7	1 - ♭3 - 5 - ♭7	D^{min7}	D F A C	D^{min7}, D^{-7}
Half-Diminished 7	1 - ♭3 - ♭5 - ♭7	$D^{ø7}$	D F A♭ C	$D^{min7(b5)}$
Fully Diminshed 7	1 - ♭3 - ♭5 - ♭♭7	D^{o7}	D F A♭ C♭	D^{dim7}
Less Common 7th Chords				
Min$^{(maj7)}$	1 - ♭3 - 5 - 7	$D^{min(maj7)}$	D F A C#	$D^{min(maj7)}$
Sus 4 Dominant 7	1 - 4 - 5 - ♭7	D^{sus7}	D G A C	$D^{sus7}, D^{7(sus4)}$
Augmented 7	1 - 3 - #5 - ♭7	D^{aug7}	D F# A# C	D^{aug7}, D^{+7}

7th Chord Building

Build the given chords four ways: letter names, keyboard, treble staff, and bass staff.

Example:
C^{min7}:   C E♭ G B♭

G^7:

E^{dim7}:

$E^{♭maj7}$:

B^{min7}:

$B^{♭maj7}$:

$C^{ø7}$:

Unit 5

C°7:

C#min7:

Abmaj7:

Eb7:

Bsus7:

Emin(maj7):

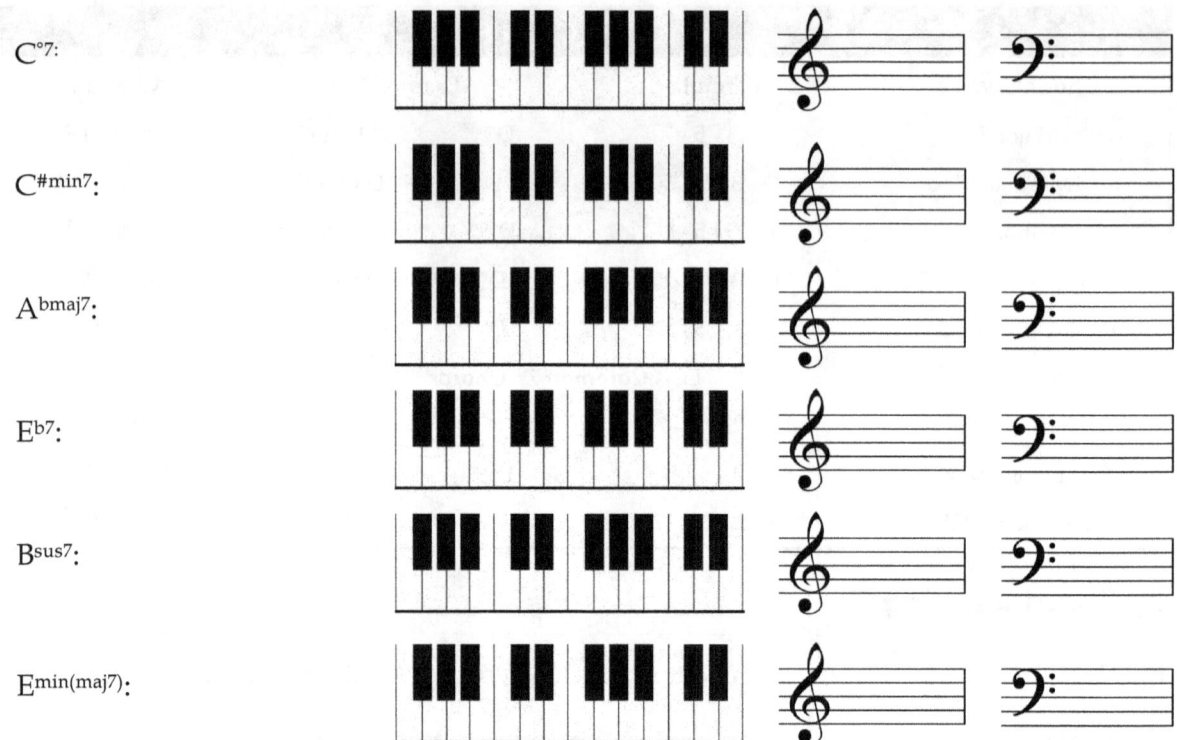

Identifying 7th Chords

Name the following triads from their given notation.

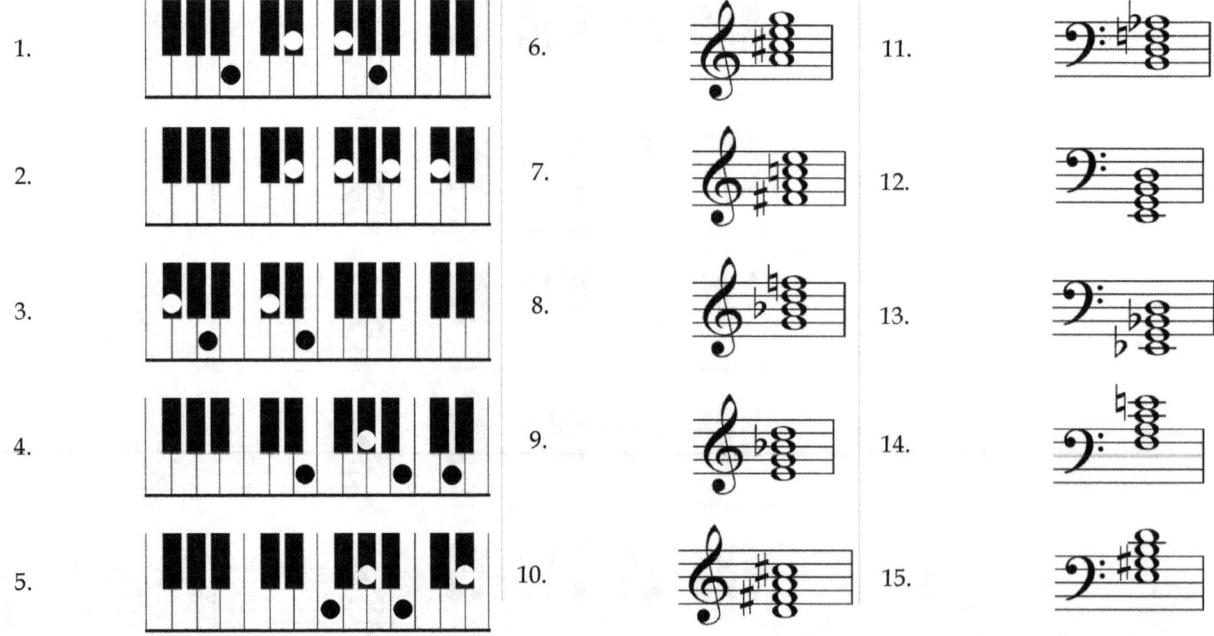

150 Unit 5

 **Practicing 7th Chords**

Drilling the Primary Chord Qualities

Use this chord progression to cycle through all five types of seventh chords built on the same root note. All seventh chords will use fingers *1-2-3-5* (LH *5-3-2-1*) in each hand. Practice playing through this progression on all twelve notes starting hands separately.

Example: 7th Chords Built on D
  Use fingers 1-2-3-5 (RH) or 5-3-2-1 (LH) for all root position seventh chords.

Drilling One Quality at a Time

This drill leans into one chord quality at a time. Pick one of the primary seventh chord qualities. Practice going up chromatically through all twelve root notes playing the same quality. Start hands separately. Variations of this exercise could include going *down* chromatically, practicing the chords broken instead of blocked, or a combination of the two.

Example: All Maj7 chords starting with C moving up chromatically

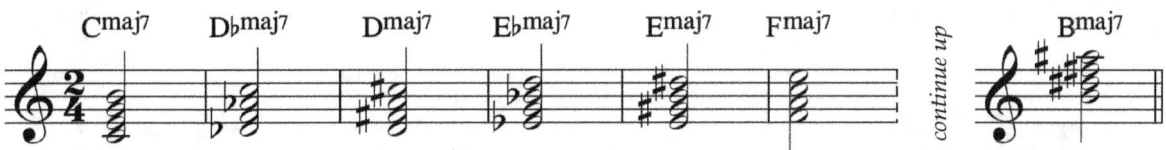

Example: All Min7 chords starting with G moving up chromatically

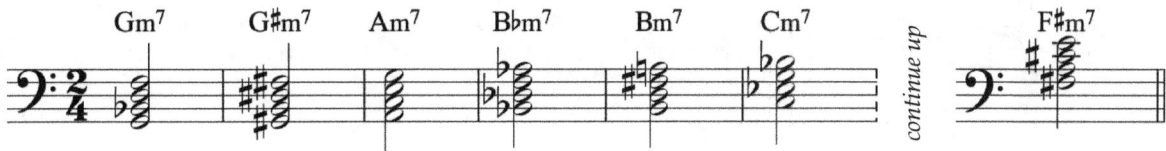

Lead Sheets with 7th Chords

Practice the following lead sheets with the RH playing the given melody, and the LH playing blocked chords in root position unless otherwise indicated with a slash chord.

Example:

What you SEE

What you could PLAY

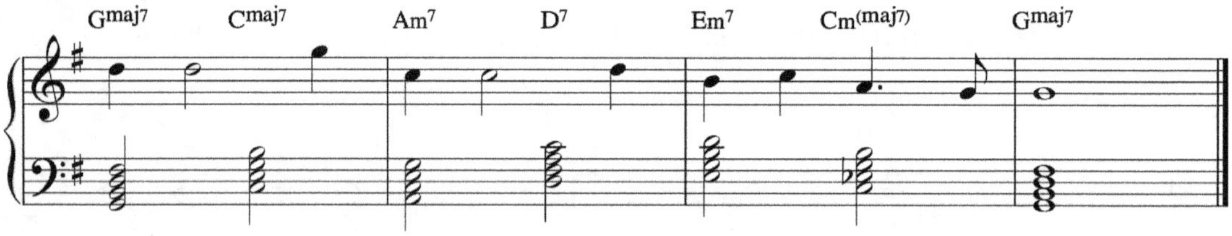

1 50s Rock (♩ = 96)

2 Medium Ballade (♩ = 66)

3 Contemporary R&B (♩ = 108)

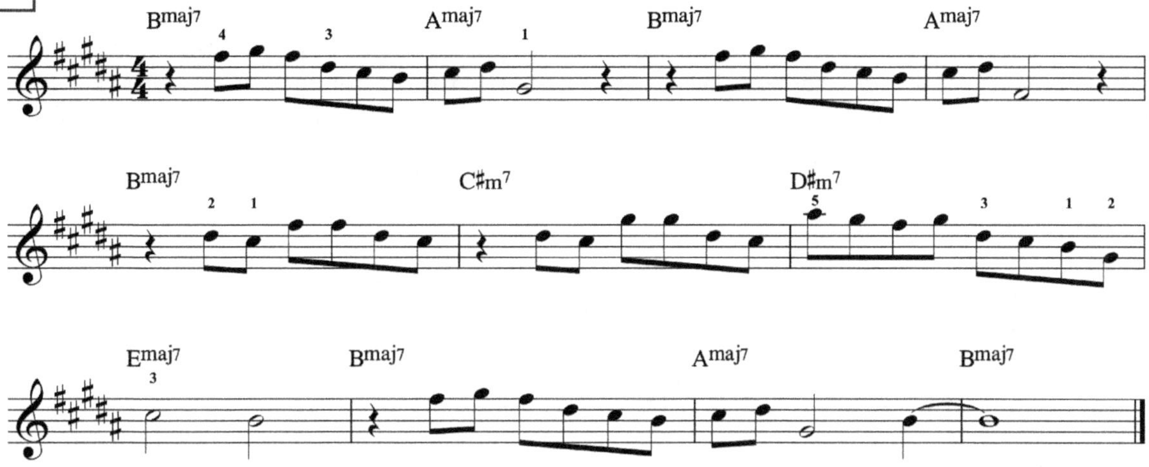

4 Medium Waltz (♩ = 88)

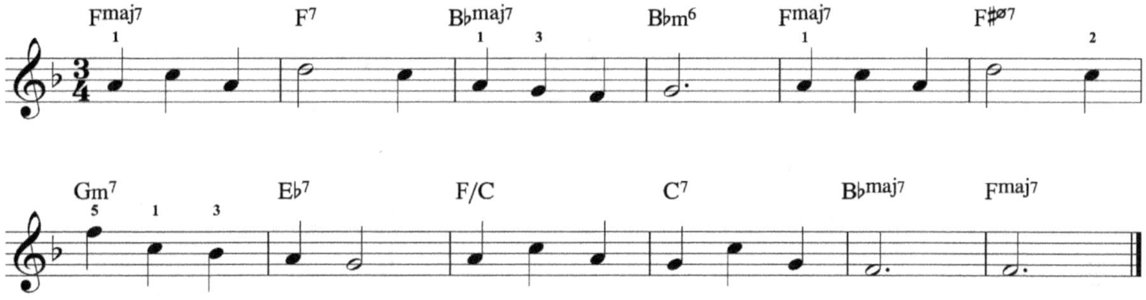

5 Medium Swing (♩ = 120)

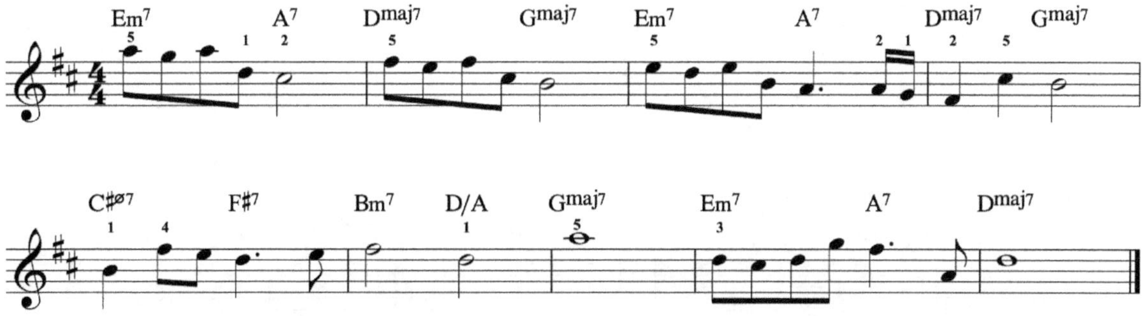

Keyboard Style with 7th Chords

As a review, keyboard style puts the root or bass note in the LH, the melodic note on the top of the RH, and other chord tones falling underneath the melodic note in the RH. When seventh chords are thrown into the mix, players will have to decide the best voicing in the RH especially if any chord tones should be doubled or left out depending on the melody note. See examples below.

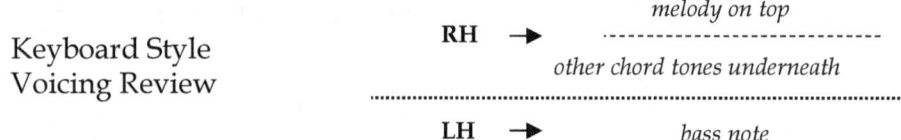

Basic Voicings with 7th Chords

EXAMPLE 1:
  What you might *SEE*

  What you could *PLAY*

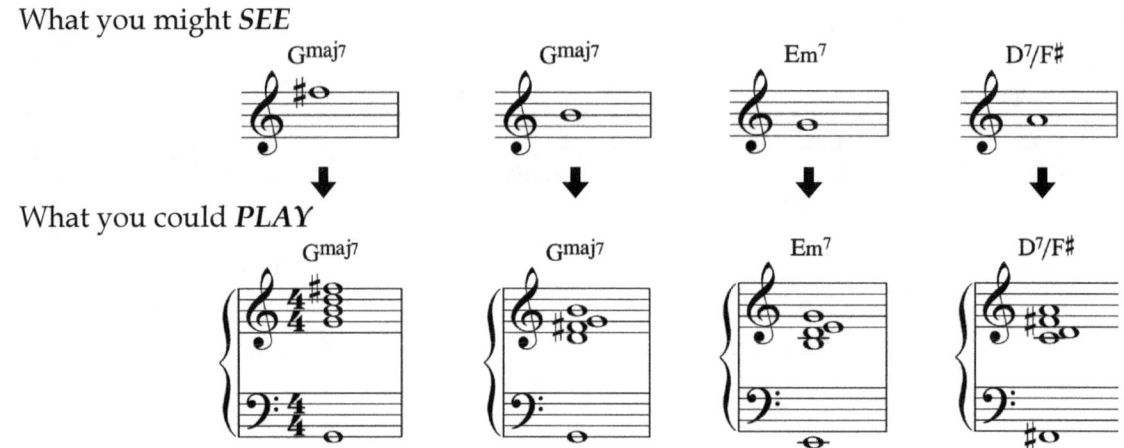

EXAMPLE 2:
  What you might *SEE*

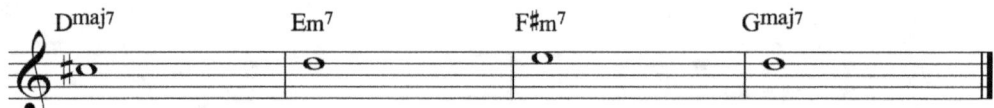

  What you could *PLAY*

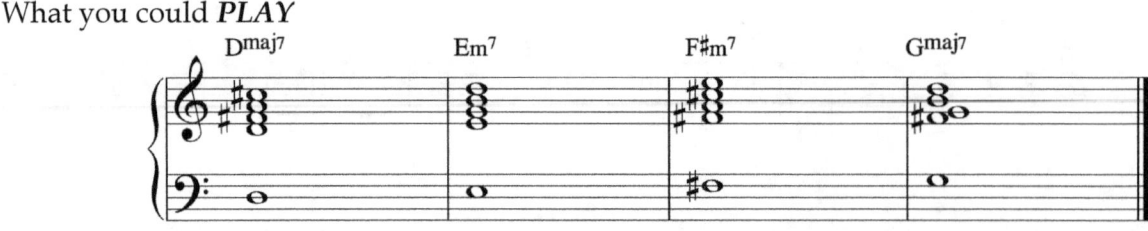

Voicings Without Doublings

Not all realizations of seventh chords will require playing four notes in your RH. The example below shows voicings that double the root note unnecessarily except for the B♭7 where the root note is also the melody note. Below is also a more efficient way of realizing the original lead sheet notation without doubling roots when the root is not the melody.

Realizations with non-chord tones in the melody

The example below demonstrates how you can interpret a lead-sheet melody that has non-chord tones at the change of harmony. Each realized harmony avoids doubling in the RH and uses only essential chord tones underneath when the melody is a non-chord tone.

Using the guidelines on the previous pages, practice the examples below in **keyboard style.** *Notate the specific chord voicings you use.*

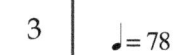

Blue Skies

Irving Berlin

Notate the realization of the above lead sheet using efficient chord voicings.

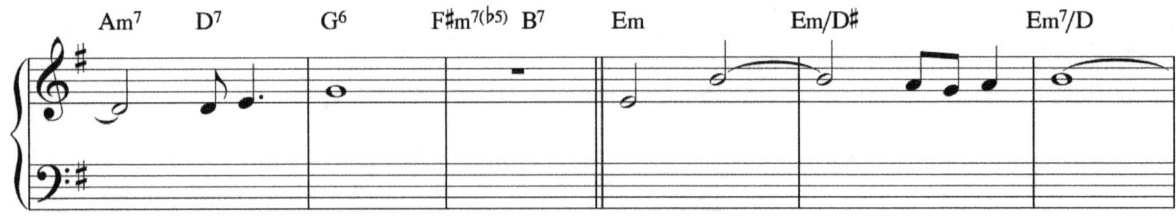

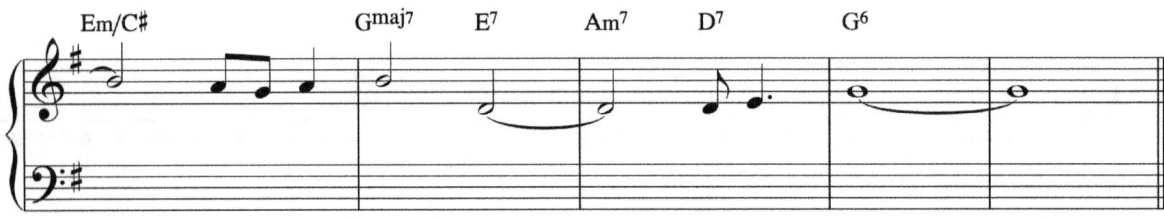

The "New World"

Adagio (♩ = 58)

Antonin Dvorak
arr. A. Villemez

Notate the realization of the above lead sheet using efficient chord voicings.

Adagio (♩ = 58)

Unit 5   159

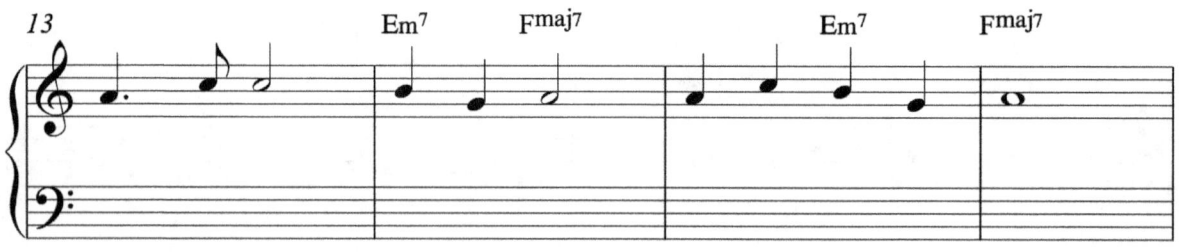

Chord Charts with 7th Chords

The following chord chart exercises are examples of common chord progressions with 7th chords in various styles. Play the following exercises in **keyboard style** with smooth voice leading.

| EX | You can hear a chord progression like the example below in the song "Wait a Minute!" as performed by Willow. |

KEY: Gb   Alternative/Indie (♩ = 101)

Use a blocked chord accompaniment with the harmonic rhythm notated below.

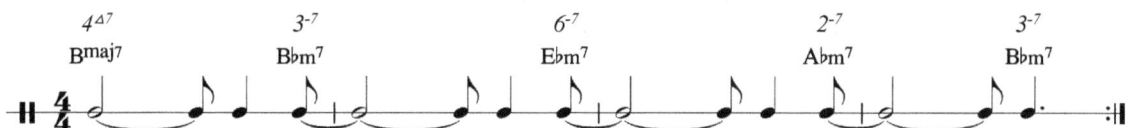

Example of possible realization:

| 1 | You can hear a chord progression like exercise 1 in the song "my future" as performed by Billie Eilish. |

KEY: Eb   Pop Ballad (♩ = 53)   Suggested Patch: E. Piano

Use a blocked chord accompaniment pattern throughout.

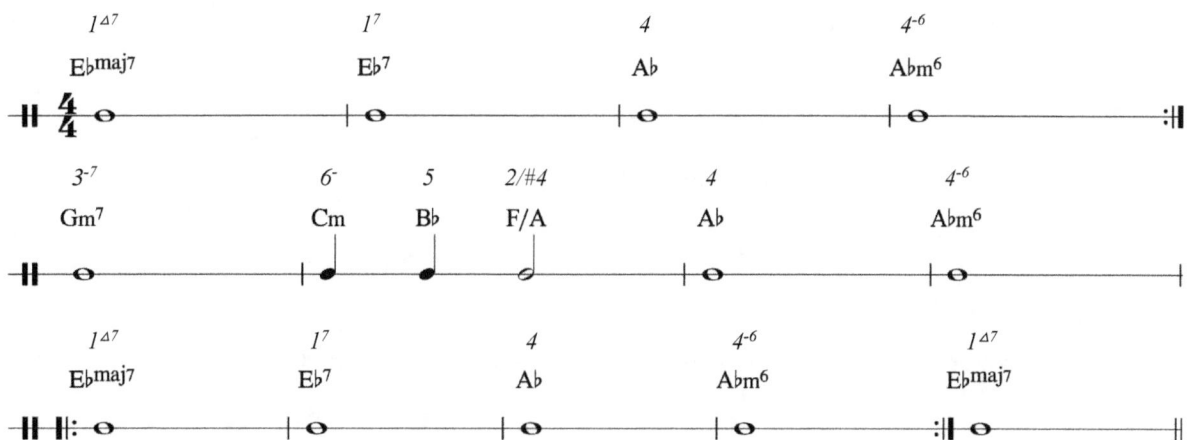

Unit 5   161

2. You can hear a chord progression like exercise 2 in the song "Going to a Town" as performed by Rufus Wainwright.

KEY: C   Pop/Rock (♩ = 62)   Suggested Patch: Piano

Use a blocked chord accompaniment pattern throughout.

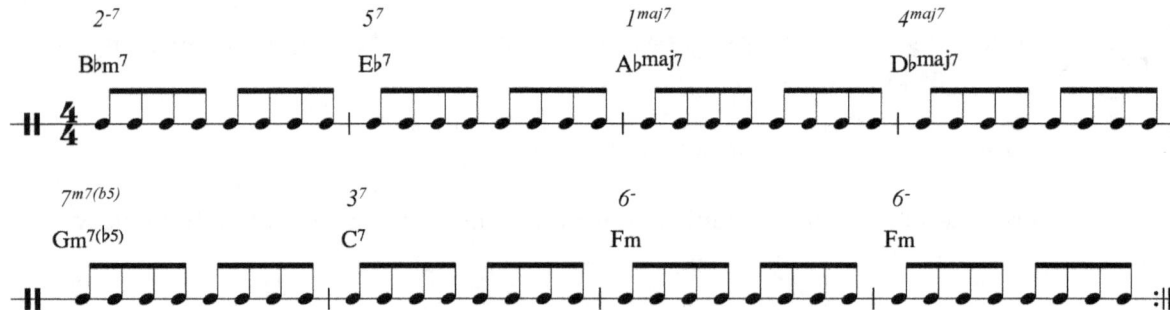

3. You can hear a chord progression like exercise 3 in the song "Do You Wanna Do Nothing With Me?" as performed by Lawrence.

Accompaniment Pattern:

KEY: B   Pop R&B/Soul (♩ = 102)

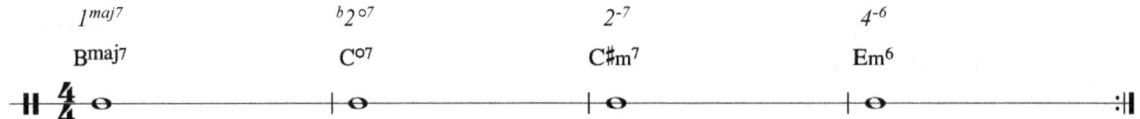

4. You can hear a chord progression like exercise 4 in the song "Lovefool" as performed by the Cardigans.

KEY: C   Indie Pop (♩ = 112)   Suggested Patch: E. Piano

Use blocked chords with the notated rhythm below.

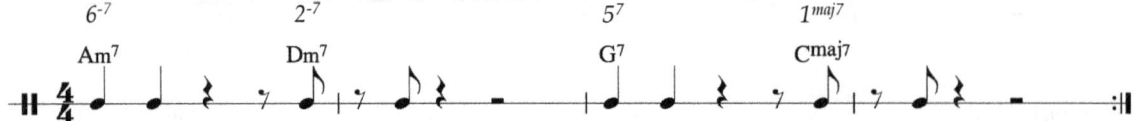

Common Chord Progressions with 7th Chords

Practice these exercises in the keys indicated using keyboard style with smooth voice leading. Use the sustain pedal to make transitions between chords sound smooth. Practice in a variety of accompaniment patterns and tempos.

1 $\frac{4}{4}$ 6⁻⁷ | 2⁻⁷ | 5⁷ | 1△⁷ :||

Write in chord names and practice in the following keys:

F:

E♭:

B♭:

2 $\frac{4}{4}$ 1△⁷ | 5⁷ | 4△⁷ | ♭7⁷ :||

Write in chord names and practice in the following keys:

C:

B:

D:

3 $\frac{4}{4}$ 1△⁷ | #1°⁷ | 2⁻⁷ | 4/5 :||

Write in chord names and practice in the following keys:

E:

A:

G:

Unit 5

Diatonic 7th Chords in Major Keys

As we found in Unit 2, the word **diatonic** means a group of notes that are associated with a given key. Below shows what building 7th chords based on each note of a scale looks like. A third, fifth, *and* seventh is added to each note of the scale making sure to use notes found only in the given key. (As a reminder, all chords use the interval of a 3rd as their building block.)

C Major

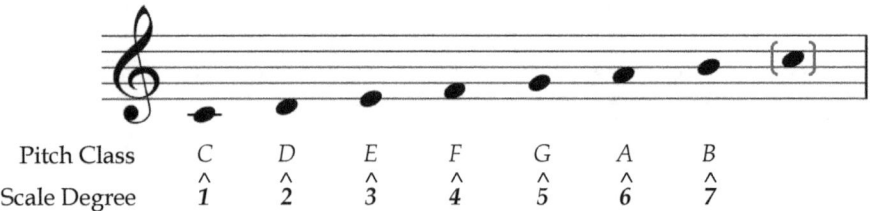

Pitch Class	C	D	E	F	G	A	B
Scale Degree	$\hat{1}$	$\hat{2}$	$\hat{3}$	$\hat{4}$	$\hat{5}$	$\hat{6}$	$\hat{7}$

C Major Diatonic 7th Chords

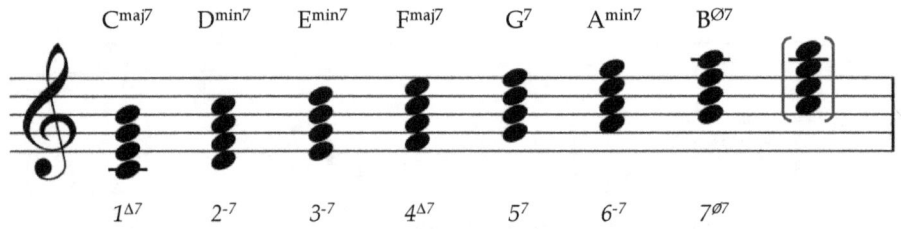

$1^{\Delta 7}$ 2^{-7} 3^{-7} $4^{\Delta 7}$ 5^{7} 6^{-7} $7^{\emptyset 7}$

Major Key Diatonic 7th Chord Chart

Tonic	1 Major 7	2- Minor 7	3- Minor 7	4 Major 7	5 Dominant 7	6- Minor 7	$7^{7(b5)}$ Half- Diminished 7
C	$C^{\Delta 7}$	D^{-7}	E^{-7}	$F^{\Delta 7}$	G^{7}	A^{-7}	$B^{\emptyset}$
Db	$D^{b\Delta 7}$	E^{b-7}	F^{-7}	$G^{b\Delta 7}$	A^{b7}	B^{b-7}	$C^{\emptyset}$
D	$D^{\Delta 7}$	E^{-7}	$F^{\#-7}$	$G^{\Delta 7}$	A^{7}	B^{-7}	$C^{\#\emptyset}$
Eb	$E^{b\Delta 7}$	F^{-7}	G^{-7}	$A^{b\Delta 7}$	B^{b7}	C^{-7}	$D^{\emptyset}$
E	$E^{\Delta 7}$	$F^{\#-7}$	$G^{\#-7}$	$A^{\Delta 7}$	B^{7}	$C^{\#-7}$	$D^{\#\emptyset}$
F	$F^{\Delta 7}$	G^{-7}	A^{-7}	$B^{b\Delta 7}$	C^{7}	D^{-7}	$E^{\emptyset}$
F#/Gb	$F^{\#}/G^{b\Delta 7}$	$G^{\#-7}$	$A^{\#-7}$	$B^{\Delta 7}$	$C^{\#7}$	$D^{\#-7}$	$E^{\#\emptyset}$
G	$G^{\Delta 7}$	A^{-7}	B^{-7}	$C^{\Delta 7}$	D^{7}	E^{-7}	$F^{\#\emptyset}$
Ab	$A^{b\Delta 7}$	B^{b-7}	C^{-7}	$D^{b\Delta 7}$	E^{b7}	F^{-7}	$G^{\emptyset}$
A	$A^{\Delta 7}$	B^{-7}	$C^{\#-7}$	$D^{\Delta 7}$	E^{7}	$F^{\#-7}$	$G^{\#\emptyset}$
Bb	$B^{b\Delta 7}$	C^{-7}	D^{-7}	$E^{b\Delta 7}$	F^{7}	G^{-7}	$A^{\emptyset}$
B	$B^{\Delta 7}$	$C^{\#-7}$	$D^{\#-7}$	$E^{\Delta 7}$	$F^{\#7}$	$G^{\#-7}$	$A^{\#\emptyset}$

7th Chord Functions and Harmonization

As a review from Unit 2, music is a cyclical pattern of increased and decreased energy, or tension and resolution. Understanding how chords affect energy will help you make thoughtful choices when harmonizing a melody. Chords fall into three basic functions: **tonic** (T), **predominant** (P), and **dominant** (D). Seventh chords are no exception to this principle. When you practice and use seventh chords in a diatonic context, you want to reflect on how that extra note (the 7th of the chord) affects energy and "color." For example, a 1^{maj7} chord still feels like a point of rest or resolution so the energy is not as affected, but the added 7th gives it a shimmering or glassy quality. On the other hand, a 5^7 chord has a more noticeable change in energy than color; it has slightly more energy to resolve than a 5 without the added 7th.

These are the qualities you are paying attention to as you use 7th chords and larger extensions in the future. How do the extensions of a basic triad affect its energy and color? The melody on the following page is the same example as used in Unit 2 harmonized with diatonic 7th chords.

HARMONIC FUNCTION	TONIC	PREDOMINANT	DOMINANT
COMMON TRAITS	• Points of Rest • Resolutions	• Maintain or slight increase/decrease in energy	• Highest energy • leads to resolution
DIATONIC TRAIDS	1$^{\triangle 7}$, 3^{-7}, and 6^{-7}	2^{-7}, 4$^{\triangle 7}$, and 6^{-7}	5^7, 7$^{7(b5)}$, and 3^{-7}

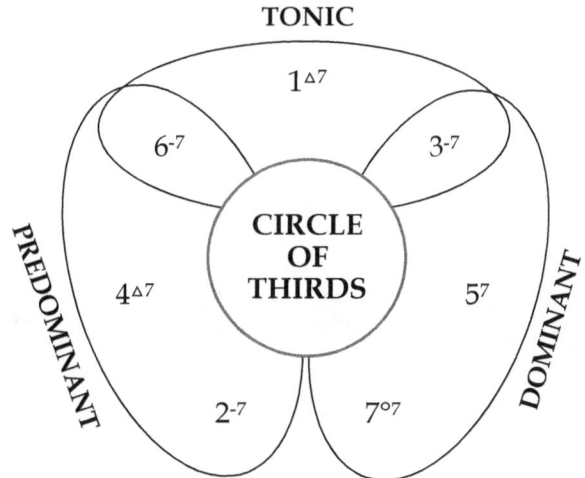

Example Melody:

Key: C Major

As you play and listen to the three harmonizations below, reflect on the following questions.

1. How do the different harmonizations with 7th chords affect how we hear the melody?
2. Which chords support melody notes that are non-chord tones?
3. Where do chords add, suspend, or take away energy? Where are there points of rest?
4. How do the 7th chords (as opposed to triads) add subtlety or depth?

Example Harmonizations:

Your Harmonization:

Chord Names

NNS

Harmonize each melody two ways. The first harmonization should consist of diatonic chords only. The second harmonization of the same melody should explore reharmonization techniques using seventh chords. Practice each harmonization by playing the melody in the RH and root position chords in the LH.

| 1 | Key: C Major |

Diatonic Harmonization:

Chord Names

Nashville Numbers

Reharmonization:

Chord Names

Nashville Numbers

| 2 | Key: A Major |

Diatonic Harmonization:

Chord Names

Nashville Numbers

Reharmonization:

Chord Names

Nashville Numbers

Compose and notate two melodies. Harmonize each two ways. The first harmonization should consist of diatonic chords only. The second harmonization of the same melody should explore reharmonization techniques using triads and/or seventh chords. Practice each harmonization by playing the melody in the RH and root position chords in the LH.

1 Key:

Diatonic Harmonization:

Chord Names

Reharmonization:

Chord Names

2 Key:

Diatonic Harmonization:

Chord Names

Reharmonization:

Chord Names

Unit Five Rhythm Training

The following rhythm drills prepare you to play simple and repetitive beat patterns for performance or production. Instruments are notated so that you can use drum pads or a percussion patch on a keyboard. Focus on the overall feel of these patterns and your relationship to the pulse. Don't let mistakes derail the groove.

The patterns for Unit 5 are notated in four parts: kick drum, snare, high hat, and open high hat. However, feel free to replace those parts with other sounds that still function similarly.

Practice at a variety of tempos.
($\quarternote$ = 56–140)

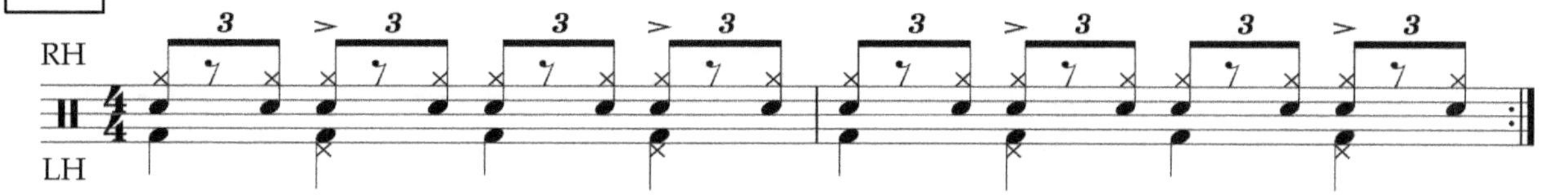

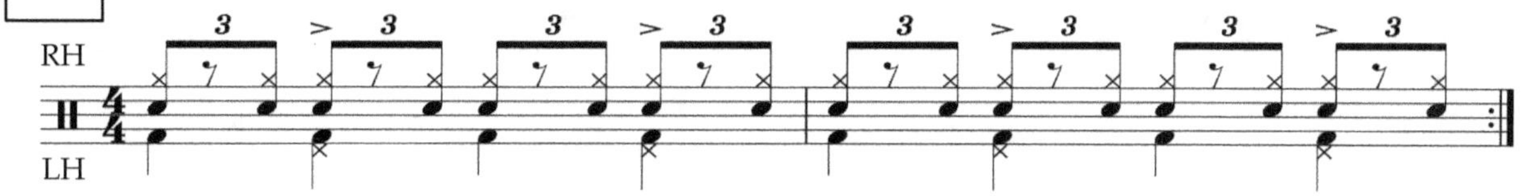

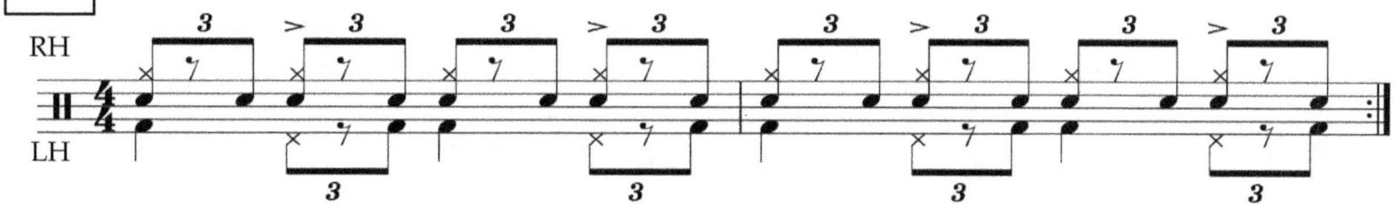

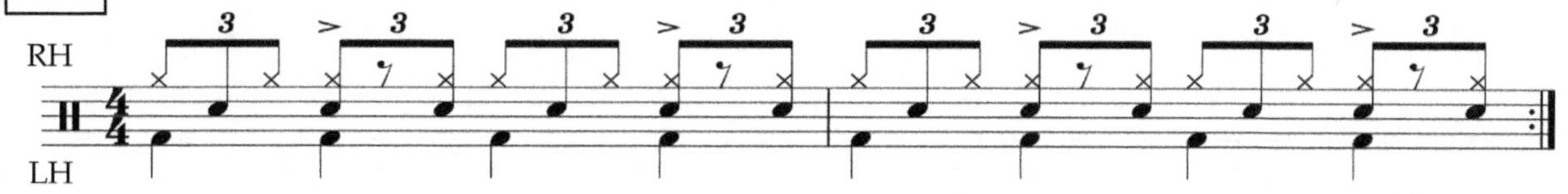

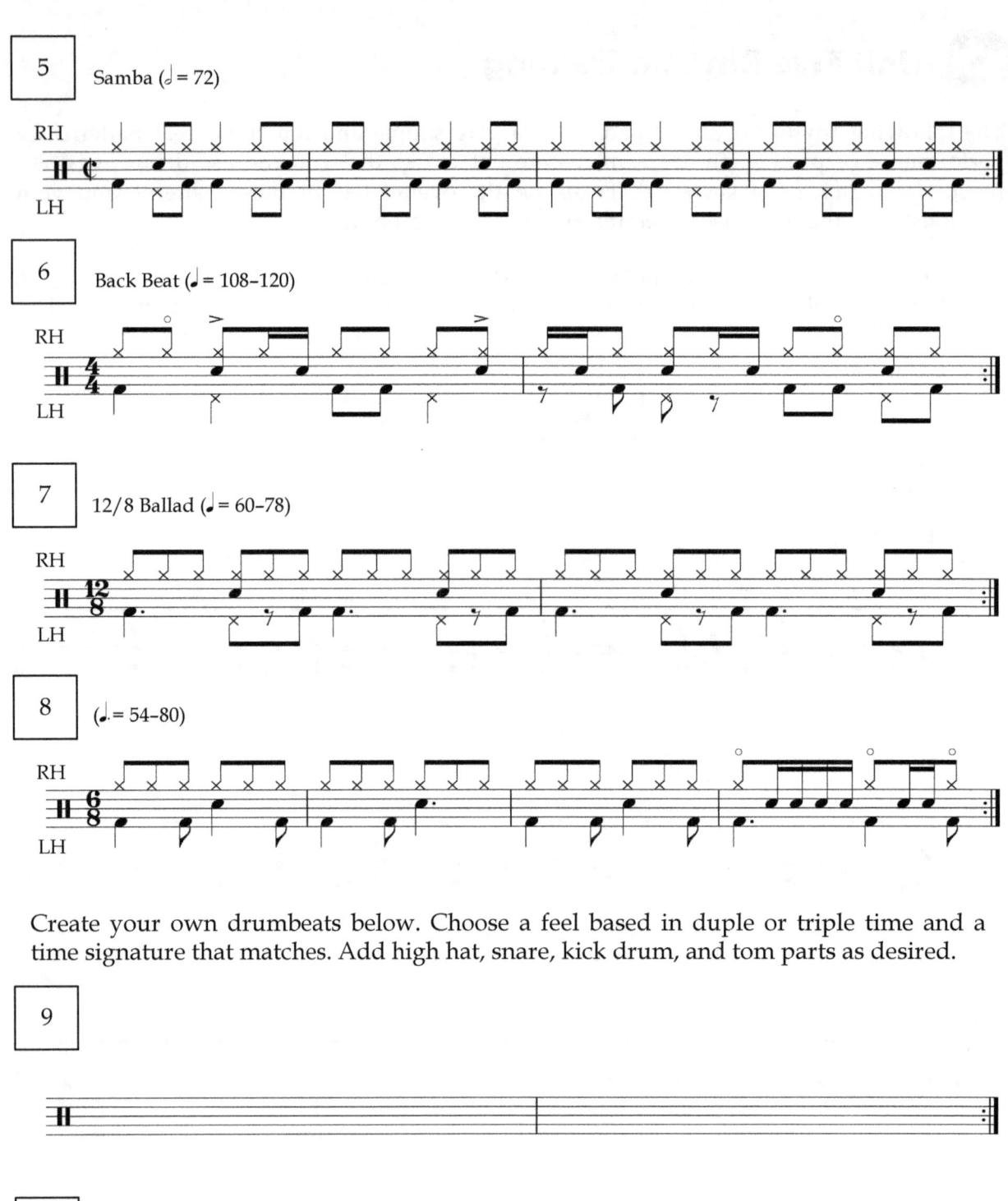

Create your own drumbeats below. Choose a feel based in duple or triple time and a time signature that matches. Add high hat, snare, kick drum, and tom parts as desired.

Part Two: Rhythm Reading

For all rhythm reading exercises:
1. Your primary is goal is fluency, not perfection.
2. Prioritize the pulse.
3. Don't stop.

Practice at a variety of tempos.

Rhythm Ensemble

12

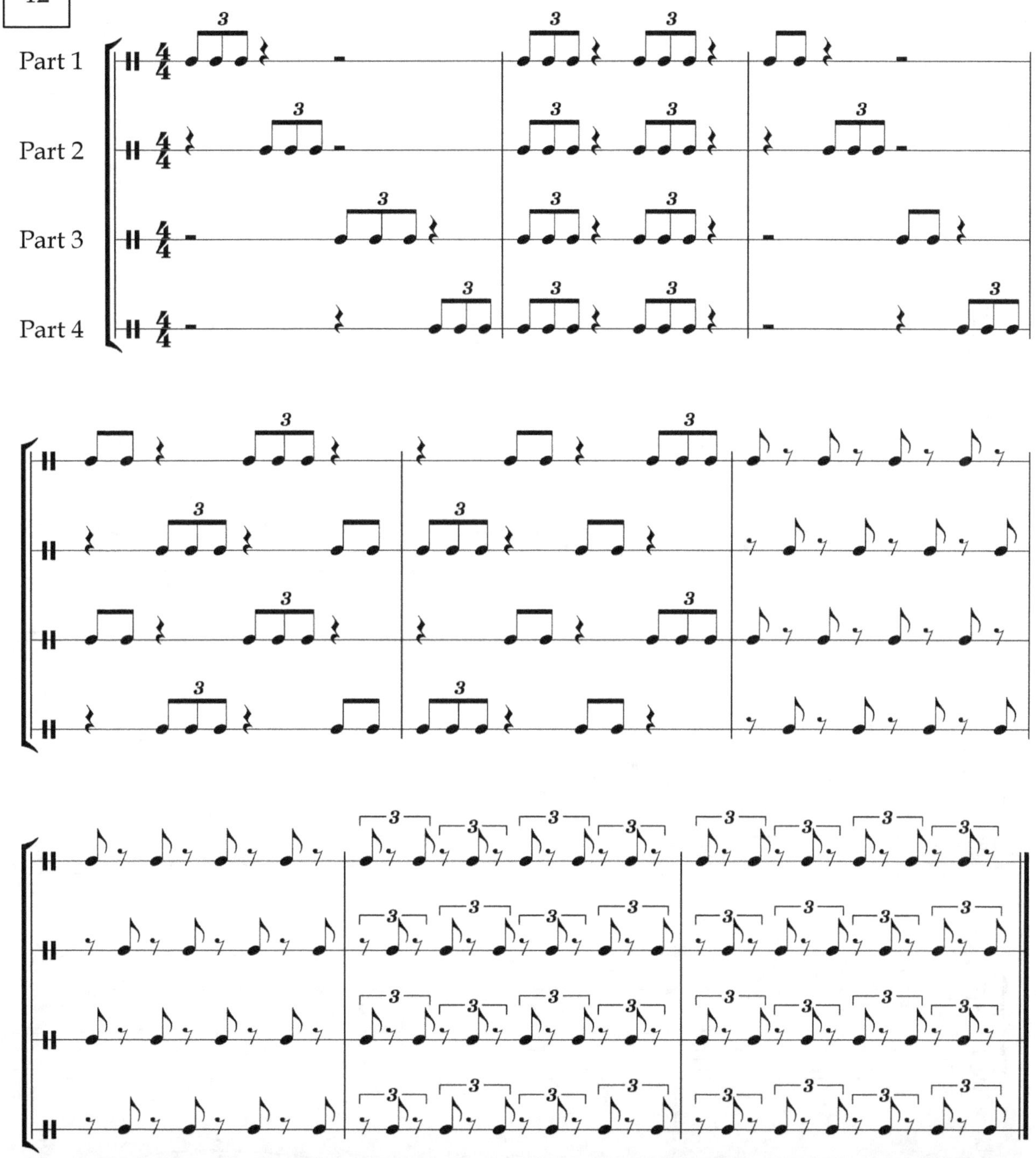

Practice Variations and Challenges:
1. For individual work, practice different two-part combinations.
2. For paired or group work, assign alternating measures.

Unit 5

Piazza

Flowing, not too fast (♩ = 110)

Andy Villemez

Adieu

Andy Villemez

Andantino (♩ = 80)

Unit Five Harmonic Playback   INSTRUCTOR PAGE

Guidelines for drilling playback:
1. Play the following chord progression in the key of the exercise before each row of examples.
2. Before playing, students should say the Nashville Number of each chord in the exercise. (EX: "1 – minor 3 – 1")
3. Play all triads in root position and keyboard style **with smooth voice leading in the RH.**

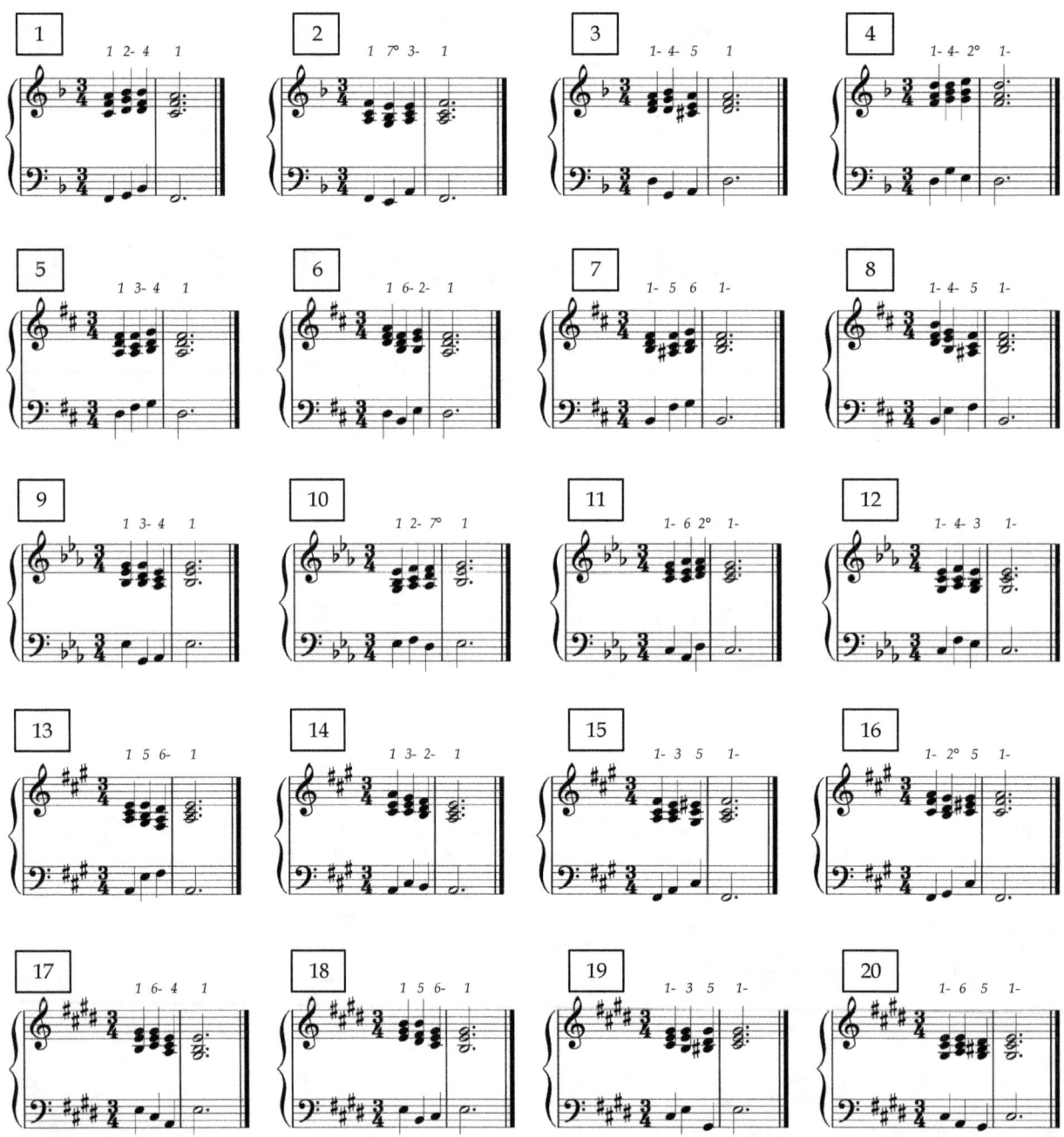

Unit Five Melodies for Playback

INSTRUCTOR PAGE

Guidelines for drilling playback:
1. Give the hand position (but not major/minor) of the example along with playing the tonic chord.
2. Count in one measure before playing.

ADVANCED TOPICS III: WRITING GREAT MELODIES

"Melody is the heart of music. It's what stays with you long after the song is over." – Rick Rubin

While there's no single way to create an interesting and memorable melody, an analysis of some of your favorite tunes would reveal they share similar characteristics. The principles below can help you internalize and recreate those characteristics in your own compositions and improvisations.

Before reading through these shared attributes of memorable melodies, open the music-streaming platform of your choice and listen to a chorus of one of your favorite songs. Take the time to transcribe the melody for that section of the song on the keyboard. Reflect on the following questions:

1. How would you describe the structure of the melody?
2. What patterns do you observe?
3. What elements repeat exactly (intervals, rhythms, etc.)? What elements repeat with some variation?
4. How large is the range of the melody (from the lowest to the highest note of the phrase)?
5. How difficult (or easy) is the melody to sing yourself?
6. Is the melody diatonic or does it also have chromatic elements?

After you've answered these questions for one melody, try it for another. The more melodies you analyze through the lens of these questions, the more you will see characteristics that unite them.

Common Characteristics of Good Melodies

1. **Shape**
   Contour, the overall shape, is an important aspect to think about while creating a melodic line. Melodies should reveal a natural *direction* throughout. Even if subtle, every melody will either be increasing or decreasing in energy to achieve a ***climax or point of arrival***. Melodies that successfully achieve clear senses of direction have a **unique high and/or low point**.

2. **Supportive Repetition**

   Different elements of a melody, i.e. motive, rhythm, and intervals, can and should be used in a supportive way. Without any elements of repetition, a melody can sound disjunct and wandering. An overly repetitive melody can sound boring and bland. The right kind of repetition is the key to having your melody be memorable while sounding fresh and purposeful.

3. **Sing-ability**

   A good guideline for testing a melody is seeing how easy it is to **sing**. This will give you instant feedback on obvious weaknesses or awkward spots. For similar reasons, the **range** of a melody is usually limited to a 12th and most often a 9th with most of the intervals within that melody being **steps with well-timed larger intervals**.

4. **Playing With Expectations**

   A core aspect of composition is a repeated process of establishing a pattern and breaking that pattern. The subtlety (or lack thereof) in how you **establish *and* break patterns** has a significant effect on the listening experience. When listening to and analyzing melodies, ask yourself how the composer surprised you or subverted your expectations.

Practicing Melody Writing

The activities below help you address each principle individually so you may begin to internalize these characteristics. However, **do not think of these characteristics as rules**; they are simply a way of providing structure and guidance for melody writing. You can also experiment with purposefully avoiding some of these characteristics to see what the opposite effect would be.

Similar to practicing a lead sheet or repertoire, creative activities require you to define your own structure, boundaries, or guidelines for an exercise. Below are suggestions that you can adapt for your own use.

Activity 1: Shape and Contour Exploration

Objective: Understand and create melodies with clear direction and contour.

Instructions:
1. Choose a starting note and decide on the overall shape of your melody (ascending, descending, arch, wave, etc.).
2. Write a melody that reflects this shape. Ensure it has a clear sense of direction and a unique high or low point.
3. Play or sing your melody to see if the contour is apparent and if it achieves a climax or point of arrival.

Activity 2: Supportive Repetition
Objective: Use repetition effectively to create memorable melodies.

Guidelines:
1. Write a short melodic motif (2–4 measures).
2. Use this motif as the foundation for a longer melody (8–16 measures).
3. Incorporate variations of the motif through rhythmic changes, interval alterations, or transpositions while ensuring the motif remains recognizable.
4. Play or sing the melody to ensure it is cohesive but not overly repetitive.

Activity 3: The Sing-ability Test
Objective: Create melodies that are easy and natural to sing.

Guidelines:
1. Write a melody within a range of a 9th to 12th, primarily using stepwise motion.
2. Sing the melody yourself or have a peer sing it.
3. Identify any awkward intervals or difficult leaps. Revise the melody to make it smoother and more singable.
4. Repeat the process until the melody feels comfortable to sing.

Activity 4: Patterns and Expectations
Objective: Learn to establish and break patterns to create interest in melodies.

Guidelines:
1. Write a simple melodic phrase that establishes a clear pattern (e.g., a specific rhythmic motif or interval pattern).
2. Write a second phrase that slightly alters the established pattern to create a surprise or subvert expectations.
3. Continue writing a few more phrases, alternating between establishing patterns and breaking them.
4. Analyze your melody to ensure it maintains listener interest through this technique.

Activity 5: Melody Expansion
Objective: Develop a short motif into a full melody.

Guidelines:
1. Start with a 2-measure motif.
2. Expand the motif into an 8-measure melody by repeating, varying, and developing it.
3. Ensure the expanded melody has a clear shape, effective repetition, is singable, and includes interesting pattern manipulation.
4. Play or sing the final melody and make any necessary adjustments.

PRACTICE: Composing Melodies

Instead of attempting to improvise a melody in your "mind's voice," try to write a few down while using the keyboard sparingly to facilitate transcribing. Try to notate as much of the melody before using the keyboard. Troubleshoot with the keyboard after you've attempted to write as much as possible without it.

Unit Six

- ❏ Transilient Scales
- ❏ Practicing Transilient Scales
- ❏ Riffs and Melodies with Transilient Scales
- ❏ 7th Chord Inversions
- ❏ Lead Sheets with 7th Chords
- ❏ Chord Charts with 7th Chords
- ❏ Diatonic Chord Exercises and Secondary Chords
- ❏ Harmonization Using Secondary Chords and Displacement
- ❏ Unit Six Rhythm Training with Beat Patterns
- ❏ Lead Sheet Ensembles
- ❏ Solo Repertoire
- ❏ Final Project: Arranging a Tune

Notes:

Transilient Scales

In contemporary Western music, some frequently used scales have less than eight notes. These scales are part of a category called **transilient scales**. Transilient scales "skip" certain notes when compared to a typical major or natural minor scale. The most common transilient scales are the pentatonic and blues scales (and their alterations).

The Pentatonic Scale

What is distinctly absent from both the major and minor pentatonic scales are the use of half steps. The notes that are "skipped" in the major or minor scale are those that would result in a half step from one note to the next.

Deriving the **major pentatonic scale** from a regular major scale involves removing the 4th and 7th notes of the scale.

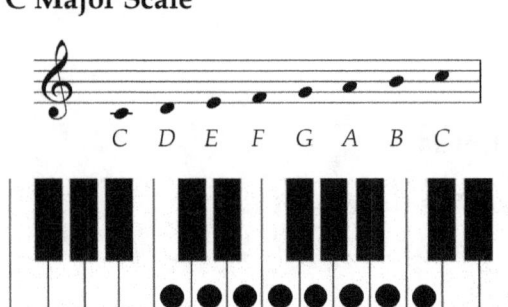
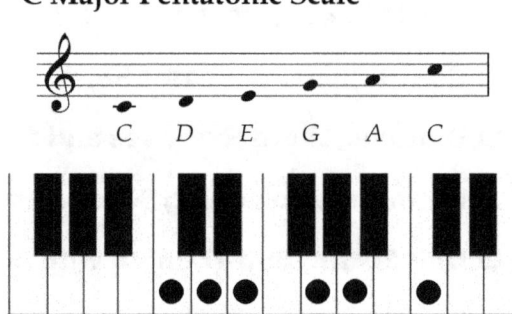

Deriving the **minor pentatonic scale** from the natural minor involves removing the 2th and 6th notes of the scale.

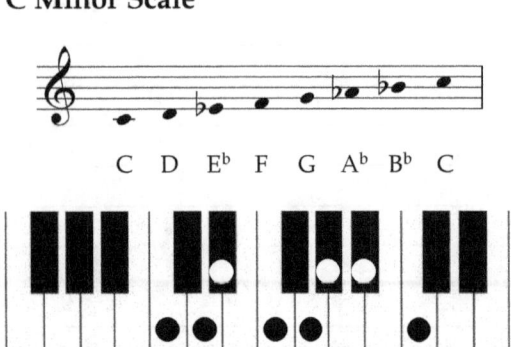
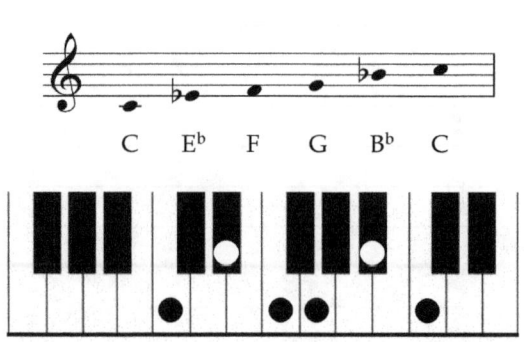

The Blues Scale

Blues scales also belong in the transilient scale category. However, the major and minor blues scales do not avoid half steps. In addition to skipping some scale degrees, they have added "blue notes" that do not belong in the corresponding major or minor key.

Building the **major blues scale** involves adding a lowered 3rd scale degree to the major pentatonic scale, creating the scale formula below.

$$\hat{1} - \hat{2} - {}^{\flat}\hat{3} - \hat{3} - \hat{5} - \hat{6}$$

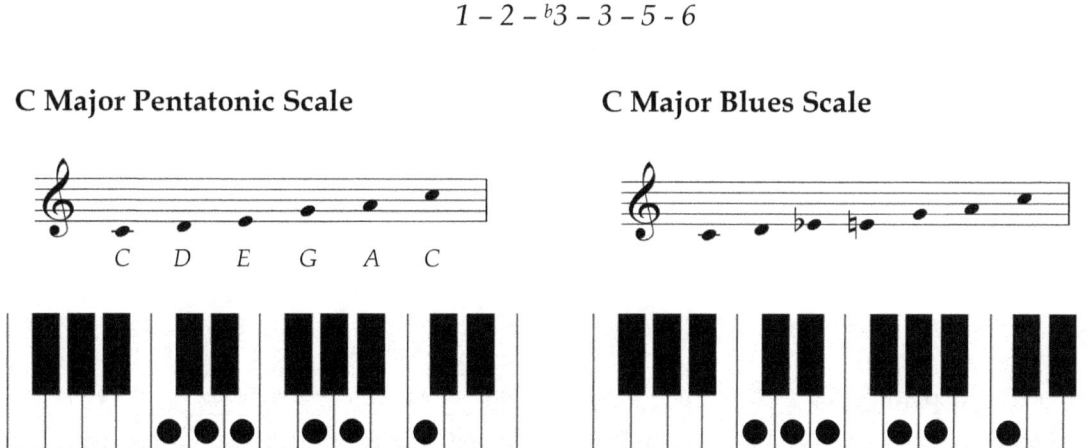

Building the **major blues scale** involves adding a lowered 3rd scale degree to the major pentatonic scale creating the scale formula below.

$$\hat{1} - {}^{\flat}\hat{3} - \hat{4} - {}^{\sharp}\hat{4} - \hat{5} - {}^{\flat}\hat{7}$$

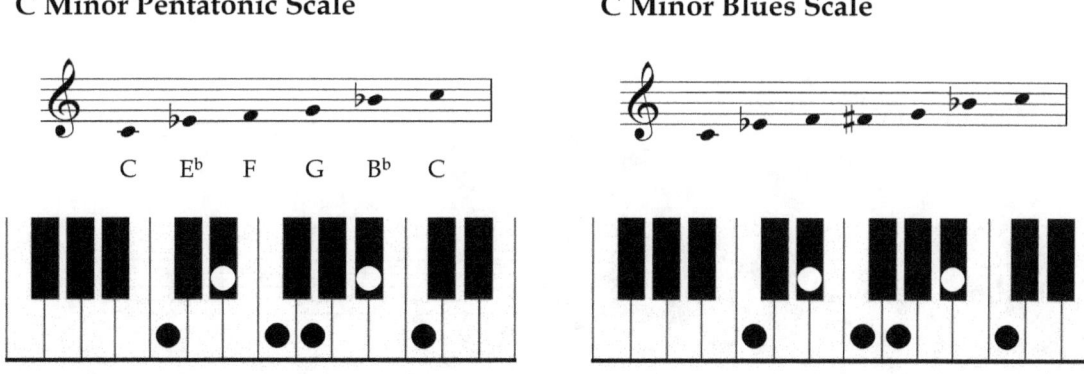

Building Pentatonic Scales

Notate the following pentatonic scales using the scale formulas on the previous pages. Use key signatures and accidentals where appropriate.

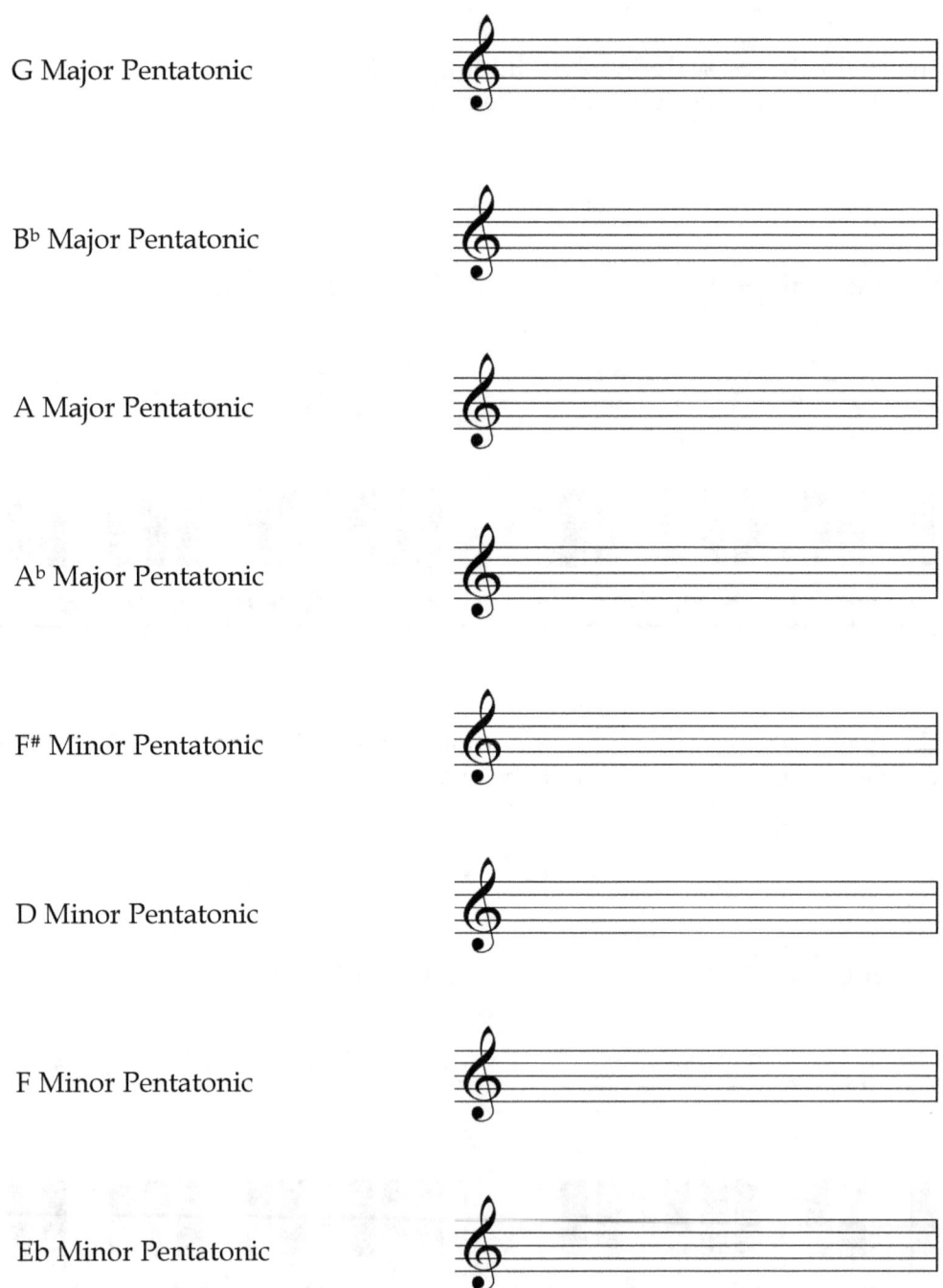

G Major Pentatonic

B♭ Major Pentatonic

A Major Pentatonic

A♭ Major Pentatonic

F♯ Minor Pentatonic

D Minor Pentatonic

F Minor Pentatonic

E♭ Minor Pentatonic

Building Blues Scales

Notate the following blues scales using the scale formulas on the previous pages. Use key signatures and accidentals where appropriate.

F Major Blues

D Major Blues

E♭ Major Blues

A Major Blues

G Minor Blues

F# Minor Blues

E Minor Blues

A Minor Blues

Practicing Transilient Scales

Because transilient scales have "skipped" notes, finding a comfortable fingering can be a challenge. Below are principles that will help you navigate what fingering you should use for exercises and riffs that use these scales.

1. **Avoid playing black keys with the thumb.** While it's not possible to *completely* avoid using the thumb on black notes, it is a good guiding principle. The thumb should gravitate towards white notes and let the other fingers play black notes.
2. **Practice beyond the limits of an octave.** Exercises often have the negative effect of training us to "stop" at an octave when this rarely (if ever) happens in a riff or melody from a song. You can avoid this by practicing larger portions of the scale that go beyond the octave.
3. **Practice in rhythms.** Your brain and fingers need rhythmic variety in exercises. Place different rhythmic emphases on different notes of the scale for a solid foundation.
4. **Create and drill riffs with comfortable fingering.** Take the time to experiment with different fingerings and find the most comfortable for your hand. There are basic principles of good fingering, but ultimately, it will take dedicated time exploring various options for fingering to become a healthy unconscious decision.

Example Two-Octave Fingerings

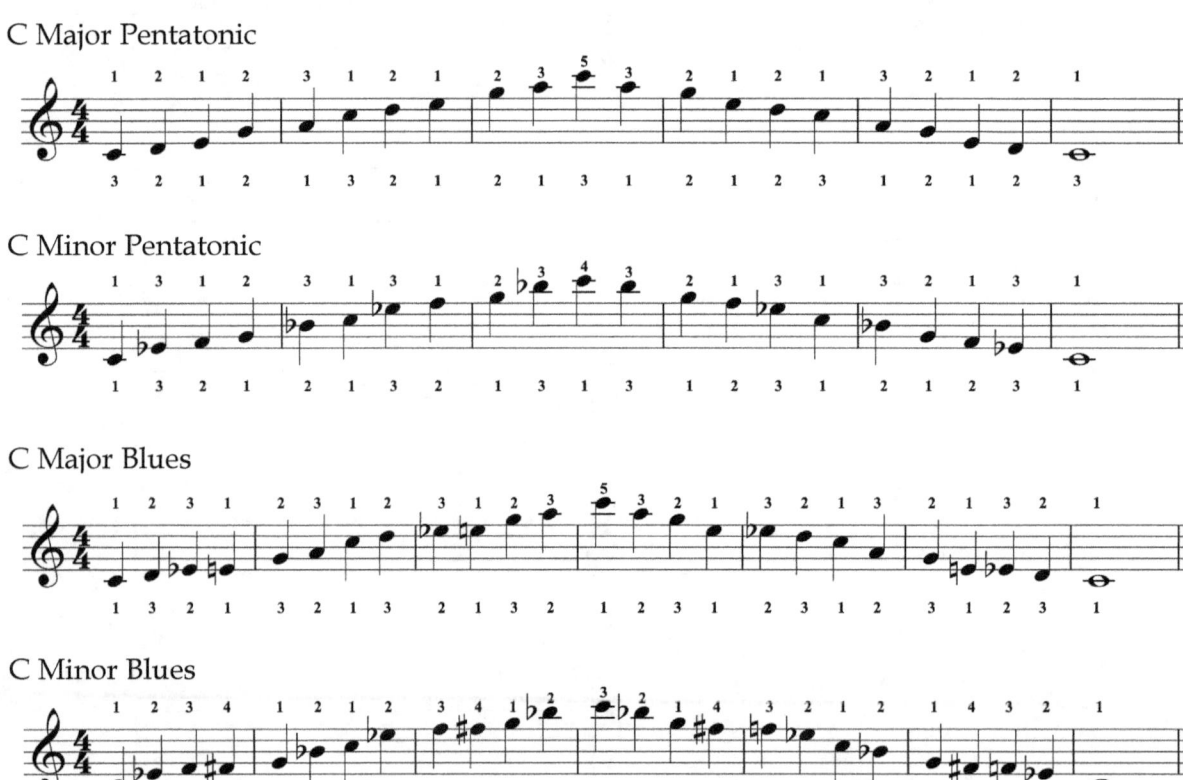

Essential Patterns and Variations

Rhythmic Variations

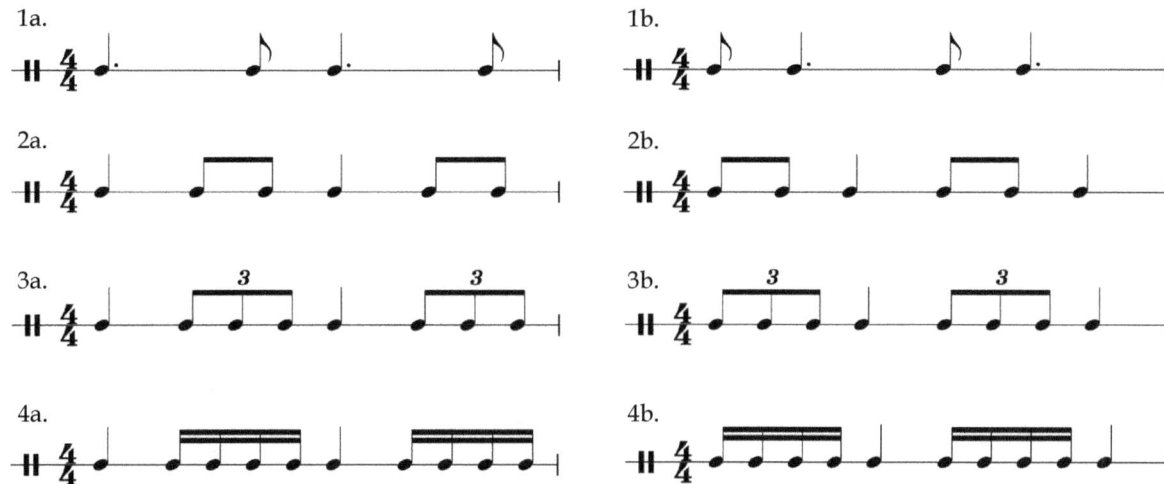

Accent Variations

Melodic Patterns

Riffs and Melodies with Transilient Scales

The exercises below are built using the blues scale and its variants (in the key of each example). Practice the first riff in all three keys. A different key will "feel" different to play, so pay close attention to how the fingerings are different for each key.

1a

1b

1c

Create your own riff or melody using blues scales.

Example 2 is built using the pentatonic scale (in the key of each example). Practice the riff in all three keys. A different key will "feel" different to play, so pay close attention to how the fingerings are different for each key.

1a ($\dot{\partial} = 60$)

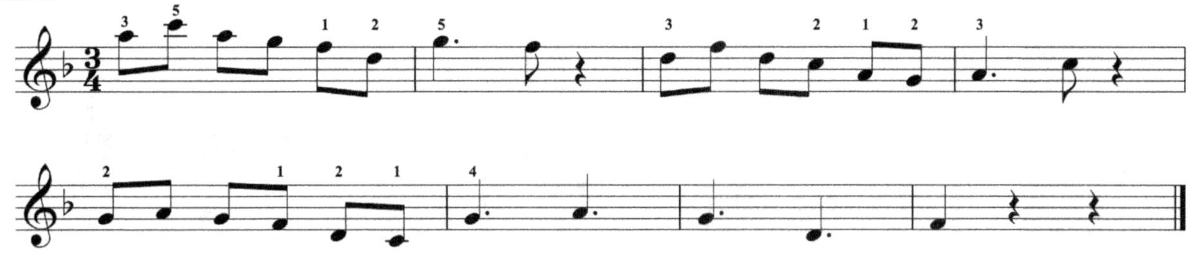

1b

1c

Create your own riff or melody using pentatonic scales.

Unit 6 191

7th Chord Inversions

Just like triads, the notes of a 7th chord will often be rearranged creating different voicings of a chord. Keyboards and composers use different inversions of 7th chords depending on their context. Since 7th chords have four notes instead of three, they will have an extra inversion.

Example: E♭ Major 7

Root Position
- root of the chord is the lowest note

E♭ – G – B♭ – D

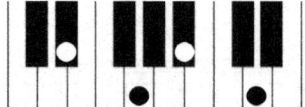

First Inversion
- 3rd of the chord is the lowest note

E♭ – G – B♭ – D – E♭

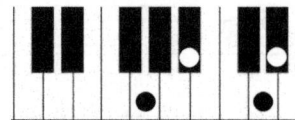

Second Inversion
- 5th of the chord is the lowest note

G – B♭ – D – E♭ – G

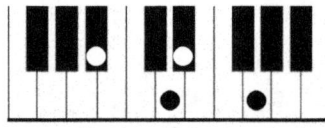

Third Inversions
- 7th of the chord is the lowest note

B♭ – D – E♭ – G – B♭

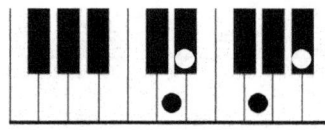

An important note: inversions are defined by the lowest note arranged in a chord. The examples above use a **closed voicing** where the notes are compacted as closely as possible. In other voicings, you would still identify a chord inversion by the lowest note.

Practicing 7th Chord Inversions

The most optimal fingering to use for a 7th chord ultimately comes down to context. For these inversion exercises, you will always use fingers 1, 2, and 5 to play three notes of the chords. The remaining note will be played by finger 3 or 4. Look at the fingering for each hand in Example 1.

Example 6.1: C^{min7} Chord Inversions

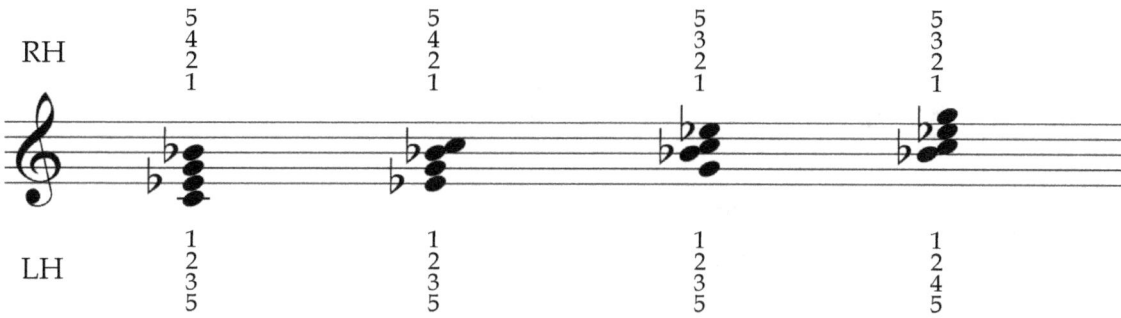

While all 7th chords will use this pattern of fingers 1, 2, and 5, whether you should use finger 3 or 4 for the remaining note will be up to your hand and what you find most comfortable and efficient.

Besides fingering, 7th chord inversions can be practiced the same as triads. Your "go-to" exercises for inversions are blocked, half-blocked, and broken. Gain fluency hands separately before attempting hands together.

> **PRO TIP**
>
> Professional performers often have custom-made warm-up routines and technical exercises that few other people use. This is usually because professionals have found or created exercises that combine multiple concepts. For example, how do you think you could expand and adapt the 7th chord exercises from Unit 5 on page 151 to include working on 7th chord inversions?

Lead Sheets with Seventh Chords

Practice the following lead sheets with the RH playing the melody, and the LH interpreting chord symbols with the given accompaniment pattern.

4 ♩= 120

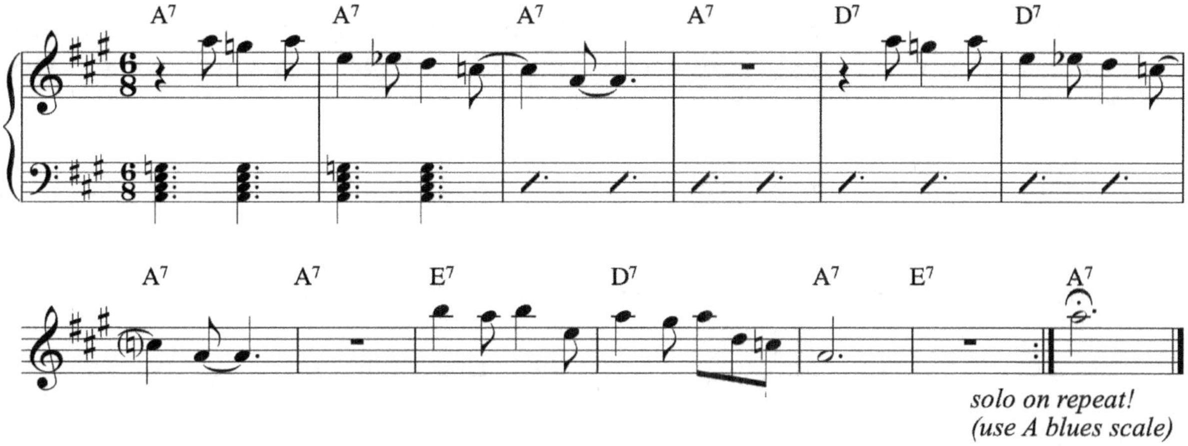
A7 A7 A7 A7 D7 D7
A7 A7 E7 D7 A7 E7 A7
solo on repeat!
(use A blues scale)

5 ♩= 90

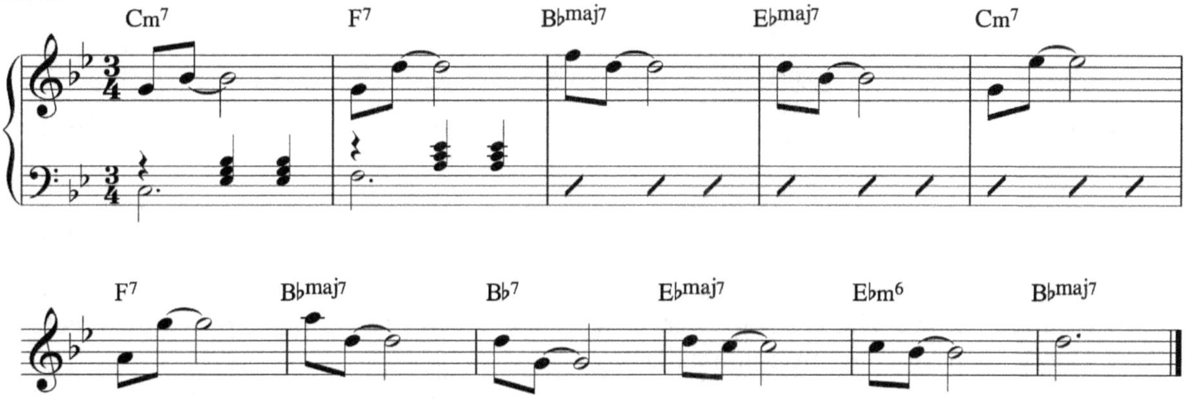
Cm7 F7 B♭maj7 E♭maj7 Cm7
F7 B♭maj7 B♭7 E♭maj7 E♭m6 B♭maj7

6 ♩= 80

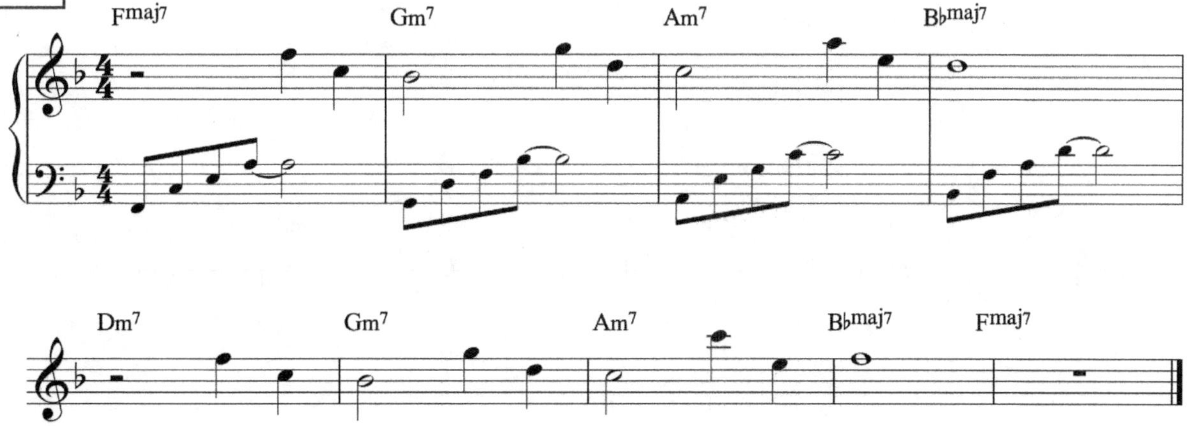
Fmaj7 Gm7 Am7 B♭maj7
Dm7 Gm7 Am7 B♭maj7 Fmaj7

Chord Charts with 7th Chords

The following chord chart exercises are examples of common chord progressions with 7th chords in various styles. Play the following exercises in **keyboard style** with smooth voice leading.

1 You can hear a chord progression like the example below in the song "Love On Top" as performed by Beyoncé.

KEY: C   R&B/Pop ($\quarternote = 94$)   Suggested Patch: E. Piano

Use a blocked chord accompaniment with the harmonic rhythm notated below.

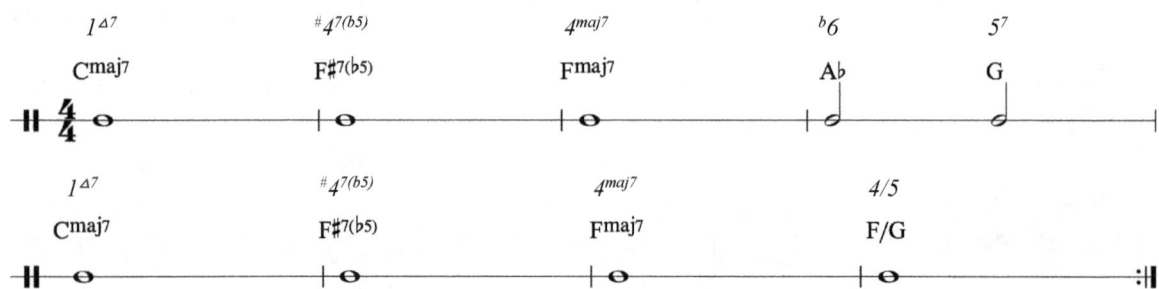

2 You can hear a chord progression like exercise 2 in the song "Love Never Felt So Good" as performed by Michael Jackson.

KEY: F   Pop Soul ($\quarternote = 120$)   Suggested Patch: E. Piano

Accompaniment Pattern:

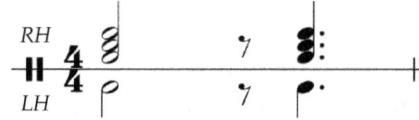

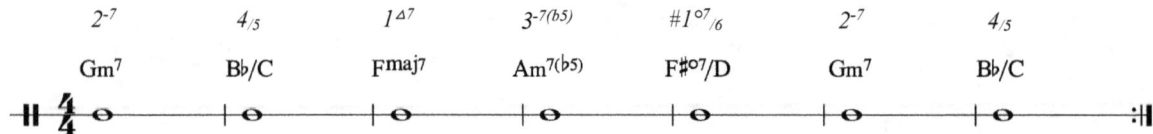

196   Unit 6

| 3 | You can hear a chord progression like exercise 3 in the song "South of the River" as performed by Tom Misch. |

KEY: C   Contemporary R&B (♩ = 113)   Suggested Patch: Synth Pad

Use a blocked chord accompaniment pattern throughout.

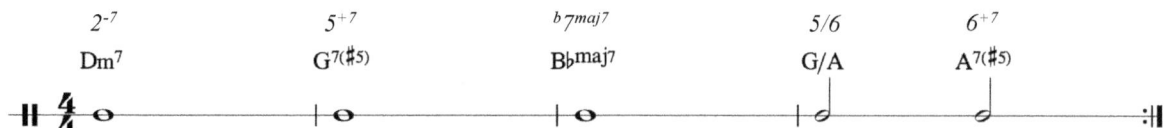

| 4 | You can hear a chord progression like exercise 4 in the song "Animal Spirits" as performed by Vulfpeck. |

KEY: D♭   Funk (♩ = 102)   Suggested Patch: Upright Piano

Use a blocked chord accompaniment pattern with the notated rhythm below.

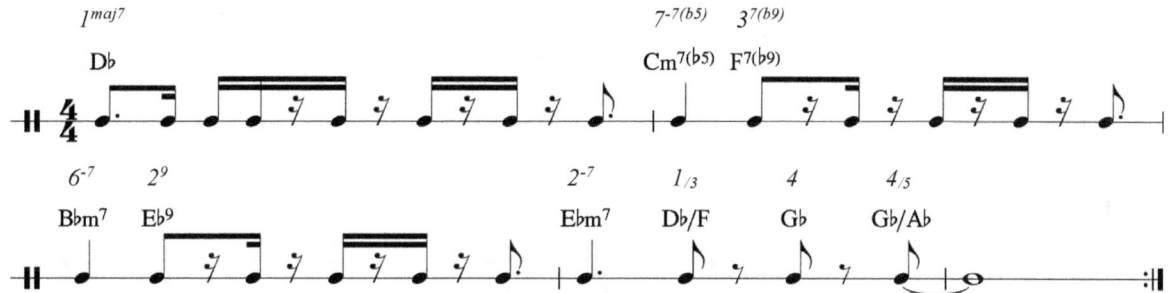

| 5 | You can hear a chord progression like exercise 5 in the song "Everything In Its Right Place" as performed by Radiohead. |

KEY: C   Alternative/Indie (♩ = 124)   Suggested Patch: E. Piano

Use a blocked chord accompaniment pattern with the notated rhythm below.

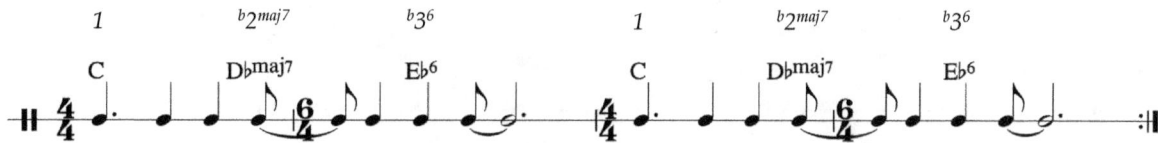

6 You can hear a chord progression like exercise 6 in the song "Isn't She Lovely" as performed by Stevie Wonder.

KEY: C   Soul (♩ = 119)   Suggested Patch: E. Piano

Use a blocked chord accompaniment pattern throughout.

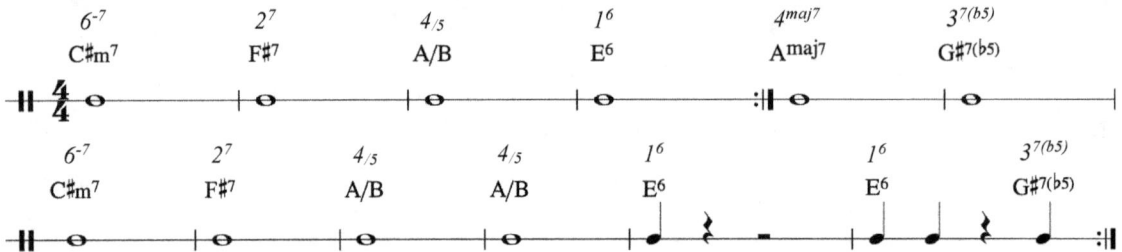

7 You can hear a chord progression like exercise 7 in the song "Leave the Door Open" as performed by Silk Sonic.

KEY: C   Soul (♩ = 74)   Suggested Patch: Upright Piano

Use a blocked chord accompaniment pattern with the notated rhythm below.

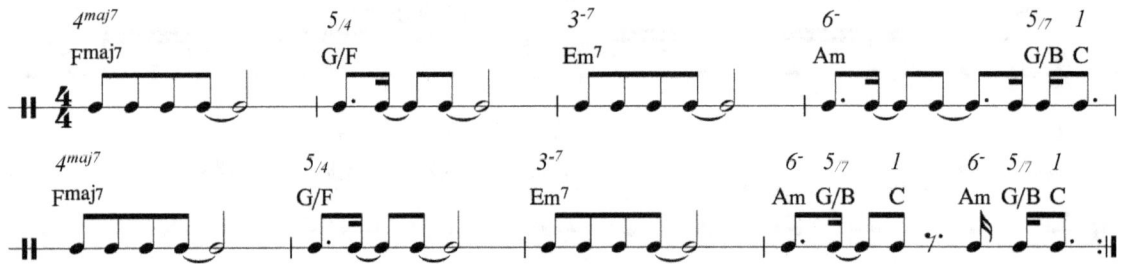

8 You can hear a chord progression like exercise 8 in the song "How Deep Is Your Love" as performed by PJ Morton.

KEY: G♭   Soul Ballad (♩ = 88)   Suggested Patch: E. Piano

Use blocked chords *or create your own accompaniment pattern* with the notated harmonic rhythm below..

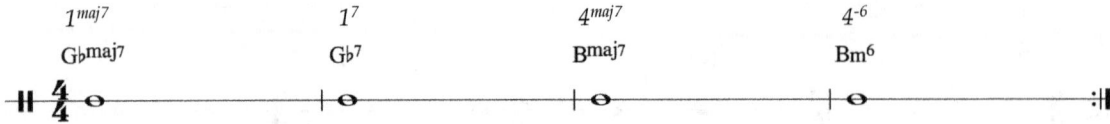

Diatonic Chord Exercises and Secondary Chords

The following exercises help you become familiar with diatonic triads in a particular key while using smooth voice leading. This first exercise becomes a base for later variation, as well.

Drilling Diatonic Triads

Play the following chord progressions in keyboard style with smooth voice leading.

Ascending Diatonic Triads

| 4/4 | 1 | 2- | 3- | 4 | |
| 5 | 6- | 7° | 1 | ||

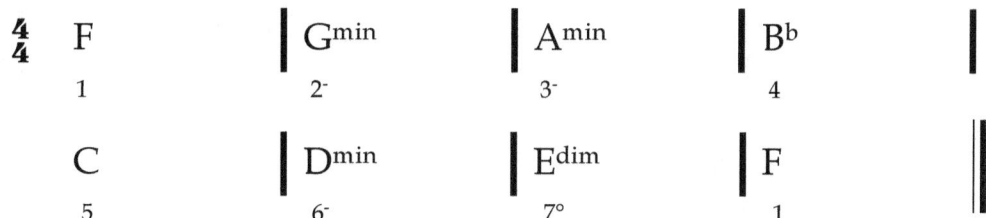

Example with chord names in F major:

4/4	F	Gmin	Amin	B♭	
	1	2-	3-	4	
	C	Dmin	Edim	F	
	5	6-	7°	1		

Possible realizations:

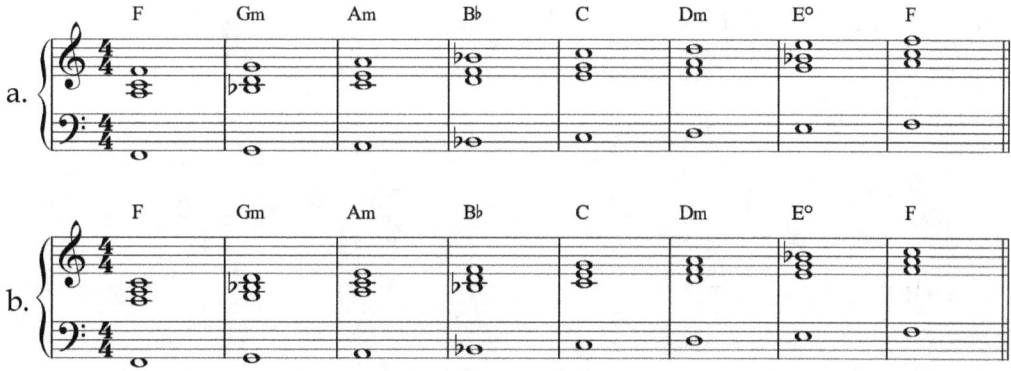

Practice ascending diatonic triads in all major keys. Practice each key with different inversions in your RH. After gaining fluency with different RH voicings, you can practice with various accompaniment patterns like the basic patterns on page 128 or create your own.

Unit 6

Adding Secondary Chords

Secondary chords are borrowed chords from the major and minor keys of diatonic chords other than tonic. For example, the secondary keys of C major would include D minor, E minor, F major, G major, and A minor. The most common types of secondary chords are secondary dominants, secondary subdominants, and secondary leading-tone diminished. They are identified by their function in the borrowed key.

Secondary Dominants

The most common type of secondary chord is a secondary dominant. Secondary dominants are always major triads or dominant 7 chords that function as a temporary dominant, leading to a chord other than the tonic. For example, in the key of C major, the V^7 (dominant 7 chord) is G^7; it is the V^7 of C. The V^7 of ii in the key of C major would be a dominant 7 chord built on the fifth scale degree of D minor: A^7.

Diatonic Triads with Secondary Dominants

Play the following chord progressions in keyboard style with smooth voice leading.

$\frac{4}{4}$ 1 5^7 of 2- | 2- 5^7 of 3- | 3- 5^7 of 4 | 4 5^7 of 5 |
         (6^7)   (7^7)   (1^7)   (2^7)

5   5^7 of 6- | 6-   7° | 1 ||
     (3^7)

Example with chord names in F major:

$\frac{4}{4}$ F D^7 | G^{min} E^7 | A^{min} F^7 | $B^\flat$ G^7 |

C A^7 | D^{min} E^{dim} | F ||

Possible realizations:

a.

b.

200   Unit 6

Secondary Subdominants

Different secondary chords will give you more control over the energy in a phrase. While secondary dominants offer a direct and obvious increase in energy toward a note that is not tonic, secondary subdominants are less intense. Secondary subdominants can be major or minor—the IV or iv of a diatonic chord. For example, in the key of C major, the IV (subdominant chord) is F; it is the IV of I. The IV of ii would be a major chord built on the fourth scale degree in the key of D minor: G. While this exercise uses only major triads, you can experiment with converting all secondary subdominants to minor triads or seventh chords (IV^{maj7} or iv^7).

Diatonic Triads with Secondary Subdominants (Major)

Play the following chord progressions in keyboard style with smooth voice leading.

$\frac{4}{4}$ | 1 $4_{of\ 2-}$ | 2- $4_{of\ 3-}$ | 3- $4_{of\ 4}$ | 4 $4_{of\ 5}$ |
       (5)   (6)   (b7)   (1)

| 5 $4_{of\ 6-}$ | 6- 7° | 1 ||
    (2)

Example with chord names in F major:

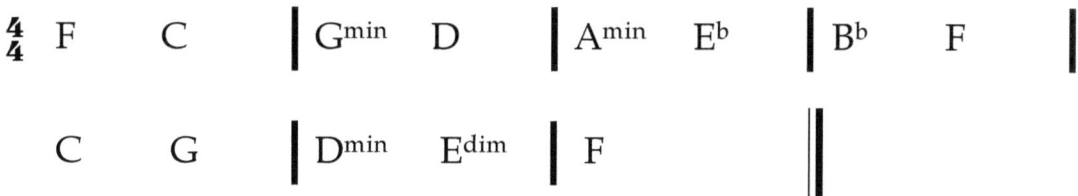

Possible realizations:

Unit 6   201

Secondary Leading-Tone Diminished Chords

Secondary leading-tone diminished chords will always be diminished triads or fully diminished seventh chords—the vii° or vii°⁷ of a diatonic chord. For example, in the key of C major, the vii° (leading-tone diminished chord) is B°; it is the vii° of I. The vii° of ii would be a diminished triad built off the leading-tone in the key of D minor: C#°. Similar to secondary dominants, secondary leading-tone diminished chords are a high-energy tool for harmonization.

Diatonic Triads with Secondary Leading-tone Diminished Chords

Play the following chord progressions in keyboard style with smooth voice leading.

4/4	1	7°of 2- (#1°)	2-	7°of 3- (#2°)	3-	7°of 4 (3°)	4	7°of 5 (#4°)
	5	7°of 6- (#5°)	6-	7°	1			

Example with chord names in F major:

4/4	F	F#°	Gmin	G#°	Amin	A°	B♭	B°
	C	C#°	Dmin	Edim	F			

Possible realizations:

a.

b.

FAQs

How do I incorporate chord progressions into my regular practice?
When you have multiple concepts to practice like scales, chord inversions, and chord progressions, it's helpful to think about organizing them by keys. Choose at least one key from each scale grouping and practice all the concepts within those keys including chord progressions.

Harmonization Using Secondary Chords and Displacement

Displacement is a harmonization tool that moves a chord earlier or later in a phrase, creating an open space for other chords to be added. Displacement can be used for small or dramatic changes. Moving a chord by a beat or less will create a sound like the original phrase. When you desires a more dramatic change, displace a chord by a measure or more. While displacement can be used in a myriad of ways, this unit focuses on using this harmonization tool in conjunction with secondary dominant and leading-tone diminished chords.

Play the example melody below with its original harmonization.

A simple starting point for using displacement is identifying phrase structure, including cadences and target chords.

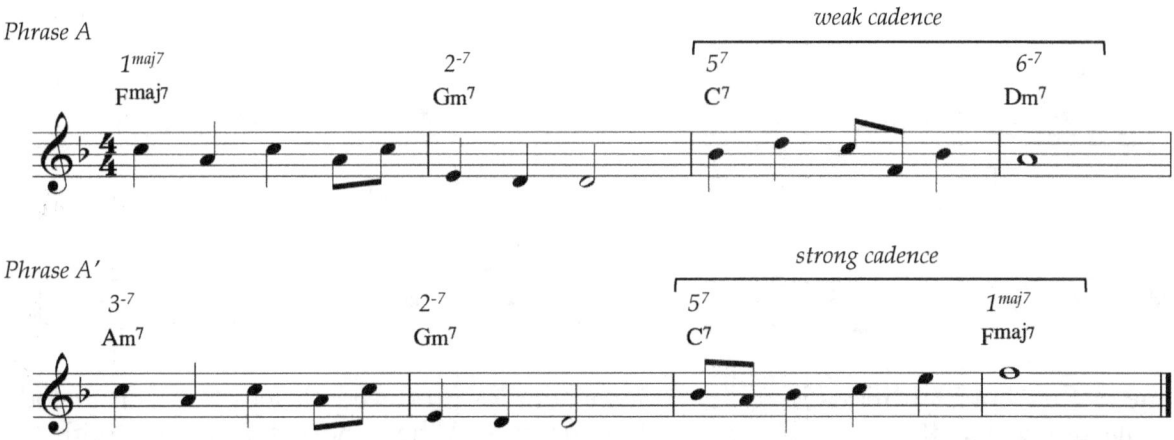

This melody has two important cadential points both containing a C^7 chord; the first phrase ending in a deceptive cadence to 6^{-7} (D^{min7}) and the second ending in an authentic cadence on I^{maj7} (F^{maj7}). Marking phrases and cadences is an important first step in using displacement so you know how your chord choices will affect the shape of the phrase.

Displacement directly addresses the harmonic space available in a phrase. It utilizes empty space or creates it own. In example 1, two minor 7 chords were shifted two beats (measure 2 and 5) which allowed the opportunity for **secondary dominants** to be put in their place. Note the location of added chords along with their melody/harmony relationships.

Example 1

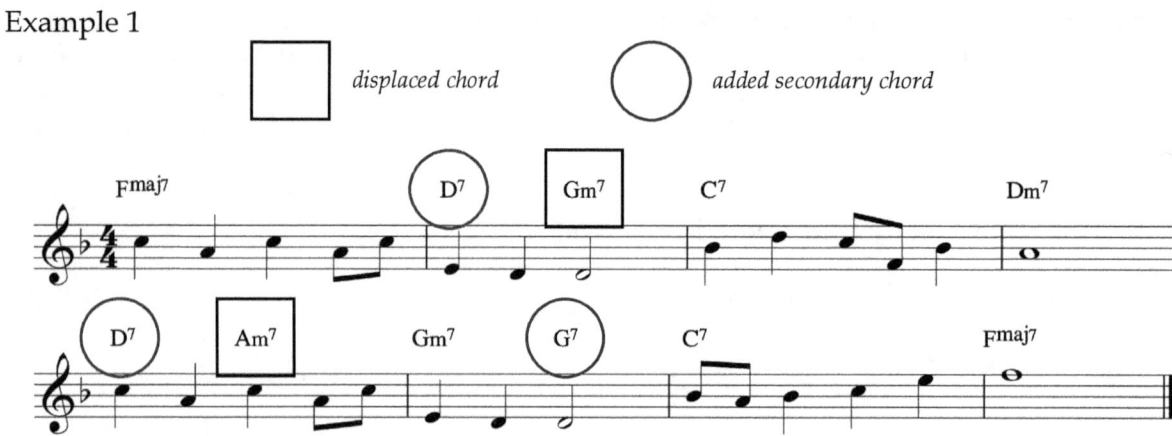

The next example shows utilizing empty space to add secondary leading-tone diminished chords.

Example 2

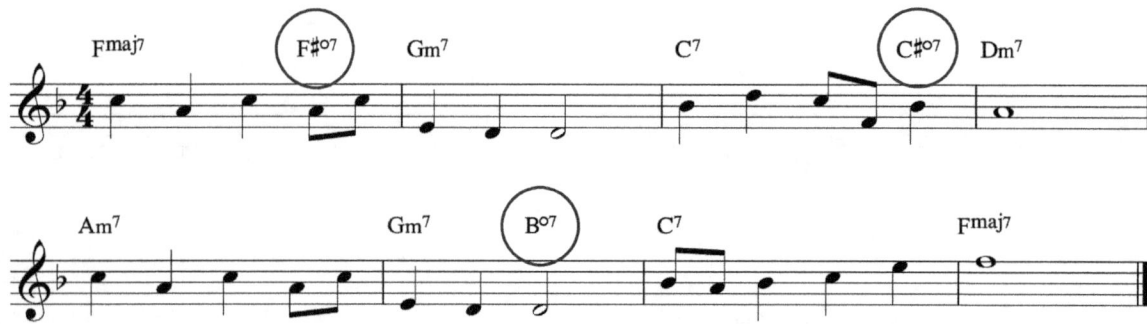

None of the chord additions in the previous examples produced clashes between melody and harmony, but that can be a frequent occurrence. When chord tones clash with the original melody, make small adjustments until you find a combination that has the effective amount of consonance or dissonance for its location in the phrase.

Play the following melodies with the RH playing the melody and the LH playing blocked root position chords. Then, use displacement to add secondary dominant or secondary leading-tone diminished chords. Create two reharmonizations using displacement for each melody. Mark displaced chords with a box around the chord name. Mark added chords with a circle around the chord name.

1

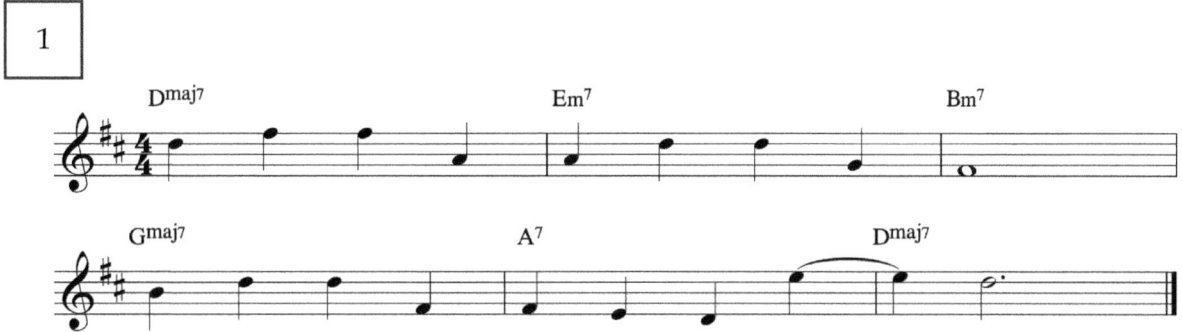

Reharmonize with displacement and added secondary chords.

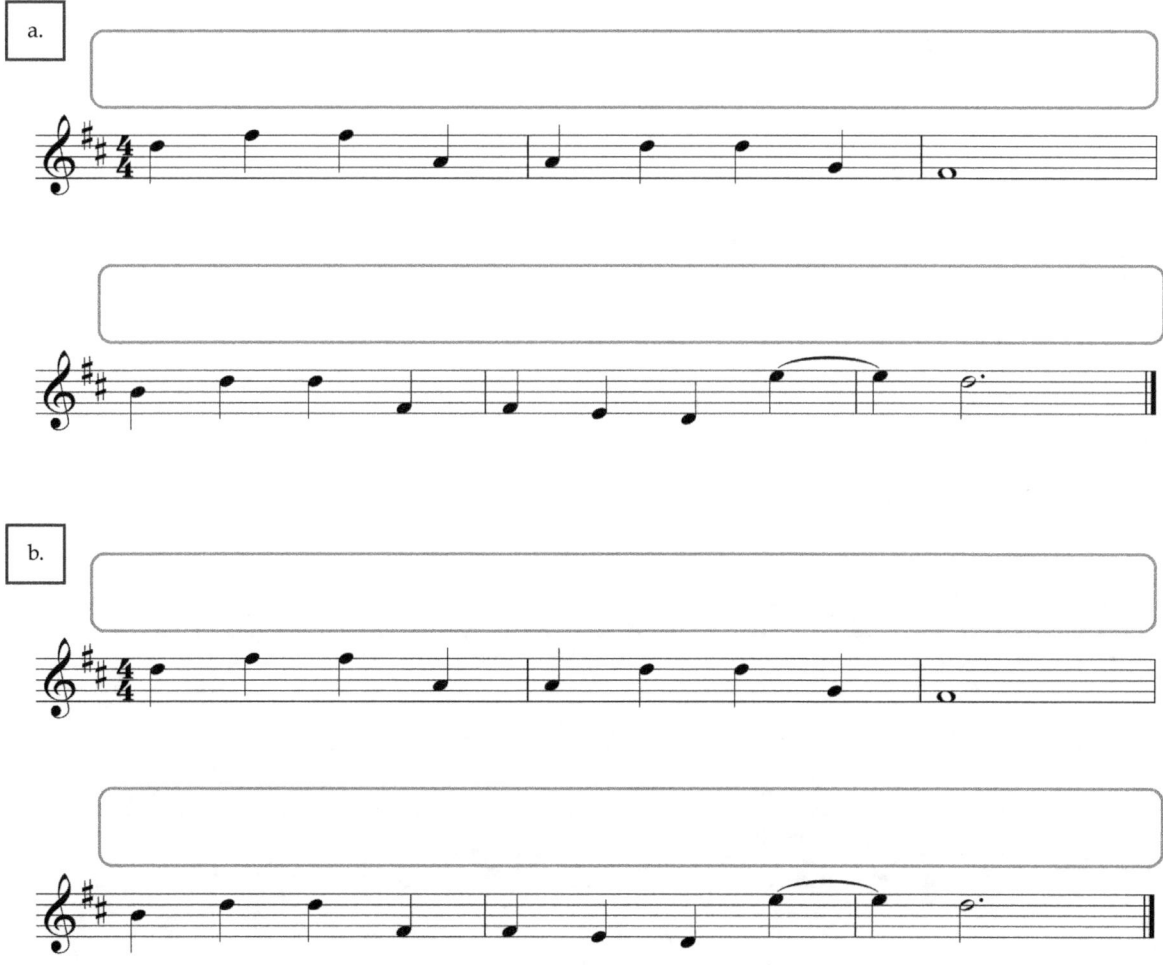

Unit 6

Reharmonize with displacement and added secondary chords.

Harmonize each melody two ways. The first harmonization should consist of diatonic chords only. The second harmonization of the same melody should explore reharmonization techniques using seventh chords. Practice each harmonization by playing the melody in the RH and root position chords in the LH.

| 1 | Key: A |

Diatonic Harmonization:

Chord Names

Nashville Numbers

Reharmonization:

Chord Names

Nashville Numbers

| 2 | Key: Bb |

Diatonic Harmonization:

Chord Names

Nashville Numbers

Reharmonization:

Chord Names

Nashville Numbers

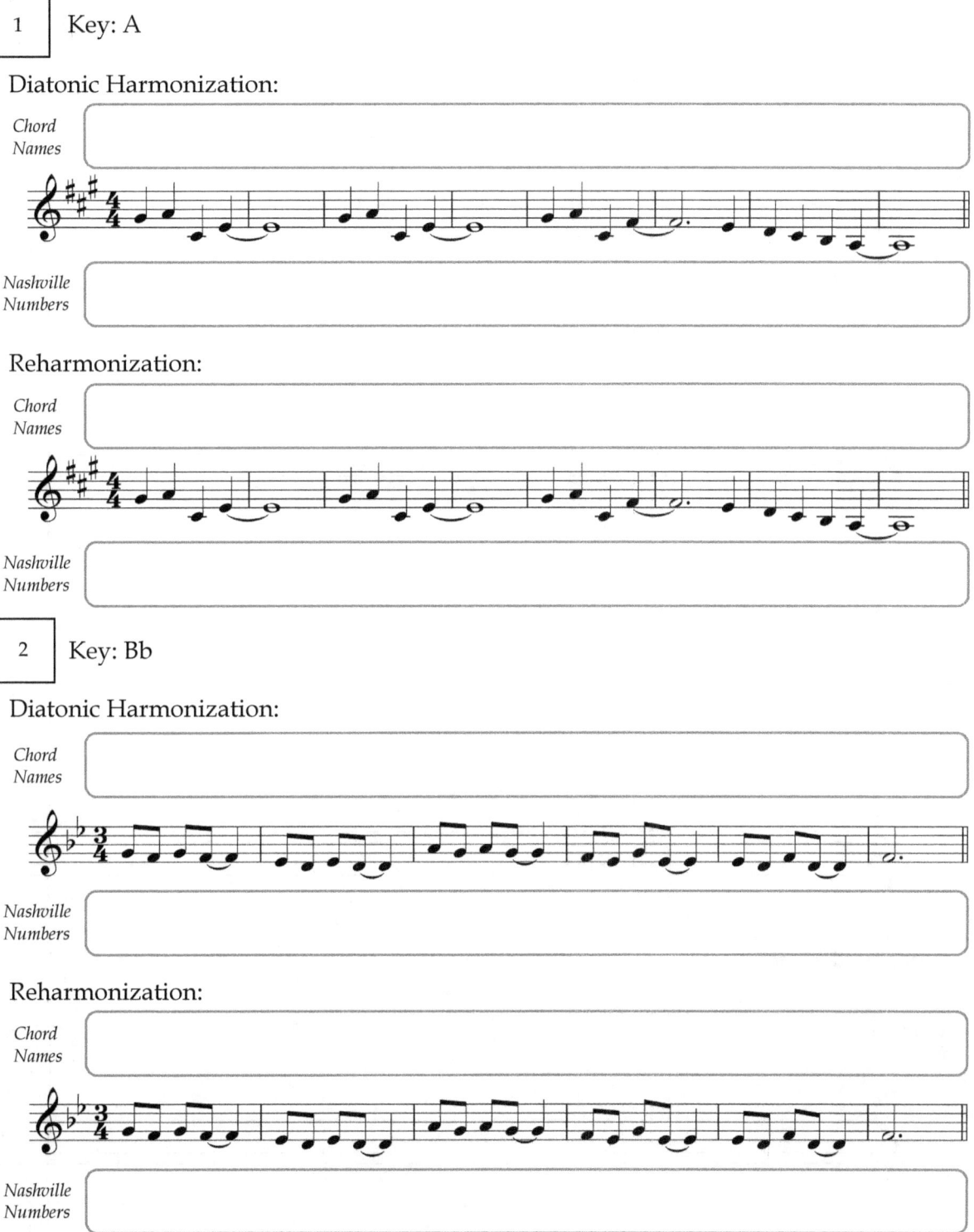

Unit 6 207

Compose and notate two melodies. Harmonize each two ways. The first harmonization should consist of diatonic chords only. The second harmonization of the same melody should explore reharmonization techniques using triads and/or seventh chords. Practice each harmonization by playing the melody in the RH and root position chords in the LH.

1 Key:

Diatonic Harmonization:

Chord Names

Reharmonization:

Chord Names

2 Key:

Diatonic Harmonization:

Chord Names

Reharmonization:

Chord Names

Unit Six Rhythm Training with Beat Patterns

The following rhythm drills prepare you to play simple and repetitive beat patterns for performance or production. Instruments are notated so that you can use drum pads or a percussion patch on a keyboard. Focus on the overall feel of these patterns and your relationship to the pulse. Don't let mistakes derail the groove.

The patterns for Unit 6 are notated in four parts: kick drum, snare, high hat, and open high hat. However, feel free to replace those parts with other sounds that still function similarly.

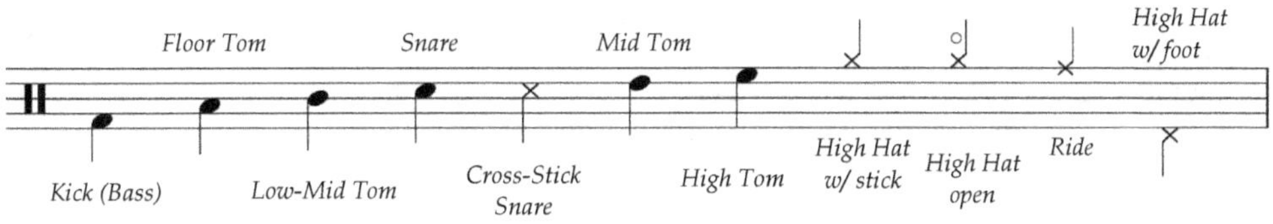

Practice at a variety of tempos.
(♩ = 56–140)

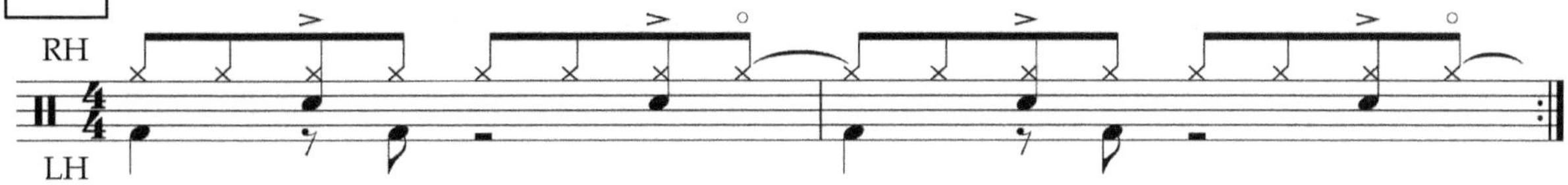

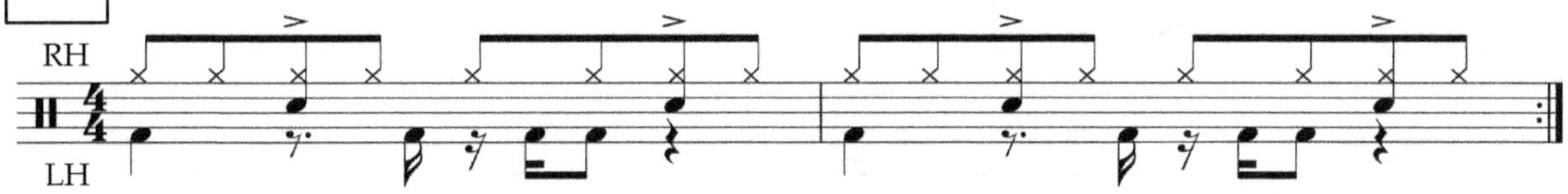

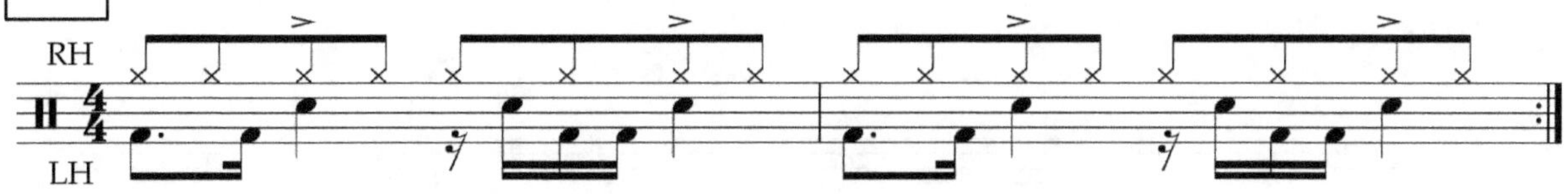

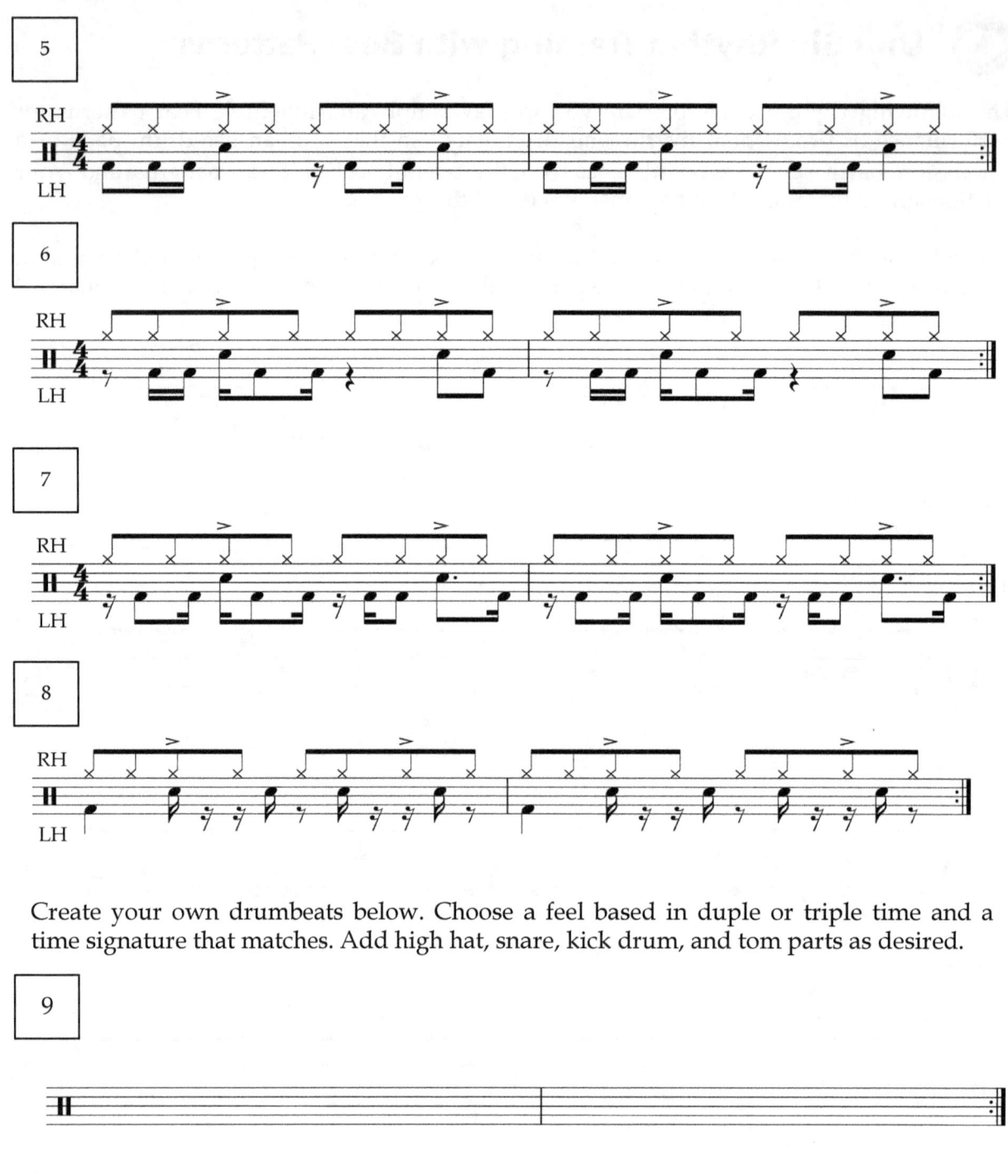

Create your own drumbeats below. Choose a feel based in duple or triple time and a time signature that matches. Add high hat, snare, kick drum, and tom parts as desired.

Lead Sheet Ensembles

The following ensembles are written in four parts: melody, harmony, keyboard accompaniment, and drumbeat. The goal of these ensembles is to become fluent in all four parts like a conductor or music director. That does not necessarily mean being able to play different parts at the same time (although that could be a way you develop intimacy with a passage), but it does mean being able to hear parts in your head in different combinations.

Take note of how your practice changes knowing you're responsible for all the parts. Below are suggestions for practicing and performing the ensembles in this text.

Part 1: Melody

This part of the ensemble can be interpreted the same way you would interpret a lead sheet with melody and chords. Students can play this line in keyboard style, with the RH playing the melody while the LH plays root position chords, or as soloist, playing the melody by itself.

Part 2: Harmony/Rhythm

This part is designed to support the harmony and groove of a tune. As a harmony/rhythm player, students do not need to worry about root notes or bass parts. A basic interpretation would be playing the notated rhythm in a closed voicing in the RH like keyboard style. Smooth voice leading should be emphasized.

Part 3: Keyboard Accompaniment

Interpret Part 3 just like you would a chord chart in this text—keyboard style with the indicated harmonic rhythm and accompaniment pattern.

Part 4: Drum Pattern

Refer to the drum notation key in this unit to interpret the notated drum pattern in part 4.

A Note on Practicing Ensembles:

These ensembles are a combination of skills addressed throughout this text. The exercises will require you to use most, if not all the practice strategies you know. While you could (and should) learn each part on its own, this exercise requires you to be thinking about each part's relationship to one another. Ultimately, you can say you're "prepared" when you can perform one of the parts while hearing another part in your head. Practice in ways that helps you internalize each part's relationship to the whole - i.e., how everything fits together.

Laying Low

Andy Villemez

Relaxed (♩ = 65)

Solo Repertoire

Good Times

Nostalgic, with some swing (♩ = 84)

Andy Villemez

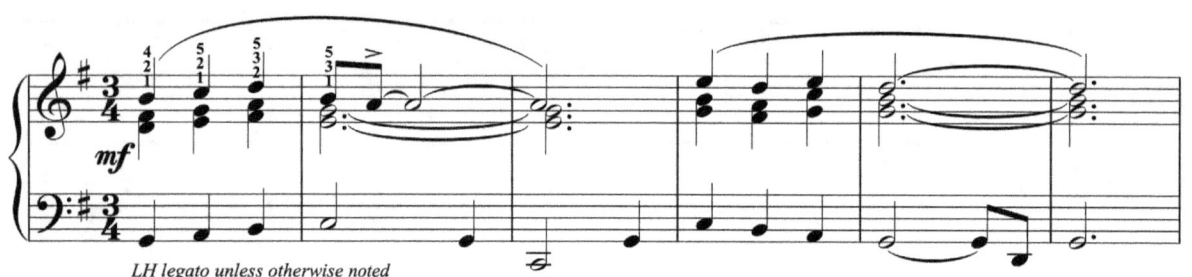

LH legato unless otherwise noted

Mini Gymnopedie

Final Project: Arranging a Tune

The steps below help you create a unique solo keyboard arrangement of a given song using concepts from previous units. This exercise is designed to take you through a workflow that encourages intentional choices on one aspect of the arrangement at a time. After choosing a song, writing a melody of your own, or receiving a song as an assignment, follow the steps below.

1. Internalize the melody.

Listen critically to the melody (or studio a capella track) until you can sing it back and hear it in your head (your mind's ear). Listen in sections taking note of the overall shape, intervals, varied repetitions (if any), rhythm and syncopation, and feel. Take the time to engage with the melody before moving forward. Your workflow will be more efficient if you put this work in on the front end.

2. Practice the melody in multiple ways.

If you're attempting to internalize the melody, you want to be able to play it on whatever instrument you have in front of you. In this case, that means your voice and the keyboard. Practice reproducing the melody by singing and also by playing it on the keyboard (at the same time or separately). Do this in smaller sections of the song that make sense to you. If you're doing this by ear (and not with a lead sheet), refer to the guidelines on melodic playback from Unit 1.

3. Add a simple harmonic structure.

This might seem like a boring step to you. You might be tempted to skip ahead to find the juiciest harmonies. However, we need a foundation before anything can be decorated. Take the time to build a basic (and potentially boring) harmonic structure using only triads. This will give you a better idea of how to be intentional with chord substitutions or embellishments. The goal in this step is to know *how* you want harmonies to function at different points in the song (i.e., higher energy, crunchy, points of rest, etc.).

4. Embellish harmonies.

After you have a simple chord structure and an awareness of how those chords function in the context of the melody, you can start to embellish harmonies with diatonic or chromatic substitutions, extensions, or adding passing harmonies where there was no chord before. *A few notes for the ambitious:*

- Choose harmonies that sound good in the context of an entire progression, not just on their own.

- You must be able to play the chords you choose. In this case, you're arranging for yourself so don't choose chords that are too difficult to play at your current level.

- Take note of the process you're taking. Whether you end up with an arrangement you like or dislike, you need to know *how* you got to that result so you can repeat it or change certain elements of it.

5. Add an accompaniment pattern.

Texture should complement the feel or energy of each section. Choose a simple rhythmic pattern to get you started. Think about what parts of the song have significant changes in energy and how the accompaniment can reflect that. Don't be afraid to steal good ideas from other tunes you've heard or practiced.

6. Share your work and ask for feedback.

Don't let your work stay in a bubble. Share your creation and ask listeners for their impressions/thoughts/opinions.

(Title)

Unit 6

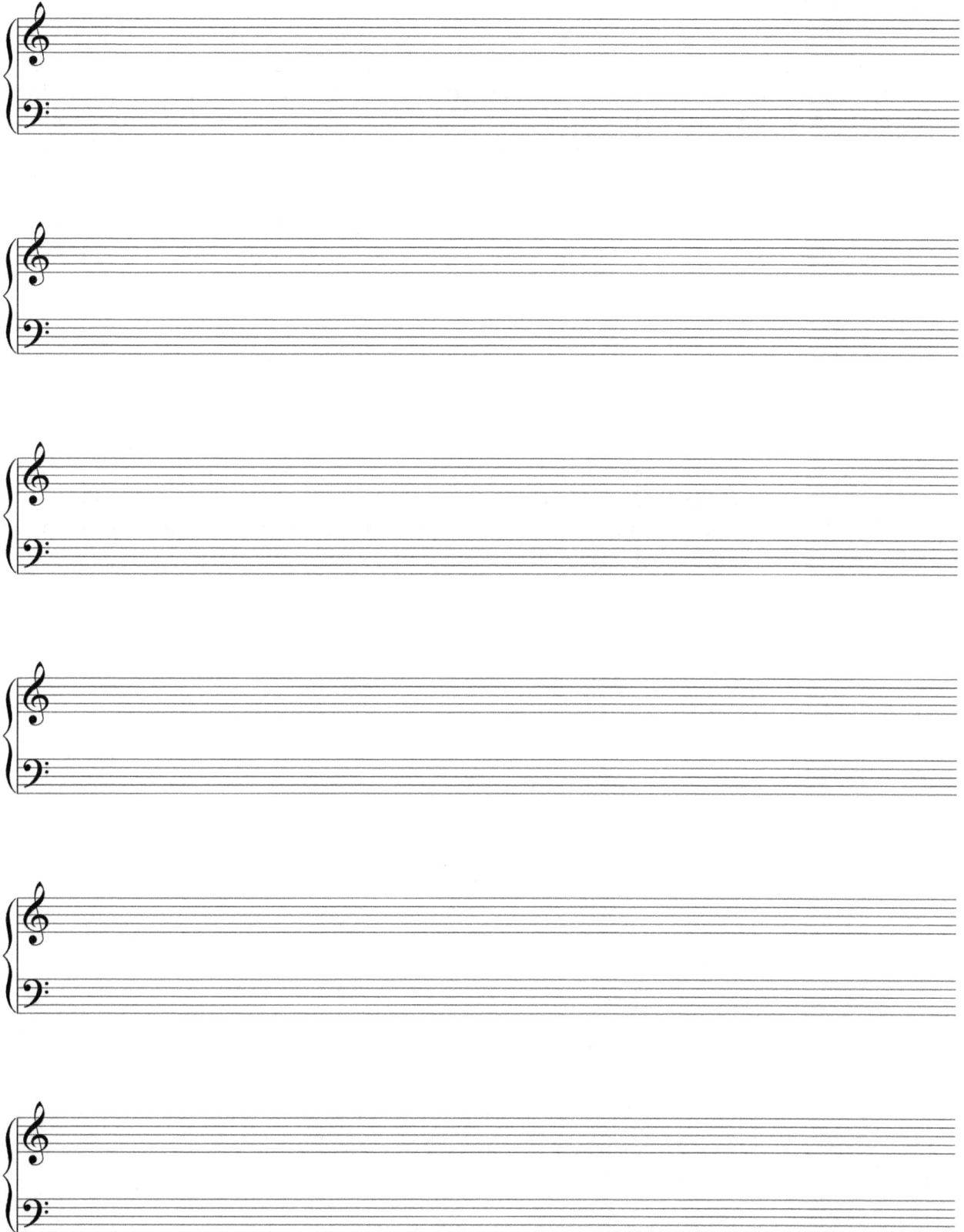

Acknowledgments

This book would not exist without the encouragement and guidance from Dr. Michelle Conda. Thank you for your long-term support of this project and all my endeavors. Thank you to the many friends and colleagues that offered to test materials and offer feedback—Rachel Hahn, Grace Ho, Leonidas Lagrimas, Chris Madden, Omar Roy, and Kevin Woosley. Thank you to all the students who have dealt with my continuous experimentation in the classroom. Your feedback has been invaluable in creating something effective and cohesive for other students. Thank you to Michael Tan for your feedback and support of this project. Lastly, thank you to my family. Your unconditional support made this possible.

About the Author

Dr. Andy Villemez is an educator, composer, author, and performer based in Cincinnati, Ohio where he serves as associate professor of piano and piano pedagogy at the University of Cincinnati College-Conservatory of Music. He teaches courses in piano literature, music pedagogy, and keyboard musicianship. His research focuses on the development of teaching strategies and educational materials that empower students with well-rounded musicianship and long-lasting creativity.